THE EVERYTHING BOOK

FOR TEACHERS OF YOUNG CHILDREN

AUTHORS:

Valerie Indenbaum
Marcia Shapiro

ILLUSTRATIONS BY:

Nancy Bishop
Rebecca Boynton

Published by

PP PARTNER PRESS
Box 124
Livonia, Michigan 48152

ISBN 0-933212-22-4

Distributed by:

Gryphon House
3706 Otis Street
Mt. Rainier, Maryland 20822

ACKNOWLEDGEMENTS

The materials used in The Everything Book have come from our accumulation of early childhood educating materials. A studious effort has been made to trace the ownership of all material included, and to make proper acknowledgement of its use. The selections not credited in the acknowledgement pages are classified as "author unknown". If any errors have been committed, they will be rectified in future editions upon notification of the publisher.

For permission to use Monkey Face by Frank Asch, grateful acknowledgement is made to Parent's Magazine Press, Division of Guner + Jahr, U.S.A.

INTRODUCTION

Many nursery school teachers and parents of pre-schoolers have expressed a desire and a need for a handbook which would include materials successfully used in a classroom.

After several years of teaching pre-schoolers, we also felt the need for such a guide in which we could incorporate many of our own ideas and experiences.

The activities we present are designed to foster a healthy child that has a positive self image and enjoys learning. We have tried to provide materials that will produce an atmosphere conducive to each child's own individual creativity and self expression.

TABLE OF CONTENTS

TABLE OF CONTENTS

(Continued)

TABLE OF CONTENTS
(Continued)

TABLE OF CONTENTS
(Continued)

ART

The following art activities are designed to be appropriate for pre-school children. We are listing activities and materials that are designed not to frustrate our little people by our expectations of a certain result. We will offer them an experience with much emphasis on process.

ART

Paint

Tempera paint, in a variety of colors, is a must for every child. To apply the paint to paper use:

1. different size brushes
2. Q-tips
3. cookie cutters
4. eye droppers
5. string (held by clothespins)
6. straw (dab paint on paper and blow through straw to move paint)
7. comb and brushes
8. toy cars
9. vegetables
10. spools and wooden pieces
11. squeeze bottles
12. roll on bottles (from roll-on deodorants)
13. spatter with toothbrushes over screen
14. marbles (spoon marbles into paint - place on paper and roll marbles around. Paper must be in a container with sides - pie pans work well.

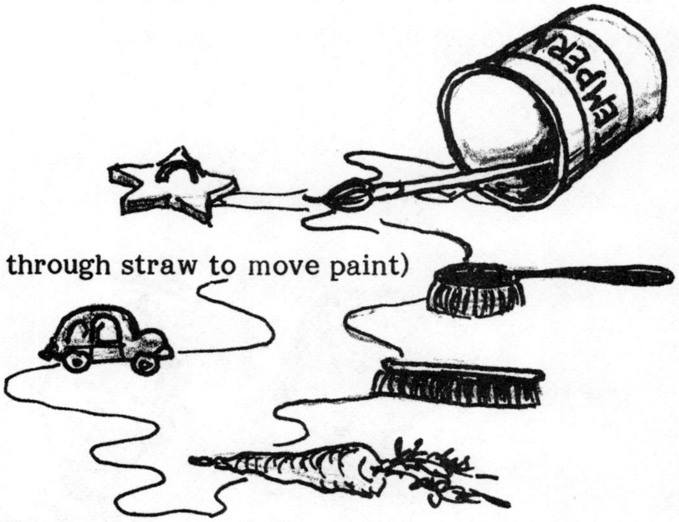

Sprinkle Painting - wet the paper first. Then use empty spice bottles to sprinkle a mixture of powder tempera and (Kosher) coarse salt on paper.

Salt Painting - (pictures sparkle when dry)

1/2 cup liquid starch
2 cups salt
1 cup water
Powder tempera or food coloring

Fingerpainting

Whipped soap flakes, Ivory flakes and water beaten well with hand or electric mixer make very clean fingerpaint material. Add tempera for color.

General Information

Liquid Starch - Add powder tempera for color.

Shaving cream

Instant pudding

Finger paint print - After completing a finger painting (press firmly for absence of paint in some areas), place a sheet of construction paper carefully on top and pat gently all over. Pull off carefully.

Folded Paper Print - Fold paper in half once. Open and place dabs of paint in two or three colors on one side. Fold over and press.

Peanut Butter Playdough

1 cup peanut butter
1 cup honey
1 cup powdered milk
1 cup oatmeal

Make something beautiful and then eat it!

Crayon Resists - Call them magic pictures! Color a picture, pressing very firmly with crayons. With watercolor, paint over the entire picture. The wax crayon "resists" the paint.

Crayon Shavings - Iron crayon shavings between two sheets of waxed paper to make a beautiful scene reflecting picture to hang in a window.

Silly Putty - Mix equal parts of Elmer's glue and liquid starch. Food coloring can be added for color. Store in an airtight container.

Goop

2 cups salt

2/3 cup water

Mix and heat 3-4 minutes. Remove from heat and quickly add mixture of:

1 cup cornstarch

1/2 cup cold water

Stir quickly. Return to heat briefly if too "goopy".

Macaroni Coloring - An easy, non-messy method of coloring macaroni. In a medium-sized, closed container, (a mayonnaise jar works well) place 3 tablespoons of water and liquid food coloring. Fill jar about 1/3 full with macaroni. When desired color is reached, remove with slotted spoon and dry on newspaper. NO SOGGY MESS! BRILLIANT COLORS!

GENERAL FINGERPLAYS

For math related fingerplays, can use felt objects.

tag board covered with
clear contact

stick

(Can use felt chickadees)

6 little chickadees sitting by a hive
1 flew away and then there were five
5 little chickadees sitting by the door
1 flew away and then there were four
4 little chickadees sitting in a tree
1 flew away and then there were three
3 little chickadees sitting by my shoe
1 flew away and then there were two
2 little chickadees sitting by my thumb
1 flew away and then there was one
1 chickadee flying around the sun
he or she flew away and then there was none

Stop, Look and Listen

Stop, look and listen
Before you cross the street
Use your eyes, use your ears,
And then use your feet

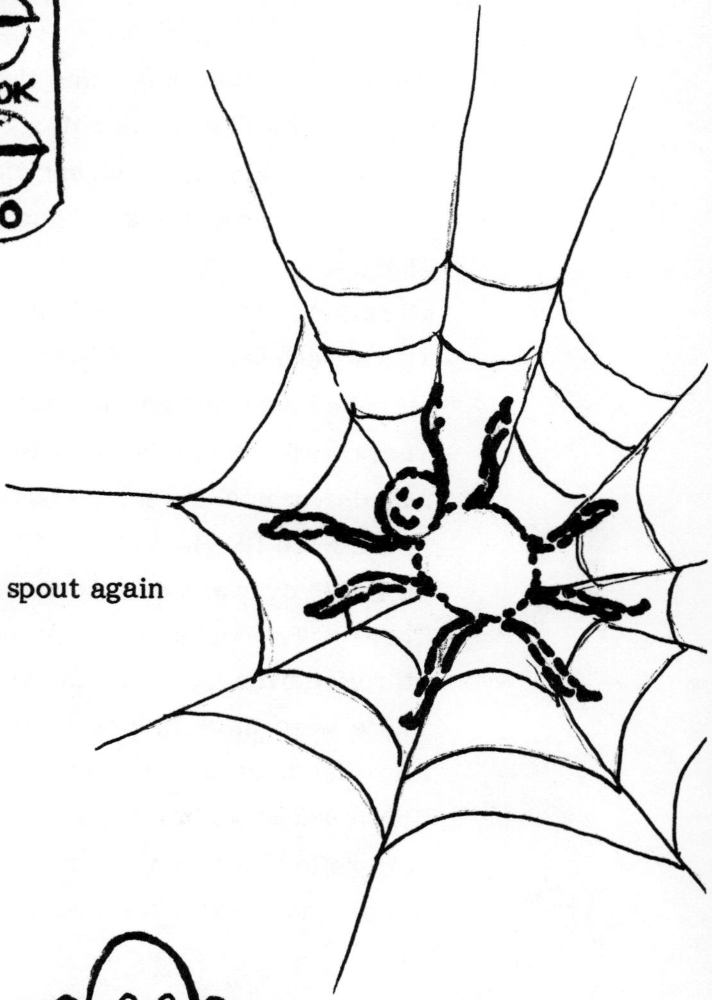

Eensie, Weensie Spider

Eensie,weensie spider
Goes up the water spout
Down comes the rain
and washes the spider out
Out came the sun and dried up all the rain
And the eensie, weenise spider goes up the spout again

Do Your Ears Hang Low?

Do your ears hang low
Do they wobble to and fro
Can you tie them in a knot
Can you tie them in a bow
Can you throw them over your shoulder
Like a continental soldier,
Do your ears hang low?

10 in a Bed (Can use felt objects)

There were ten in a bed and the little one said, "Roll over, roll over." So they all rolled over and one fell out.
There were nine in a bed and the little one said, "Roll over, roll over." So they all rolled over and one jumped out.
There were eight in a bed and the little one said, "Roll over, roll over." So they all rolled over and one hopped out.
There were seven in a bed and the little one said, "Roll over, roll over." So they all rolled over and one jumped out.
There were six in a bed and the little one said, "Roll over, roll over." So they all rolled over and one skipped out.
There were five in a bed and the little one said, "Roll over, roll over." So they all rolled over and one bumped out.
There were four in a bed and the little one said, "Roll over, roll over." So they all rolled over and one jumped out.
There were three in a bed and the little one said, "Roll over, roll over." So they all rolled over and one hopped out.
There were two in a bed and the little one said, "Roll over, roll over." So they both rolled over and one bumped out.
There was one in a bed and the little one said, "Good Night!"

Swinging in the Tree (Can use felt objects)

5 little monkeys (hold up 5 fingers)
Swingin' in the tree (lace fingers and swing)
Teasing Mr. Alligator (thumbs in ears, wave fingers)
You can't catch me!
Along came Mr. Alligator (hands together, reach forward)
Ugly as can be (make ugly face)
Snap! (clap alligator's mouth shut)

Repeat for 4 - 3 - 2 - 1 - 0 monkeys

I Had a Little Turtle

I had a little turtle
He lived in a box
He swam in a puddle
He climbed on the rocks
He snapped at a mosquito
He snapped at a flea
He snapped at a minnow
He snapped at me
He caught the mosquito
He caught the flea
He caught the minnow
But he didn't catch me.

Harry Hippopotamus (do with appropriate motions)

Harry Hippopotamus has such a heavy tread (gently pat thighs)
That when he goes to bed at night
His mother often says
Good gracious Harry (shake finger)
Your pounding hurts my head
And your little baby brother is fast asleep in bed.

People on the Bus

The wheels on the bus go round and round
Round and round, round and round
The wheels on the bus go round and round
All through the town

The people on the bus go up and down
Up and down, up and down
The people on the bus go up and down
All through the town

The wipers on the bus go swish, swish, swish
Swish, swish, swish, Swish, swish, swish
The wipers on the bus go swish, swish, swish
All through the town

The money on the bus goes clink, clink, clink
Clink, clink, clink, Clink, clink, clink
The money on the bus goes clink, clink, clink
All through the town

The driver on the bus says move on back
Move on back, move on back
The driver on the bus says move on back
All through the town

The children on the bus say waa, waa, waa
Waa, waa, waa, Waa, waa, waa
The children on the bus say waa, waa, waa
All through the town

The mommies and daddies on the bus say I love you
I love you, I love you
The mommies and daddies on the bus say I love you
All through the town

Let Everyone

Let everyone clap like me . . . clap, clap
Let everyone clap like me . . . clap, clap
Come and join in with the game
You'll find that it's always the same

Let everyone touch their head

Let everyone touch their shoulders

Let everyone touch their knees

Let everyone touch their toes

Let everyone flap their wings

Wiggles

I wiggle my fingers
I wiggle my toes
I wiggle my shoulders
I wiggle my nose
Now no more wiggles are left in me
So I will be still as still can be

5 Little Monkeys (can use felt objects)

5 little monkeys jumping on a bed
1 fell off and bumped his head
His mother called the doctor and
the doctor said, "No more monkeys
jumping on the bed!"
4 little monkeys, etc.

2 Little Blackbirds

2 little blackbirds sitting on a hill
1 named Jack
1 named Jill
Fly away Jack
Fly away Jill
Come back Jack
Come back Jill

Open, Shut Them

Open, shut them, open, shut them
Do a little clap
Open, shut them, open, shut them
Put them in your lap

The Bee Hive

Here is a bee hive
(Make a fist with fingers covering thumb)
Where are the bees?
Hidden away where nobody sees
Soon they come creeping out of the hive
1, 2, 3, 4, 5
(Open fist, one finger at a time)
Buzz - zzz

The Church

Here is a church
And there is a steeple
Open the doors
And see all the people!

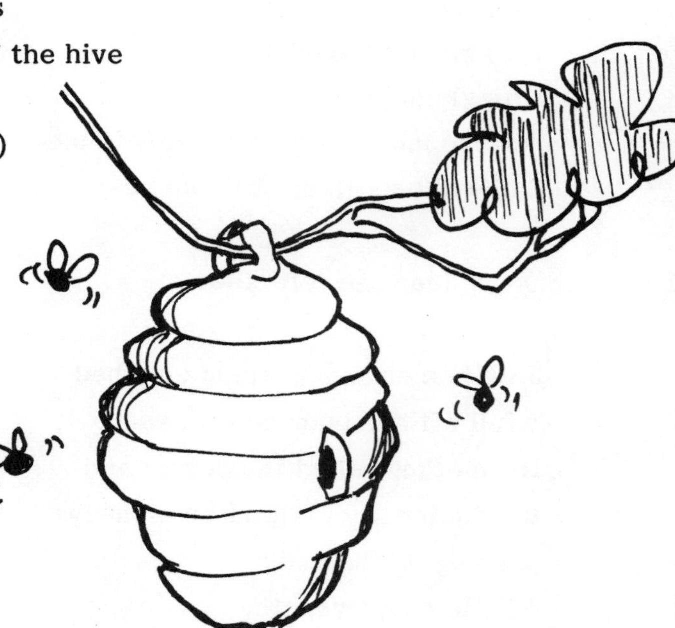

This Old Man

This old man, he played one
He played knick-knack on his drum
With a knick-knack, paddy wack,
Give a dog a bone
This old man came rolling home

Repeat -,

2	shoe
3	knee
4	floor
5	hive
6	sticks
7	heaven
8	plate
9	spine
10	den

My Hands

My hands upon my head I'll place
Upon my shoulders, on my face
At my waist, and by my side
And then behind me they will hide.
Then I will raise them way up high
And let my fingers fly, fly, fly,
Then clap, clap, clap and one, two, three
Just see how quiet they can be.

Clap Your Hands

Clap, clap, clap your hands
As slowly as you can.
Clap, clap, clap your hands
As quickly as you can.

Shake, shake, shake your hands, etc.

Rub, rub, rub your hands, etc.

Wiggle, wiggle, wiggle your fingers, etc.

Pound your fist, pound your fist, pound your fist, etc.

Wiggle

I can't keep quiet, I can't keep quiet
I can't keep quiet right now
I've got to wiggle, watch me wiggle
Wiggle my thumbs, tee da, tee dum
Ta dee, dee, dee, dum

I can't keep quiet, I can't keep quiet
I can't keep quiet right now
I've got to wiggle, watch me wiggle
Wiggle my thumbs, my fingers, my head, etc.

(Slow) I can keep quiet, I can keep quiet
I can keep quiet right now
No more wiggles, no more wiggles
Ta da dee dum
Dee da da da dee do do dum

(Sing to whatever tune seems appropriate)

The More We Are Together (Tune of "Lassie")

The more we are together, together, together
The more we are together, the happier we'll be
For your friends are my friends and my friends are your friends
The more we are together the happier we'll be

We're all in school together, together, together
We're all in school together and happy we will be
There's Mary and Peter and Janet and Joshua
There's ___ and ___ and ___ and ___
We're all in school together and happy are we

Teapot

I'm a little teapot short and stout
Here is my handle
Here is my spout
When I get all steamed up I will shout
Tip me over and pour me out.

<u>Caterpillar Crawling</u> (can use felt objects)

One little caterpillar crawled on my shoe
Another came along and then there were two

Two little caterpillars crawled on my knee
Another came along and then there were three

Three little caterpillars crawled on the floor
Another came along and then there were four

Four little caterpillars watch them crawl away
They'll all turn into butterflies some fine day.

<u>Freckled Frogs</u> (can use felt objects)

Five little freckled frogs
Sitting on a speckled log
Eating the most delicious bugs
Yum! Yum! (rub tummy)

One jumped into the pool
Where it was nice and cool
Now there's only four freckled frogs
Glum Glum

Ten little fingers

I have 10 little fingers
And they all belong to me
I can make them do things
Would you like to see
I can shut them up tight
Or open them wide
I can hold them in front
Or make them all hide
I can put them up high
Or put them down low
I can put them in my lap
And hold them just so

Where is Thumbkin?

Where is thumbkin, where is thumbkin?
Here I am, Here I am
How are you today sir? Very well I thank you
Run away, run away.

2 pointer
3 tall man
4 ringman
5 pinky
6 all men

Put Your Finger in the Air

Put your finger in the air, in the air
Put your finger in the air, in the air
Put your finger in the air and leave it about a year
Put your finger in the air, in the air

2 head   tell me is it green or red

3 cheek   leave it about a week

4 nose   wind blows

5 chest   give it a little rest

6 belly   shake like apple jelly

BINGO

There was a farmer had a dog and Bingo was his name - O
B-I-N-G-O, B-I-N-G-O, B-I-N-G-O, and
Bingo was his name - O.

Sing verse through one time. The second time, substitute a clap for the letter "B" (e.g., Clap, I - N - G - O)
In each succeeding verse, substitute a clap for the next letter until the fifth time around, when you will have 5 claps replacing all 5 letters.

Nobody Likes Me

Nobody likes me, everybody hates me
Think I'll go eat worms, big fat juicy ones.
Eeny, weeny, squeeny ones, see how they wiggle and squirm

Chop up their heads and squeeze out the juice
And throw away their tails
Nobody knows how I survive on worms three times a day

If You're Happy

If you're happy and you know it, clap your hands
If you're happy and you know it, clap your hands
If you're happy and you know it, your face will surely show it
If you're happy and you know it, clap your hands.

If you're happy . . . stamp your feet

Hokey Pokey

You put your right foot in
You put your right foot out
You put your right foot in
And you shake it all about
You do the Hokey Pokey and you turn yourself about
That's what it's all about.

Left foot
Right hand
Left hand
Right shoulder
Left shoulder
Whole self

The Donut Song

Oh I walked around the corner
And I walked around the block
And I walked right into the bakery shop

And I picked up a donut and I wiped off the grease
And I handed the lady a 5 cent piece
Thanks for the donut, Good day

Well she looked at the nickel
And she looked at me
And she said, "Hey mister, can't you plainly see?
There's a hole in the nickel, there's a hole right through."
Said I, "There's a hole in the donut too!"

SPECIAL DAYS AND SPECIAL BOOKS

Nursery school children love special days. We try to have a special day at least twice a month. Here are some days we have used and ideas to go along with them.

Teddy Bear Day - Have children bring their own Teddy Bear from home (may substitute other stuffed animal)

A. Trace parts of bear. Use glue or paper fasteners to attach parts to body. Either fill in with coffee grounds, saw dust, or glue fuzzy material to tummy.

B. "Bare" feet painting. Have one child paint bottom of another child's foot or feet, with brush. Child walks around on a long sheet of paper. Wash feet in tub.

C. Have a "Bear Show" with ribbons and/or awards for fattest bear, biggest bear, smallest bear, etc. Children can help think of awards.

D. Read book Corduroy by Don Freeman. Act out the story of Corduroy. Also, A Pocket for Corduroy. A filmstrip of Corduroy is available. Ask Mr. Bear is another excellent book to read and act out.

Songs and Games for Teddy Bear Day

Teddy Bear

Teddy bear, Teddy bear, turn around
Teddy bear, Teddy bear, touch the ground
Teddy bear, Teddy bear, show your shoe
Teddy bear, Teddy bear, that will do
Teddy bear, Teddy bear, go upstairs
Teddy bear, Teddy bear, say your prayers
Teddy bear, Teddy bear, turn out the light
Teddy bear, Teddy bear, say "good-night"

Let's Go on a Bear Hunt

(The children repeat each line after the leader)

Let's go on a bear hunt.
All right, let's go.
(Tap hands on thighs like walking)

Oh look, I see a wheat field.
Can't go around it,
Can't go under it,
Let's go through it,
All right, let's go.
Swish, swish, swish.
(Rub hands together like swishing through the wheat.)

Oh look, I see a tree.
Can't go over it,
Can't go under it,
Let's go up it,
All right, let's go.
(Pretend to climb tree. When top is reached, place hand on forehead and look around. Climb down)

Oh look, I see a swamp.
Can't go around it,
Can't go under it,
Let's swim through it,
All right let's go.
(Pretend to swim)

Oh look, I see a bridge
Can't go around it,
Can't go under it,
Let's cross over it.
All right, let's go.
(Make clicking sound with tongue and stamp feet)

Oh look, I see a cave.
Can't go around it,
Can't go under it,
Let's go in it.
All right, let's go.
(Cup hands and make hollow sound when clapping together)

Oh look, I see something.
I think - it's a bear.
(Say this with suspense in voice.)
IT IS A BEAR!
Let's go! (Repeat everything backward and
fast - wipe brow - make a big sigh of relief.)
WHEW WE MADE IT!

TEDDY BEAR

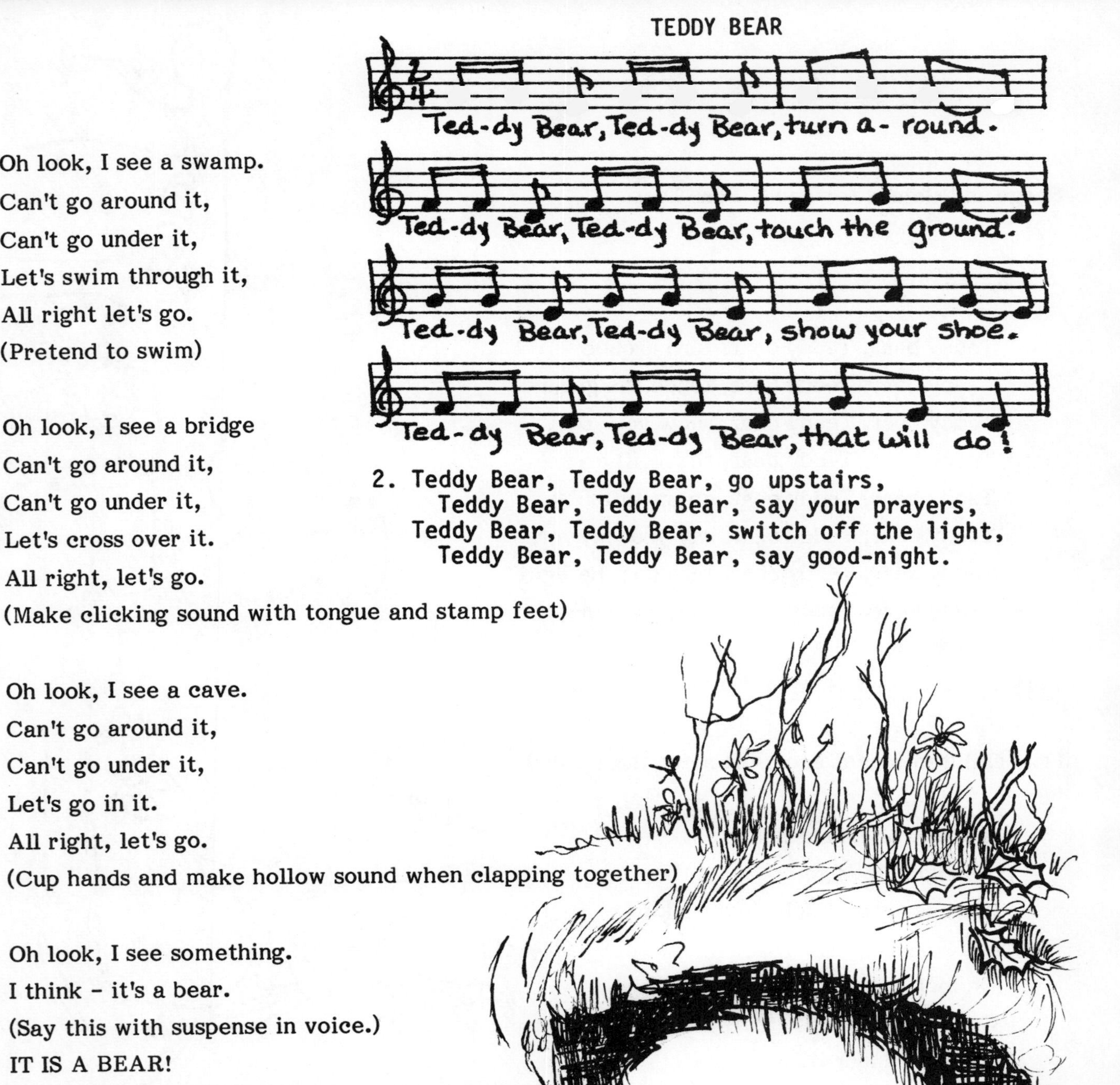

2. Teddy Bear, Teddy Bear, go upstairs,
Teddy Bear, Teddy Bear, say your prayers,
Teddy Bear, Teddy Bear, switch off the light,
Teddy Bear, Teddy Bear, say good-night.

Books for Teddy Bear Day

Barr, Catherine	Bears in - Bears out
Brown, Margaret Wise	Little Fur Family
Carroll, Ruth	The Picnic Bear
Chaffin, Lillie D.	Bear Weather
Flack, Marjorie	Ask Mr. Bear
Freeman, Don	Corduroy
	A Pocket for Corduroy
Gackenbach, Dick	Hound and Bear
Hodgson, Ida	Bernadette's Busy Morning
Janice	Little Bear's Thanksgiving
McCloskey, Robert	Blueberries for Sal
Miklowitz, Gloria	The Marshmallow Caper
Waber, Bernard	Ira Sleeps Over
Ward, Lynd	The Biggest Bear
Ylla	Two Little Bears
Walsh, Ellen Stoll	Brunus and the New Bear Benjamin gets a new stuffed bear and his old bear, Brunus, becomes jealous. Benjamin shows Brunus that two friends can happily become three.
Tobias, Tobi	Moving Day A small girl is involved in the excitement, turmoil, and sadness of moving from one house to another and keeps her toy bear close for reassurance.
Hazen, Barbara Shook	Where Do Bears Sleep? Tells where many animals sleep, in verse form.
Turkle, Brinton	Deep in the Forest A curious bear expolores a cabin in the forest with disastrous results.

Flannel Board Story: Goldilocks and the Three Bears

For lacing
on
Teddy Bear
Day

The Three Bears

Once upon a time there were three bears who lived together in a house of their own in the woods. One of them was a little-sized bear, one was a middle-sized bear, and the third was a great big bear. They each had a bowl for their porridge - a little bowl for the wee bear, a middle-sized bowl for the middle-sized bear, and a great big bowl for the great big bear. And they each had a chair to sit on - a little small chair, a medium-sized chair and a great big chair. And they each had a bed to sleep in - a little bed for the wee bear, a middle-sized bed for the middle-sized bear and a great big bed for the great big bear.

One day after they had made porridge for their breakfast and poured it into their bowls, they walked out in the woods while the porridge was cooling. A little girl named Goldilocks passed by the house and looked in at the window. And then she looked through the keyhole, and when she saw that there was no one home, she lifted the latch on the door. The door was not locked because the bears were good bears who never did anyone any harm and never thought that anyone would harm them. So Goldilocks opened the door and walked in. She was very glad to see the porridge on the table, as she was hungry from walking in the woods, and so she sat down and helped herself.

First she tasted the porridge of the great big bear and it was too hot for her. Next she tasted the porridge of the middle-sized bear but that was too cold. And then she tasted the porridge of the little wee bear and it was just right and she ate it all up.

Then Goldilocks sat on the chair of the great huge bear and it was too hard. Next she sat on the chair of the middle-sized bear and that was too soft. And then she sat on the chair of the little wee bear and that was just right. She rocked so hard that she broke the chair.

Then Goldilocks went upstairs to the bedroom where the three bears slept. And first she lay down upon the bed of the great big bear, but that was too high for her. And next she lay down upon the bed of the middle-sized bear, but that was too low for her. But when she lay down upon the bed of the little wee bear, it was neither too high nor too low, but just right. So she covered herself up comfortably and fell fast asleep.

When the three bears thought their porridge would be cool enough for them to eat, they came home for breakfast. Now, Goldilocks had left the spoon of the great big bear standing in the porridge.

"Somebody has been eating my porridge!" said the great big bear in a great, rough gruff voice.

Then the middle-sized bear looked at its porridge and saw the spoon was standing in it, too.

"Somebody has been eating my porridge!" said the middle-sized bear in a middle-sized voice.

Then the little wee bear looked at its bowl, and there was the spoon standing in the bowl, but the porridge was all gone.

"Somebody has been eating my porridge and has eaten it all up!" said the little wee bear in a little wee voice.

Upon this, the three bears, seeing that someone had come into their house and eaten up all the little wee bear's breakfast, began to look around them. Now Goldilocks had not put the cushion straight when she rose from the chair of the great big bear.

"Somebody has been sitting in my chair!" said the great big bear in a great, rough gruff voice.

And Goldilocks had squashed down the soft cushion of the middle-sized bear.

"Somebody has been sitting in my chair! said the middle-sized bear in a middle-sized voice.

"Somebody has been sitting in my chair, and has sat the bottom through!" said the little wee bear in a little wee voice.

Then the three bears thought that they had better look farther in case it was a burglar, so they went upstairs into their bedroom. Now, Goldilocks had pulled the pillow of the great big bear out of its place.

"Somebody has been lying in my bed!" said the great big bear in a great, rough gruff voice.

And Goldilocks had pulled the cover of the middle-sized bear out of its place.

"Somebody has been lying in my bed!" said the middle-sized bear in a middle-sized voice.

But when the little wee bear came to look at its bed, there was the pillow in its place. But upon the pillow? There was Goldilocks' head, which was not in its place, for she had no business there.

"Somebody has been lying in my bed, and here she is still," said the little wee bear in a little wee voice.

Now Goldilocks had heard in her sleep the great, rough gruff voice of the great big bear, but she was so fast asleep that it was no more to her than the rumbling of distant thunder. And she had heard the middle-sized voice of the middle-sized bear, but it was only as if she had heard someone speaking in a dream. But when she heard the little wee voice of the little wee bear, it was so sharp and so shrill that it woke her up at once.

Up she sat, and when she saw the three bears on one side of the bed, she tumbled out at the other and ran to the window. Now the window was open, for the bears were good, tidy bears who always opened their bedroom window in the morning to let in the fresh air and sunshine. So Goldilocks jumped out through the window and ran away, and the three bears never saw anything more of her.

Mother Goose Day (use this day far from Halloween)

A. Ask child to come as his favorite Mother Goose character. Go easy on costumes. Try several props to suggest it. Be sure and review nursery rhymes several weeks before using this day as a culmination.

B. Read Mother Goose books:
Brian Wildsmith's Mother Goose
Richard Scarry's Mother Goose

C. Have each child act out Mother Goose rhymes

D. Humpty Dumpties - scrambled eggs - each child cracks one.

E. Curds and Whey - cottage cheese - Little Miss Muffet

F. Little Jack Horner's Plum

Little Miss Muffett
Sat on a tuffet
Eating her curds and whey.
Along came a spider
And sat down beside her
And frightened Miss Muffett away.

Little Bo Peep she lost her sheep
And didn't know where to find them
Let them alone and they'll come home
Wagging their tails behind them.

Hickety-Pickety My Black Hen
She lays eggs for gentlemen
Sometimes 9, Sometimes 10
Hickety-Pickety My Black Hen

Humpty-Dumpty sat on a wall
Humpty-Dumpty had a great fall
All the king's horses and all the king's men
Couldn't put Humpty together again.

Hickory-Dickory Dock, the mouse ran up the clock
The clock struck one, and down she come
Hickory-Dickory Dock - tick-tock.

Hey Diddle-Diddle

Hey Diddle Diddle, the Cat and the Fiddle,
The Cow jumped over the moon,
The little dog laughed to see such a sight,
And the dish ran away with the spoon.

Monkey Day

A. Cutting exercise - monkey - paint in banana shapes - make newspaper hats (caps) for later drama of Caps for Sale. Monkey feet, fingerprints, paint with toes (monkey do!)

B. Good Monkey Books: Caps for Sale
Curious George
(key filmstrips are available on both of these books)

C. Have a peanut hunt

D. Filmstrip or movie about monkeys

Circus Day/Clown Day

Preparation - It would be super it you could find a "real" clown to visit and show the children how to dress, put on makeup, etc., as a clown.

A. Balloons

Clown hats

Animal hats from paper bags

Cut out elephant

Circus train - shoe boxes with pictures of animals

Hobby horses to show from rolled newspaper

B. Circus Books

Circus Baby, Petersham Circus, B. Wildsmith

Look, a Parade

Put Me in the Zoo, Laphire

Pierre, Maurice Sendak

C. Provide makeup for animal and clown faces. Have children act out animals and circus acts. Tight rope can be laid on floor, hula hoops to jump through.

D. Group activity - give each child one crayon and a sheet of white paper.

Then:

Draw a circle round and big
Add a few hairs as a wig
Make a circle for a nose
Now a smile, broad and wide
Put an ear on either side
Add some eyes, but not a frown
Now you have your very own clown.

E. Draw cage and paste on animal crackers

Today I ate a tiger
And then a tall giraffe
And when I ate an elephant
It really made me laugh
Now if I think it's funny
That I ate such a meal
They're animal crackers that I ate
And none of them were real.

Pretzel Day

Preparation - have ingredients ready. Here is the recipe that can be made with the children. Children can be taught to measure, stir, knead and shape dough into pretzel.

1 pkg. dry yeast, dissolve in cold water
3 cups flour
1 t sugar
1 t salt

Mix yeast mixture in flour mixture. Add about one more cup flour until it can be kneaded. Knead on floured counter top. Shape. Sprinkle with Kosher salt. 20 pretzels. Bake at 350° for about 20 minutes.

Read book, Pretzel by Rey.

Winter Picnic Day

Preparation - Be sure there is snow on the ground. Read book Winter Picnic by Robert Welber. Then have children make their own lunch in a bag. Dress warmly, go outside and have lots of fun.

Menu

peanut butter and jelly sandwich
fruit
hot chocolate
vegetable sticks

Beach Day

Preparation - This day is especially fun in the middle of winter. Have children bring in bathing suits, towels, sandals, etc., and prepare for a day at the beach in the middle of the winter. Spread out your towels and make a picnic lunch, eat on the floor of your room.

Menu

hot dogs
lemonade
chips
fruit

Peanut Day

This is a wonderful day that you can celebrate George Washington Carver's birthday. Make sketch of George Washington Carver. Then talk about the peanut plant, how it grows, etc. Bring in peanuts in shells for children to shell

A. Make peanut butter with the peanuts in a blender - add oil.
B. Make Mr. Peanut for a craft activity

put shells on fingertips - draw faces and use as puppets

C. Make a peanut shell collage from the leftover shells

Pancake Day

Preparation: read story, The Pancake Man, Pancakes for Breakfast by Tomie De Paolo

Then mix up pancakes in class and serve with milk and fruit for a delicious breakfast

Pancake

Mix a pancake
Stir a pancake
Put it in a pan
Fry the pancake
Toss the pancake
Catch it if you can

Clifford Day

Clifford is a favorite book among preschool children. There are many in the series and the children love them all. This book can be used along with red day as Clifford is a big red dog.

Clifford can be cut out and used on the easel.

Craft: triangle Clifford Dog. Cut a piece of red construction paper in half the long way, fold, color.

"Clifford" books by Bredwell.

Apple Day

This is particularly good for the fall. Bring in many different kinds of apples. Discuss different ways apples can be used for different things.

Make apple prints

Make apples out of tissue paper

Applesauce

Apple math

Read "10 Apples on Top"

Way up high on the apple tree
Two little apples smiled at me
I shook the tree as hard as I could
Down came the apples
mmmm, mmmm, mmmm, mmmm, were they good!

Gingerbread Day

We will read story of gingerbread man, bake large gingerbread boy. Put him in the oven to bake. When we come back to get him out, he will have mysteriously disappeared, leaving a note behind him. We will go from place to place looking until we find him and then we will eat him up.

Recipe for Gingerbread Boys

1 box butterscotch pudding mix
½ cup shortening
½ cup brown sugar
1 egg
1½ cups flour
1½ tsp. ginger
½ tsp. cinnamon
½ tsp. baking soda

Cream shortening and sugar, add egg and mix well. Add dry pudding mix and flour and spices. Mix well. Roll dough 1/8th to 1/4 inch thick and cut with cookie cutter - or give each child small balls of dough to use for molding body, head, two arms, two legs. This dough is EASY to work with. Bake on greased sheet, 350° for 10 minutes.
(This is enough dough for 6-7 children)

Sesame Street Day

Have children bring in Sesame Street books, records, puppets, etc. Can make "Cookie Monster" cookies.

Pajama Day

Have children come to school in pajamas. Can bring their favorite blanket or sleep toy. Read Good Night Moon by Brown or Ira Sleeps Over by Weber. A fun day!

Backward Day - Good for April 1

Have children wear their clothes backwards - reverse day.

SEPTEMBER

I. ARTS AND CRAFTS

Objective: All these activities are developed to improve small motor coordination.
Evaluation: The children will tear, paste, cut, rub, color, paint, grate and string.

A. Have available several pieces of colored scraps that children can tear and put into a paper bag to take home.

B. Draw tree trunks on large white paper.
   1. Have children tear red pieces (apple) green (leaves). May use construction paper or tissue squares to be wadded and glued on branches.
   2. Dip small sponges in red, green, orange, or yellow paint and dapple on paper to form leaves (clothespins may be clipped on for easier handling).
   3. Fold large paper in half - open with eyedropper and red paint, squeeze on apples and fold and blot.

C. Leaf rubbing: Tape leaves to table. Lay typing paper over and rub with side of peeled crayon.

D. Shave peeled crayons (using potato peeler) on waxed paper. Cover with another sheet of waxed paper. Run warm iron over. Cut in leaf shape. Punch hole, add string and hang.

E. Create leaf creatures or people. Glue a fall leaf on piece of paper. Make different people or animals by using the leaf for the body and crayons, magic markers or twigs to make limbs, heads, tails, or wings.

F. Beautiful fall leaf: Cut large white paper in leaf shape. With dropper drop fall-colored paint all over and fold in half.

Read Marmalade's Yellow Leaf - Wheeler.

G. Seasonal tree: Find a large branch that is shaped like a small tree. Anchor it in a pot of sand. During the year this can be decorated with fall leaves, Halloween shapes, snowmen, Easter eggs, spring flowers and birds according to the season. These decorations can be colored, painted, molded or pasted together.

H. Use small paper plate - have children tear red construction paper into small pieces and paste over entire plate, paste on green stem.

I. Papier-mache apple - Use 2-1/2 sheets of newspaper and wad into a paper ball, two to three strips masking tape. Hold firm and wrap around. Dip strips of newspaper into liquid papier-mache glue (can buy instant in a package), let dry overnight. Children paint it red next day and stick in real twig for stem.

J. Apple prints (Refer to story Little House With No Windows and No Doors): Cut apple in half to show star. Remove seeds, dip in thin paint and print all over white paper, try to show star.

K. Apple pigs: See book Apple Pigs by Ruth Orback. (Children will need teacher's help). You will need: 2 red apples, 1 small and 1 large; 6 toothpicks, 6 silver balls (cake decorations), 1 slice lemon, 1 pipe cleaner, scissors, apple corer or knife.

1. Hold large apple on its side and insert 4 toothpick legs.
2. Cut small apple in half. Attach one-half to body with 5 toothpicks. Make sure cut side is facing outwards to make face. Rub with lemon slice to keep cut surface from turning brown.
3. For snout cut a cylindrical shape from other half of second apple (use corer or knife). Fasten snout to face with toothpicks. Make holes for nostrils using another toothpick.

4. Using toothpick or pencil make 2 very small holes for eyes and insert silver balls. Make slits in top of head and insert leaves to make ears. If the apple had no leaves, the ears can be cut from what's left of apple skin.

L. Easel paper: Provide a variety of fall colors with which to paint. Use white or brown paper. Grocery sacks may be used. Paper may be cut into a variety of shapes--apples, leaves, etc.

M. Stringing: May use long shoelaces or yarn with large plastic needles. String with cereals (Fruit Loops, Cheerios), macaroni, snipped colored straws. Let children sit around tables and choose material to string. Let them have a choice.

N. Leaves: Roll tempera onto leaf using small brayer. Place leaf between folded newsprint and press.

II. COLOR DAY - RED

Objective: To recognize color red.
Evaluation: The following day the children will be able to find red objects on their clothes and in the room.

Have children wear something red. Bring a bag of various red objects, discuss red things around room. Try to use red in craft snack (red Knox Blox). Read Clifford, The Big Red Dog by Bridwell. Sing "Mary Wore a Red Dress". Apple prints, apple rubbings.

BLUE DAY

Blue fingerpaint

Make blueberry pancakes

Read "Blueberries for Sal"

Play "Song, Sung Blue" by Neil Diamond

MARY WORE A RED DRESS

Mary wore a red dress, red dress, red dress
Mary wore a red dress all day long.

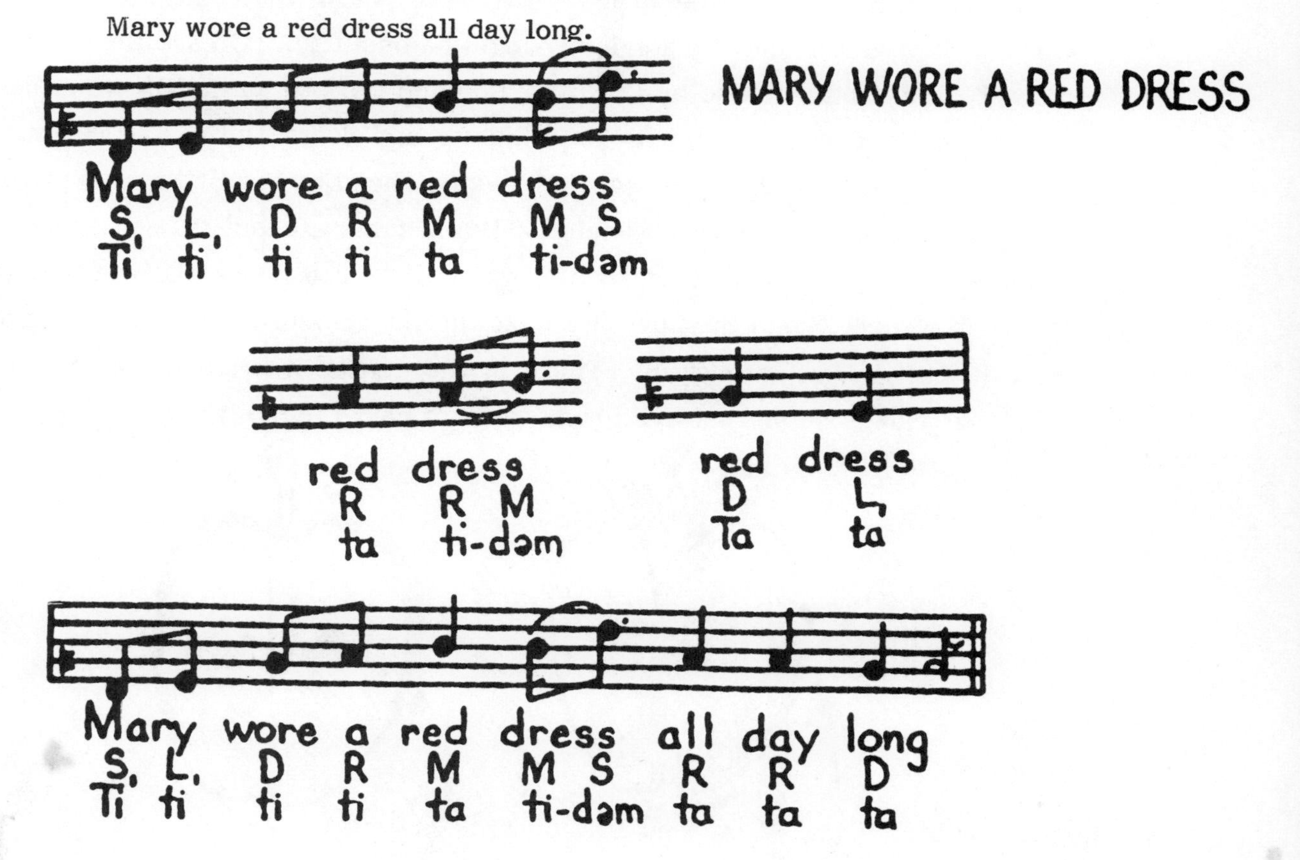

III. STORY

Objective: The teacher will emphasize the joy of storytelling. Use felt objects in telling this story.

Evaluation: The children listened and enjoyed the story very much.

"The Little Red House With No Doors"

Once upon a time there was a little boy who grew tired of all his toys and games. He asked his mother, "What shall I do?" "You shall go on a journey and find a little red house with no windows or doors and a star inside. Come back as soon as you can." So the boy started out on his journey and he found a beautiful little girl and he asked her, "Do you know where I can find a little red house with no windows and doors and a star inside?" "Ask my father, the farmer, he may know." So the little boy found the farmer and asked him, "Do you know where I can find a little red house with no windows and no doors and a star inside?" The farmer laughed and said, "I've lived many years but I've never seen anthing like it--go ask Granny--she knows everything!" So the little boy asked Granny, "Please Granny, where can I find a house with no windows and doors and a star inside." "I'd like to find that house myself, it would be warm in the winter and the starlight would be beautiful. Go ask the wind--maybe he knows." The wind whistled by the little boy and the boy said, "Oh wind, can you help me find a little red house with no windows and doors and a star inside. The wind cannot speak any words but it went on singing ahead of the little boy until it came to an apple tree and shook the branches. Down came a beautiful red apple. The little boy picked it up and looked at it. It was a little red house that had no windows or doors. "I wonder," said the boy. He took out his jackknife from his pocket and cut the apple in half. How wonderful! There in the center was a star holding little brown seeds. He ran home and showed his mother. "Look, I found it!"

THE LITTLE POT

There was once a poor but good little girl who lived alone with her mother, and they no longer had anything to eat. The little girl went into the forest, and there she met an old woman who felt sorry for her.

So the old woman gave her a little pot which when she said, "Cook, little pot, cook," would cook good sweet porridge. And when she said, "Stop, little pot," it would stop cooking. The child took the pot home to her mother, and now they were no longer hungry, for they ate sweet porridge as often as they wished.

One day the little girl had gone out, and her mother said, "Cook, little pot, Cook." And the pot did cook, and she ate until she was full. Then she wanted the pot to stop cooking, but she did not know the right words to say to make it stop. Only the little girl knew that, and she was not at home. So the pot went on cooking, and porridge bubbled over the edge, and still it cooked on until the kitchen and the whole house were full of porridge, and then the next house, and then the whole street. And everyone in town wanted the pot to stop cooking, but no one knew how to stop it.

At last, when only one single house remained that was not covered with porridge, the little girl came home. She said, "Stop, little pot," and it stopped cooking. And whoever wanted to return to town had to eat his way back.

IV. COOKING

Objective: To develop fine motor coordination through peeling, cutting, grating, and mashing--also to develop math skills by counting and measuring ingredients.
Evaluation: The children cut, grated, peeled, and mashed using a variety of utensils. They also counted and measured ingredients.

COOKING ACTIVITIES

A. Make applesauce: Wash hands and apples. Have children cut apples with plastic knives. Put in electric fry pan, cover with cider. Cover pan and bring to a boil. Simmer until apples are soft. Cool. Have on hand several food mills. Let children take turns grinding. Add sugar and cinnamon to taste.

B. Peeling carrots: Have a potato peeler for each child. Show them how carrots are peeled. When peeled, cut them into strips and serve for snack (can add raisins and a little mayonnaise and make a carrot salad).

C. Play dough: (triple for class)
1 c. flour
1/2 c. salt
1 tsp. oil
1 tsp. cream of tartar
1 tsp. alum
Enough warm water
Food coloring

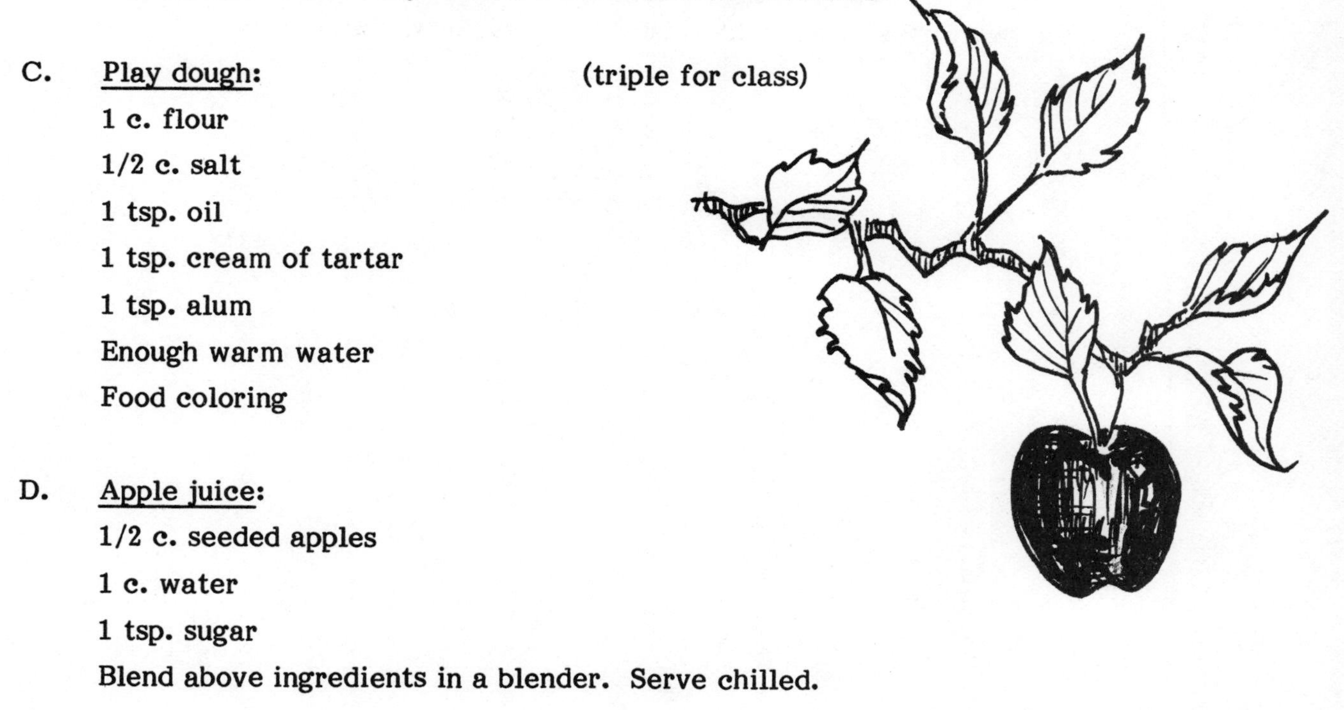

D. Apple juice:
1/2 c. seeded apples
1 c. water
1 tsp. sugar
Blend above ingredients in a blender. Serve chilled.

E. Apple crisp:

4-5 apples (peeled and sliced)

1 c. oatmeal

1-1/3 c. brown sugar

2/3 c. margarine

1 tsp. cinnamon

Place apples in a 9" x 13" greased pan. Mix remaining ingredients together to make crumbly topping. Place evenly on top of apples. Bake at 375° for 30 to 45 minutes.

F. Knox Blox

1 envelope Knox gelatin dissolved in 1/3 c. cold water

1 small box Jello dissolved in 1 c. boiling water

Mix together. Pour into 9" x 13" pan and cool. Cut into squares.

G. Dry apple rings

Peel, core, and cut apples into rings. Dip into salted water for 15 minutes. Dry for two weeks. Can make raisins from grapes the same way.

V. MATH

Objective: To develop/increase counting skills.
Evaluation: The following day we repeated activities and observed that most were counting.

A. 5 Little Ducks (can use felt objects)

5 little ducks went out to play
Over the hills and far away
Mother duck said, "Quack, quack, quack"
4 little ducks came waddling back.
Repeat with 4, 3, 2, 1, No little ...
The father duck said, "Quack, quack, quack"
5 little ducks came waddling back.

Make 5 ducks, a mother and a father out of different colored pieces of felt. Use for color recognition, counting and subtraction.

B. Bakery Shop

Down around the corner at the bakery shop
There were 10 little doughnuts with sugar on top
Along came (child's name) all alone
And she took a red one home.

Make doughnuts out of tagboard, color different colors. Cover with clear contact and glue tongue depressor on for handle. Have one for each child. Make circle with doughnuts on floor in center. Hold hands and walk around circle saying above verse.

C. <u>5 Little Monkeys</u>

5 little monkeys sitting in a tree
Teasing Mr. Alligator who can't catch me (put thumbs in ears and wave fingers)
Along came Mr. Alligator as quiet as can be (fingers walk) (clap hands)
4 little monkeys.

Make felt monkeys and alligator. Use for subtraction.

D. <u>Beans in a Basket</u>

Number the bottom of each cup in an egg carton from 1-12. Place 80 beans in the lid of the opened egg carton. Place one bean in the cup marked 1, two beans in the cup marked 2, etc.

E. <u>Matched cards</u>

Make a set of numbered cards and a set of object cards. Match each number card with object card.

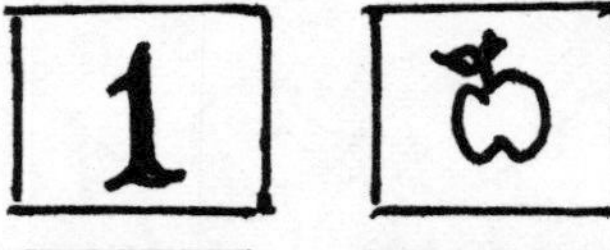

F. Record "Counting"
Classroom Materials Company
93 Myrtle Drive
Great Neck, New York
This record provides the beginning learner with excellent experiences in counting.

VI. FINGERPLAYS - SONGS

<u>Objective</u>: To improve memory skills through repetition.

<u>Evaluation</u>: During the following week we observed that most children remembered the words and actions and were able to repeat them.

Fingerplays (use action)

A. Wiggle your fingers, wiggle your toes
Wiggle your shoulders, wiggle your nose
Now all the wiggles are out of me
And I'm as quiet as I can be.

B. Way up high in the apple tree (arms up)
2 big red apples smiled at me
I shook that tree as hard as I could
And down came the apples
Ummm were they good (rubs stomach).
(Can use as a math experience - make felt tree and 5 apples. Start with "5 big apples" one fell down and then there were 4, etc.)

C. "Frere Jacques"
Hello boys, hello girls
How are you? How are you?
Hope you are just fine, hope you are just fine.
Happy too--Happy too.

D. "Frere Jacques"
Perfect posture, perfect posture
Do not slump, do not slump
You must grow up handsome, you must grow up handsome
Hide that hump, hide that hump.

E. Two little houses all closed up tight (make fists)
Open up the windows and let in the light (open fists)
10 little finger people tall and straight (10 fingers)
Ready for school at half past eight (walk with fingers).

F. Two little blackbirds sitting on a hill (hold up pointer fingers)
One named Jack (raise on pointer)
One named Jill (raise other pointer)
Fly away Jack (put pointer behind back)
Fly away Jill (put pointer behind back)
Come back Jack (bring pointer back)
Come back Jill (bring pointer back).
May substitute children's names for Jack and Jill.

G. 5 little leaves so bright and gay
Were dancing about a tree one day
The wind came blowing through the town
1 little leaf came tumbling down.
4 little leaves, etc.
(May also be used as a math experience. Can make colored leaves out of felt or tagboard on tongue depressors.)
"10 Little Indians" (tune)
1 little, 2 little, 3 little leaves
4 little, 5 little, 6 little leaves
7 little, 8 little, 9 little leaves
Blow them all away—whoof!

H. <u>5 Little Squirrels</u>
5 little squirrels
Playing in a tree
The first one said, "What's that I see?"
The second one said, "I smell a gun."
The third one said, "We all better run."
The fourth one said, "Let's sit in the shade."
The fifth one said, "I'm not afraid."
Bang! Clap goes the gun
And away they all run (put hands behind back).

"On Top of Spaghetti" by Tom Glazer (Record)

On top of spaghetti
All covered with cheese
I lost my poor meatball
When somebody sneezed.
It rolled off the table
And onto the floor
And then my poor meatball
Rolled out of the door.
It rolled in the garden
And under a bush,
And then my poor meatball
Was nothing but mush.
The mush was as tasty
As tasty could be,
And early next summer,
It grew to a tree.
The tree was all covered
With beautiful mess,
It grew great big meatballs
And tomato sauce.
So if you eat spaghetti
All covered with cheese
Hold onto your meatballs
And don't even sneeze (Ahhhhh Choo)

Book—<u>On Top of Spaghetti</u> by Tom Glazer

This is a wonderful book to accompany a terrific song. This can be used with felt board, etc.

<u>Good Morning</u>

Good morning, Good morning, and how do you do?
Good morning, Good morning, I'm fine, how are you?

GOOD MORNING

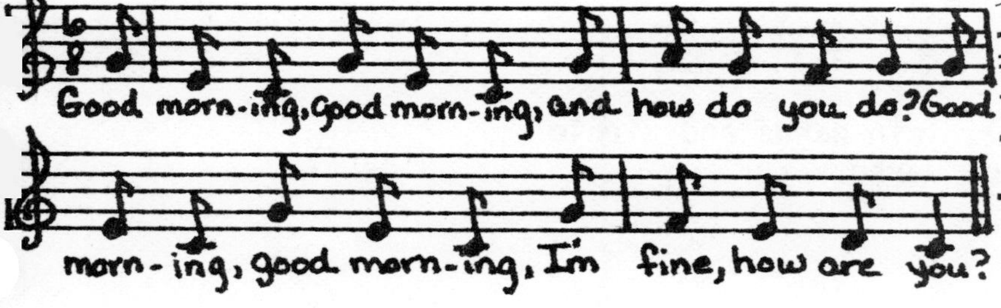

Good morn-ing, good morn-ing, and how do you do? Good
morn-ing, good morn-ing, I'm fine, how are you?

What are you Wearing?

Sally's wearing a red dress, red dress, red dress.

Sally's wearing a red dress all day long.

(Use child's name and articles of clothing.)

The Mulberry Bush

Here we go 'round the Mulberry bush,

the Mulberry bush, the Mulberry bush,

Here we go 'round the Mulberry bush,

So early in the morning.

1. This is the way we wash our face ...
2. Comb our hair
3. Brush our teeth
4. Put on our clothes
5. Etc.

(Suggestion: For circle game, join hands and circle around on chorus after each verse.)

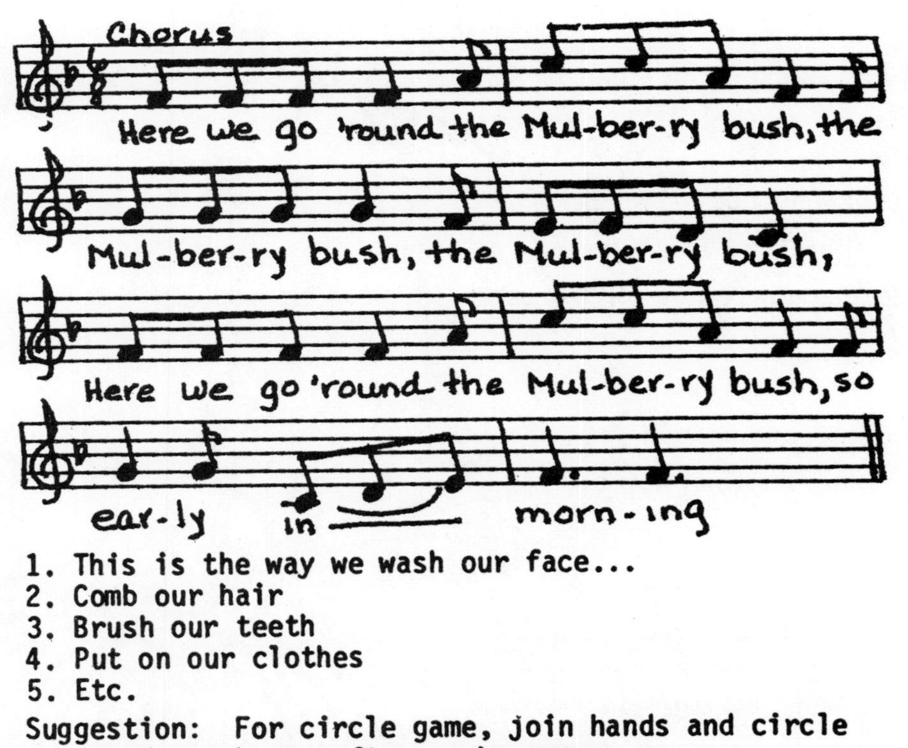

VII. SCIENCE

Objective: Children will observe seasonal changes of a special tree.
Evaluation: Children enjoyed observing the tree through the year.

A. Together pick a nearby tree (not evergreen) to be your Special Tree for the year. See what discoveries the children make about the tree. Keep returning to the tree as the seasons pass and notice the changes. Children might put birdfeeders on the tree in winter.

Help children draw their tree on brown wrapping paper keeping branches bare. As they watch their tree change, they can show the changes with cut or torn pieces of construction paper pasted on their paper. Start out with large green leaves of summer and gradually replace these with yellow and red ones and then begin to strip the colors as winter comes. Some winter day they could tear white pieces of paper for snow for their branches. As spring begins to appear, let them add green leaves. Will make good bulletin board or wall hanging.

Objective: Children will relax and enjoy playing in water.
Evaluation: Children relaxed.

B. Waterplay

Place warm water in shallow containters. Can add a few drops of red food coloring while children are playing. After a short time, add yellow food coloring. Discuss change.

Objective: To help children understand hibernation of different animals.
Evaluation: Children understood animal habits.

C. Hibernation

When the weather turns cold, many animals find sheltered places to hibernate and almost appear to be dead. Their heartbeat slows down and their bodies become very cold. To experiment, place a frog in a deep container of water and slowly add ice. The frog will become less active as his body temperature drops and he will become still as if he is hibernating. Slowly take the frog from the water and put it in a warm place - frog will become active again.

Objective: To help children observe forms of seeds.

Evaluation: Children collected and discussed various seeds.

D. Collecting seeds

Fall walk. Give each child a small bag. Look for pine cones (seeds under cone), apples, acorn, milkweed, maple seed, flowers going to seed. Inside seeds: apple, orange, avocado, pear, lemon, grape. Also collect fall leaves.

Objective: To increase knowledge of our senses.

Evaluation: Children began to better understand function of ears, eyes, nose, hands, etc.

E. Senses play an important part in this adventure.

Ears: Stand still and listen: Chattering of squirrels, the plop of falling nuts and acorns, the soft sound of leaves falling gently to the ground, the sound of wind through the trees, an airplane overhead, a dog barking, cars.

Eyes: Look carefully for: tree stump, shadows cast by the trees, squirrels nest, birds, clouds, leaves, colors and shapes, bare trees, breathe in nippy autumn air, mushrooms, berries (don't eat any!).

Nose: Can you smell? The crumbled dry leaves, the evergreen trees, the damp earth, leaves and pine needles on the ground. Different things have different smells. We can use smells to identify substances.

Hands: Feel tree bark, rough or smooth (can do bark rubbings with side of crayon on paper. You can feel softness of the moss, feel velvet, sandpaper, cotton, etc.

Legs and Feet: For running up and down hills, for picking up leaves, for jumping into leaves.

F. Shadows can be measured with preschoolers by having the children go outside on a sunny day early in the class period. Take chalk and draw around placement of child's feet and then around child's shadow. Run off to play for about an hour and then come back and have child stand in their exact feet placement. See how shadow has moved. Mention earth's movement. Remember to be sure and put child's name in shadow place. Accompany with poem, "Shadow" by Robert Louis Stevenson.

SHADOW

I have a little shadow
that goes in and out with me-
And what can be the use of him
is more than I can see-
He is very very like me
from the heels up to the head-
And I see him jump before me
When I jump into my bed.

Fun with Shadows

Materials:
flashlight or lamp
old sheet
popsicle sticks
paper or cardboard
glue

1) Make shadows on the wall using hands to make different animals.
2) You should be between light source and wall.

Shadows: Play a Shadow Guessing Game

Directions for shadow game - String a rope across the room and hang the sheet over it. Have the children sit on one side and shine light on the other side. Darken the room. Choose one child to stand so his or her shadow shows on the other side of the sheet. Have children guess who it is.

This same thing can be done by using different objects, such as spoon, scissors, starfish, cup, ball, etc.

Make a shadow picture: Have child stand or sit near a wall and shine a light so the shadow of the face's profile appears on the wall.

Tape a sheet of paper on the wall and adjust the light and child so shadow fits on the paper.

Trace the outline of the shadow with pencil or felt-tipped pen.

Remove paper, can be mounted. This is excellent at any time of the year but is especially good for a gift for a special occasion. Example: Mother's Day, Christmas gift.

VIII. PHYSICAL DEVELOPMENT

Objective: To increase social interaction, develop good sportsmanship and have fun.
Evaluation: The children played well with each other, learned to take turns, be a better loser or winner and had fun.

Physical Development Games

A. Worm Through Apple

Have children stand close together in a line with feet about 12 inches apart. One child is the worm who wiggles through the hole made between legs.

B. Football Player Aerobics

1. Click heels together and jump.
2. Running in place.
3. Jumping Jacks
4. Body Bends

C. Balancing Beam

Use a long piece of wood or regular balancing beam, or use chalk or tape on floor. Walk forwards, backwards, walk holding an umbrella, walk with arms out at sides, arms up over head, walk with beanbag or book on head.

D. Jumping

As high as possible, as far as possible, backwards, forwards, sideways, jump and turn around in air, jump and clap hands, jump and land as quietly as possible.

E. Elastics

Have one for each child (one yard of elastic sewn together forming a circle). Stretch with hands and arms, step on it and pull up, place around bent knees and pull up, stretch to music (disco).

IX. FIELD TRIPS

Objective: To develop awareness of their surroundings.

Evaluation: Children became more familiar with their surroundings outside their neighborhood.

Field Trips

A. Nature walk

B. Cider mill

C. Apple orchard

X. BOOKS AND RELATED ACTIVITIES

Apple Pigs	Ruth Orbach
A Tree is Nice	Udry
Down Come the Leaves	Bancroft
Andy and the School Bus	Bein
Seasons	Burmingham
The Bingity-Bangity School Bus	Conkling
Little Red Hen	Domanska
Betsey's 1st Day in Nursery School	Gunilla Wolde
House of Four Seasons	Duvoisen
When Autumn Comes	Fox
All for Fall	Kessler
Follow the Fall	Keemin
The Curious Chipmunk	Lakey
Now It's Fall	Lenski
The Apple Book	Martin
Day of Autumn	Miles
Let's Find Out About School	Shapp
Let's Find Out About Fall	Shapp
Apples	Nonny Hogrogian
Autumn's Harvest	Tresselt
Johnny Maple Leaf	Tresselt
Emily's Autumn	Udry
Goodbye Hello	Welber
Autumn	Wood
All Falling Down	Zion
It's Time Now	Tresselt
The Squirrel Levins	Wing
What is a Color	Alice & Martin Provensen
Big and Little, Up and Down	Ethel Berkley
Willy Bear	Kantrowitz
Benjy's Blanket	Myra Brown
Sleepy Heads	Aileen Fisher
My Five Senses	Aliki
Chicken Little	Mouskin Books
Squirrel Book	Mouskin Books

Favorite Fall Book	Mouskin Books
Marmalade's Yellow Leaf	Wheeler
Going for a Walk	Schenk de Regniers
Apple Pie	Wellington
Happy Birthday, Sam	Hutchins

OCTOBER

I. ARTS AND CRAFTS

Objectives: All these activities are developed to enhance small motor coordination.
Evaluation: The children will paste, trace, shape, paint, cut in order to develop small motor coordination.

A. Scrap Paper Jack-O-Lanterns

On black construction paper, draw a circle and paint it with glue. Tear scraps of orange paper into small pieces and arrange on glue. Add torn scraps of yellow paper for eyes, nose and mouth.

B. Paper Plate Pumpkin

Use small paper plate. Cover with glue. Have cut several pieces of orange tissue paper for each child (about 2" x 2" square). Have children crinkle up each piece and stick on. Cut out green stem and glue on.

C. Foot Ghost

Have children step on white paper and trace around their shoes. Use crayon or felt tip pen to make face or use black construction paper with white chalk.

D. Kleenex Ghost

Roll a Kleenex or piece of aluminum foil into a ball and place in center of another tissue. Attach rubber band or twister seal below ball to secure head and leave the ends free. Use felt tip pen to make eyes. Ghost can be called "Georgie" or "Casper" and can coincide with book or filmstrips.

E. Clothespin Ghost

Paint wooden clothespin white and make two dots for eyes with magic marker. For robe, glue the sleeves cut from paper to the body. Prongs of clothespin can fit over side of nut cup filled with treats.

F. Moon Painting

Use circular shaped objects - lids, spools or sponges cut into half circles or crescent shapes. Dip into thick orange, yellow, or white tempera and press on dark paper.

G. Paper Plate Masks

Give each child a large paper plate and a tongue depressor or popsicle stick. Have in center of table crayons, paper, fabric, buttons, scissors, yarn. Children can make faces using yarn or strips of paper for hair, buttons for eyes, etc. Cut holes for the eyes.

H. Shape Witch (Discuss shapes)

Older children may cut out their own shapes if you draw them. For younger children, take a large piece of white construction paper. Have them paste on orange moon, give them two black triangles, one white circle and yarn for hair. Make face with magic markers.

I. Black Cat

Fold piece of black construction paper in half, draw cat with chalk. Have children cut out half circle. Have children cut out face and tail and paste on. Cat stands up.

J. Giant-size Cottage Cheese or Yogurt Trick or Treat Container

Cover cottage cheese or yogurt container with Halloween colored paper and decorate with Halloween figures. Punch holes for handle.

K. Halloween Bags

Use medium-sized paper bag. Cut off $1\frac{1}{2}$" strip across bottom (for handle) and staple on. Draw and cut out cat ears and whiskers. Give children scissors and black and orange paper. Let them cut out eyes, nose and mouth and decorate all over with scraps.

L. Owl

Use brown construction paper for body.

M. Paper Bag Pumpkin

Small or large grocery bag. Crumple newspaper and stuff. Twist top of paper bag and secure with rubber band. Paint the bag orange. Paint the features black. Paint stem green.

N. Pumpkin Decorating

For a pumpkin which will last for days, add on the eyes, ears, nose and mouth instead of carving them in the usual way. Using toothpicks, stick on carrots, cucumbers, radishes, small gourds, raisins or other fall vegetables and fruits. You might add straw, yarn, leaves or shreds of crepe paper for the hair and top it with a funny hat. Can be used as a centerpiece for Halloween Party.

II. COLOR DAY

Objective: To recognize color orange.
Evaluation: The following day, children were able to find orange in their clothes and around room.

Orange Day
Have children wear something orange. Bring and hold up bag of different orange objects. Use orange in craft, easel paint, and in snack (oranges, orange juice, carrots, etc.) With paints, show how color orange is made from mixing red and yellow.

Black Day
Same as orange day.

Can read The Color Kittens.

III. STORIES

Objective: The teacher will emphasize the storytelling.

Evaluation: The children listened and enjoyed the story very much.

PERKY PUMPKIN

Once upon a time there was a little man who liked pumpkins so much he even looked like one. He had bright orange skin, all shiny and smooth. Everybody called him Perky Pumpkin.

Perky liked everything about pumpkins. He enjoyed eating them, whether cooked as a vegetable or baked as a pie. And he especially enjoyed the pumpkin seeds. Sometimes he made pretty designs with them and sometimes he made funny pictures with them. Sometimes he even did number work with them. He spent hours making sets of two, three, four and five.

Perky's best friend was Kate the cat. She was black and silky and had a soft, contented purr.

Perky began to think how nice it would be to have a warm, snug house of his own, instead of sleeping out in the fields among the pumpkin vines. He mentioned it to Kate and they decided to find a house together.

One crisp fall morning they set out. In front of a school, they found a large piece of orange paper. "My favorite color," said Perky. "It's just what we need."

With Kate's help, Perky tugged and pushed and pulled until he put the paper together like this (fold in half). With a pair of scissors, Perky carefully and slowly rounded off the corners, so the paper looked like this:

"Meow," said Kate. "Let's set it up and take a look at our work." And for a time, they just smiled in admiration.

But then Perky remembered he would need a door. He cut out a tall one, like this: "I think I'll add a window, too," he said. And he did like this:

Perky was pleased with himself . . . But not Kate . . . She was curious to know where she came in. "Meow . . . . . . meow," she grumbled.

Perky laughed. He quickly added another door--a teeny, tiny one that was just the right size for a rather thin cat. "This will always be open so you can come in and out as you like," he said. Kate purred her thanks.

On Halloween night, Perky and Kate invited all the Mother Goose and Storybook Friends to an open-house party. And when they opened the house to their friends, everyone was surprised and delighted--including Perky and Kate. For this is what they saw:

Just what Halloween needs . . . . a nice round Jack-O-Lantern.

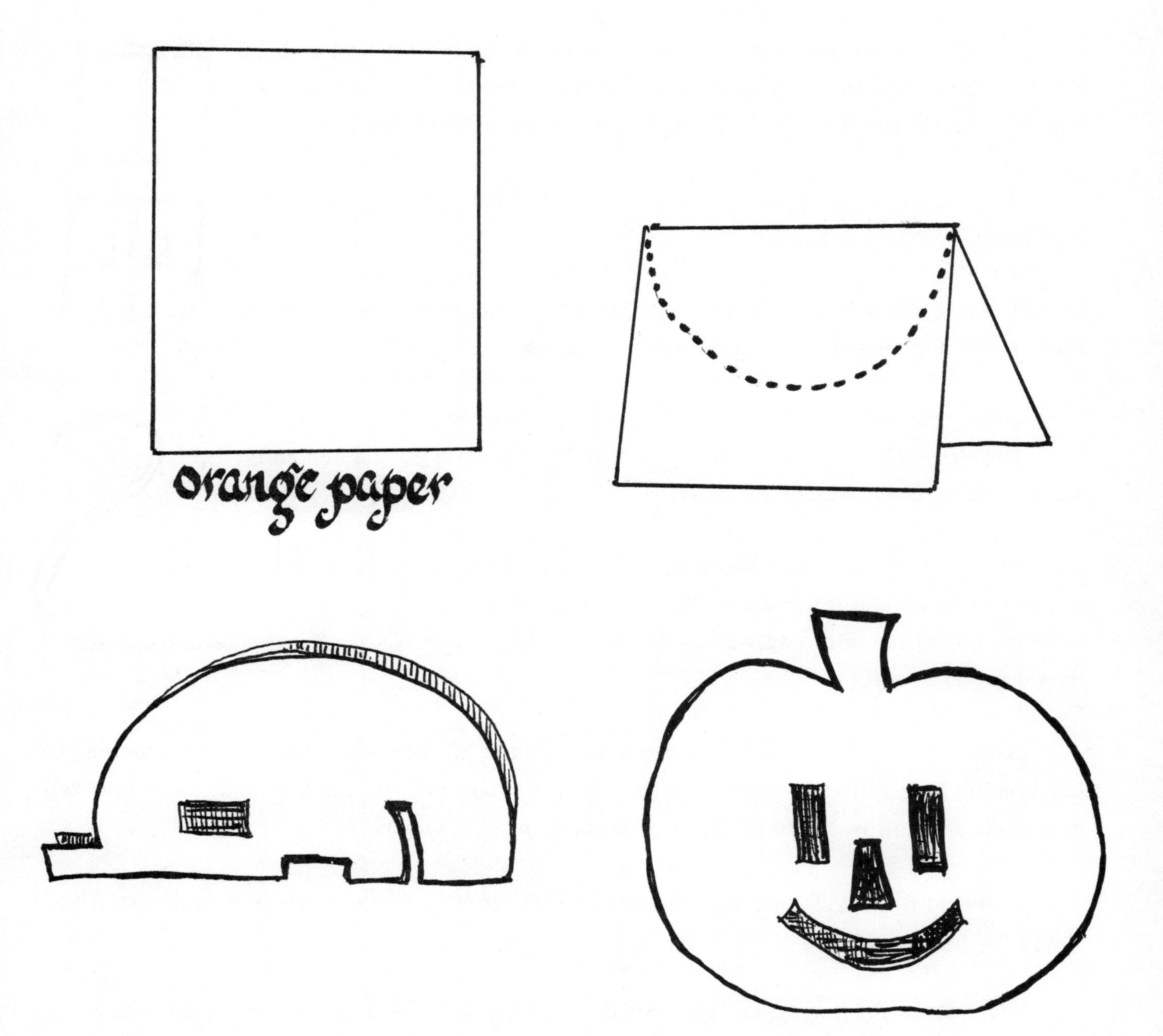

Tale of a Black Cat
(Anonymous)

Once there was a little boy named Tommy; and there's a T that stands for Tommy.

Tommy's house was not a very good one. So he built a new wall on this side of it. And then he built a new wall on that side of it. You can see now that he had two nice rooms in his house, though not very large.

Next he put in windows to look out of - one in this room - and one in that room.

Then he made a tall chimney on this side of his house. And then he made a tall chimney on the other side of his house.

After that he started some grass beside his door, like this.

Not very far away from Tommy's house lived a little girl named Sally; and there's an S that stands for Sally.

When Tommy had finished his house he thought he would like to go and tell Sally what he had been doing, so he came out of his door and walked along, this way, over to where she lived.

Sally was glad to see him, and he went into the kitchen and sat down and explained to her how he had built two new walls to his house and put in windows and made two tall chimneys, and how he had started the grass in front of his door.

"And now, Sally," said he. "I want you to come over and see how well I've fixed things."

"I'll put on my bonnet and go right back with you," said Sally; but when she was ready to start, she said, "We might go down cellar first and get some apples to eat on the way."

So they went down cellar like this.

They got some apples, and then they came up outdoors by the hatchway, like this.

Now they started for Tommy's house, but the walking was bad, and they had gone only a few steps when they tumbled down, like this.

However, they were quickly up, like this.

And they walked along until they were nearly to Tommy's house when they tumbled down again, like this.

And they were no sooner up on their feet, like this, than they tumbled down once more, like this.

But they were nearly to Tommy's house now, and they got up and were going into the yard straight toward the door, like this, when Sally pointed toward the doorstep and cried out, "O-o-o-o-o-oh! See that big Black Cat!"

<u>Objective</u>: To recognize primary colors.

<u>Evaluation</u>: The next day the children recognized the colors.

Hats Off For Olivia

(Good for flannel board; can change hats to different colors)

Olivia the witch was so very sad,
She did not like being so bad
And evil and wicked like most witches are
She would like to be happy like a bright twinkling star.

Scare-dee, her cat, said, "This just cannot be.
Olivia so sad is troubling me.
Olivia," he said, "What's the matter with you?
What's making you sad and feeling so blue?"

"It's my clothes, Scare-dee dear, Black makes me so sad,
It makes me feel evil and wicked and bad.
I would like to wear clothes that make me feel gay . . .
That would make me feel happy and good every day."

"That's silly, Olivia, feeling like that.
Mix up a potion and make a new hat
That's pretty and happy and makes you feel gay . . .
So you won't be grumpy and crabby all day."

So Olivia got busy on her hat right away.
Yellow was the color she chose . . . to be gay.
She put some bananas and corn in her pot,
Stirred them together . . . . now Ala-ga-zot!

Out came a hat so yellow and bright,
She chuckled and giggled with so much delight.
"Let's make another!" Olivia cried.
"Red is the color that has to be tried."

So into her pot some tomatoes she threw.
She stirred them and mixed them . . . . then Ala-ga-zoo!
Out came a red hat with a flower on top.
And she laughed and she laughed . . . . She just couldn't stop.

"Blue is the color next that I'll try."
So into her pot went a piece of blue sky.
She stirred it up good and said, "Ala-ga-zit!"
Out came a blue hat with clouds around it.

"Good gracious!" caried Olivia, "I need a green hat."
So with parsley and peas and an Ala-ga-zat,
She had a hum-dinger of a hat for her head.
It was tall and pointed and covered with thread.

"There must be some colors I just haven't tried.
Let's see, there's orange and purple" she cried.
So into her pot went a carrot or two
She whispered her magic words . . . . Ala-ga-zoo!

The best hat of all appeared in the air,
An orangy--carroty thing with a flair
For making Olivia scream with delight,
At that beautiful orangy-carroty sight.

Olivia was happy. Olivia was gay.
She worked making hats day after day.
She never seemed grumpy or nasty or mean.
She was the Happiest witch that ever was seen.

Now I bet you are wondering what a good witch can do
With so many hats colored red, green and blue.
Olivia and Scare-dee cat now have a shoppe.
Selling hats and happiness whenever you stop.

The Halloween Night
(Anonymous)

This is the moon that shone in the sky on Halloween night

This is the broom that sailed across the moon,
that shone in the sky on Halloween night

This is the witch who rode the broom,
that sailed across the moon,
that shone in the sky on Halloween night

This is the cat that belonged to the witch,
who rode the broom,
that sailed across the moon,
that shone in the sky on Halloween night

This is the owl who woke the cat,
that belonged to the witch,
who rode the broom,
that sailed across the moon,
that shone in the sky on Halloween night

This is the jack-o-lantern that startled the owl,
who woke the cat,
that belonged to the witch,
who rode the broom,
that sailed across the moon,
that shone in the sky on Halloween night

This is the ghost that carved the jack-o-lantern,
that startled the owl,
who woke the cat,
that belonged to the witch,
who rode the broom,
that sailed across the moon,
that shone in the sky on Halloween night.

THE STRANGE VISITOR

This story is popular at Halloween because the visitor's head can be represented as a pumpkin or jack-o-lantern. In some collections the story is titled "Queer Company" and it has a more modern vocabulary. In this version the "reel" has become a spinning wheel, "broad soles" are shoes and the refrain goes:

And still she sat
And still she spun
And still she waited for someone to come.

Cutouts needed for presentation as a felt-board story are the following parts of a man: shoes, legs, waist, shoulders, arms, hands, and a jack-o-lantern head.

A woman was sitting at her reel on night;
And still she sat, and still she reeled, and still she wished for company.
In came a pair of broad broad soles, and sat down at the fireside;
And still she sat, and still she reeled, and still she wished for company.
In came a pair of small small legs, and sat down on the broad broad soles;
And still she sat, and still she reeled, and still she wished for company.
In came a pair of thick thick knees, and sat down on the small small legs;
And still she sat, and still she reeled, and still she wished for company.
In came a pair of thin thin thighs, and sat down on the thick thick knees;
And still she sat, and still she reeled, and still she wished for company.
In came a pair of huge huge hips, and sat down on the thin thin thighs;
And still she sat, and still she reeled, and still she wished for company.
In came a wee wee waist, and sat down on the huge huge hips;
And still she sat, and still she reeled, and still she wished for company.
In came a pair of broad broad shoulders, and sat down on the wee wee waist;
And still she sat, and still she reeled, and still she wished for company.
In came a pair of small small arms, and sat down on the broad broad shoulders;
And still she sat, and still she reeled, and still she wished for company.
In came a pair of huge huge hands, and sat down on the small small arms;
And still she sat, and still she reeled, and still she wished for company.
In came a small small neck, and sat down on the broad broad shoulders;
And still she sat, and still she reeled, and still she wished for company.

In came a huge huge head, and sat down on the small small neck.
"How did you get such broad broad feet?" quoth the woman.
"Much tramping, much tramping" (gruffly).
"How did you get such small small legs?"
"Aih-h-h! . . . late . . . and wee-e-e . . . moul" (whiningly).
"How did you get such thick thick knees?"
"Much praying, much praying" (piously).
"How did you get such thin thin thighs?"
"Aih-h-h! . . . late . . . and wee-e-e . . . moul" (whiningly).
"How did you get such big big hips?"
"Much sitting, much sitting" (gruffly).
"How did you get such a wee wee waist?"
"Aih-h-h! . . . late . . . and wee-e-e . . . moul" (whiningly).
"How did you get such broad broad shoulders?"
"With carrying broom, with carrying broom" (gruffly).
"How did you get such small small arms?"
"Aih-h-h! . . . late . . . and wee-e-e . . . moul" (whiningly).
"How did you get such huge huge hands?"
"Threshing with an iron flail, threshing with an iron flail" (gruffly).
"How did you get such a small small neck?"
"Aih-h-h! . . . late . . . wee-e-e . . . moul" (pitifully).
"How did you get such a huge huge head?"
"Much knowledge, much knowledge" (keenly).
"What do you come for?"
"FOR YOU!" (At the top of the voice, with a wave of the arm and a stamp of the feet.)

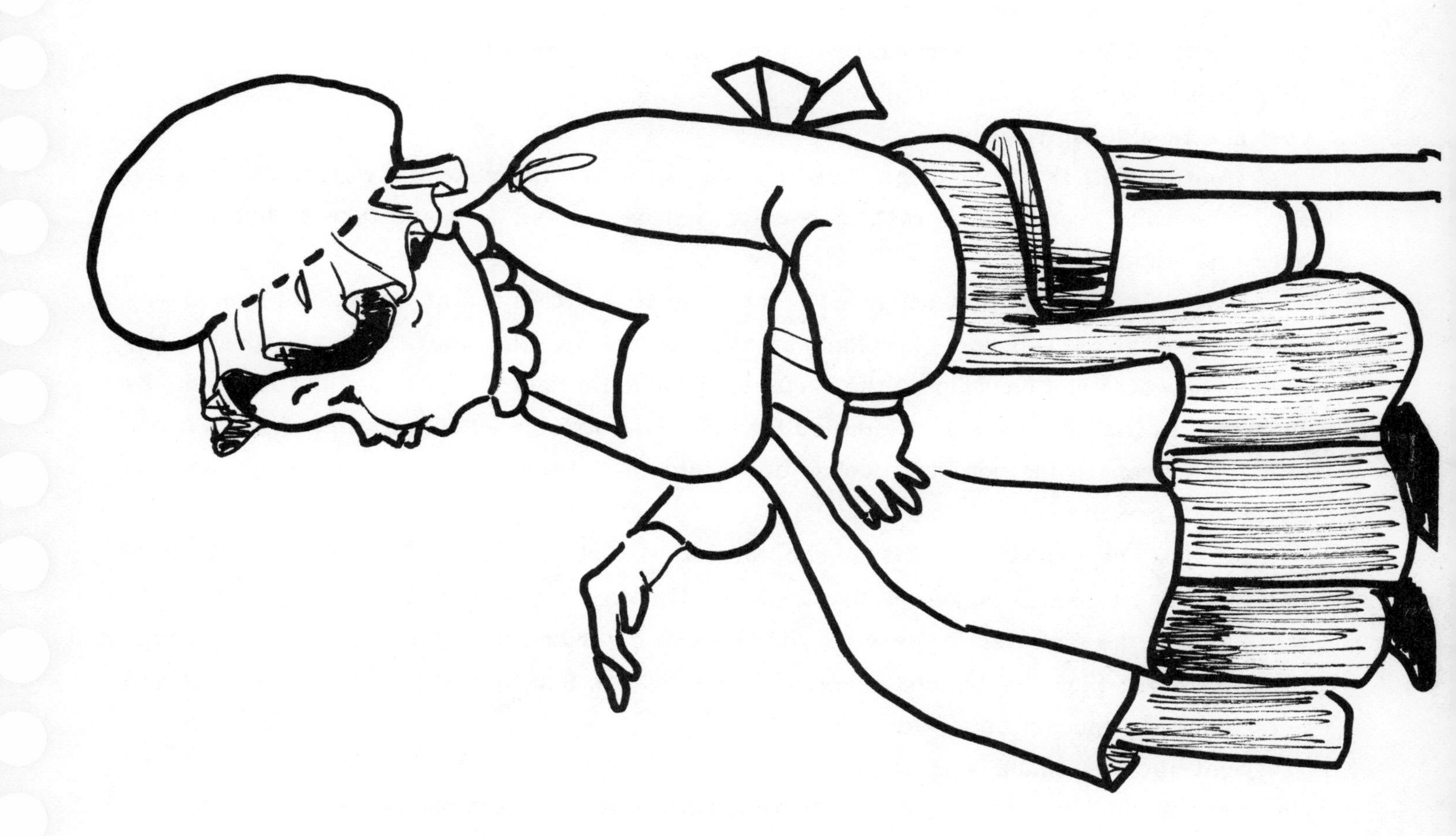

Scat - the - Cat

(Anonymous)

Once upon a time there was a little black cat whose name was Scat-the-Cat. One day he looked around and saw that all his brothers and sisters were black. He thought he would like to be some other color. So he sat up proud and said,

"I'm Scat-the-Cat (thumbs in armpits)
I'm Sassy and Fat (point finger and then shape fat figure with both hands)
And I can change my color (shake finger)
Just like that! (Snap fingers)

All of a sudden, at the snap of his fingers, he was a green cat. Green like the leaves and green like the grass. He went out to play with his friends, and what do you think happened? His friends did not see him because he was just the same color as the grass and the trees. He was so disappointed. He didn't think it was fun at all to be a green cat. So: (all join in)

"I'm Scat-the-Cat (thumbs in armpits)
I'm Sassy and Fat (point finger and then shape fat figure with both hands)
And I can change my color (shake finger)
Just like that! (Snap fingers)

And then what color was he? He was blue all over. Blue like the water, blue like the sky. He was so proud of his pretty new color that he decided he would take a walk and let everyone admire him.

But do you know what happened? He came to a little pond of water. He leaned way over to look at himself and - kerplop! Splash into the pond he went. Right down into the deep blue water and back up to the surface. Poor little Scat-the-Cat had not learned how to swim. He was frightened. He called for help. He called so loudly that his friends heard him. They ran to the pond and looked down into the blue water. They could not see him because he was blue like the water.

It just happened that his friend, Timothy Turtle came swimming by. He told Scat-the-Cat to climb up on his back. Then Timothy Turtle carried him safely back to shore. Scat-the-Cat was so grateful. He thanked his friend over and over again for saving his life. Right there he decided never to take a chance like that again. He thought he had been blue long enough so he said:

"I'm Scat-the-Cat (thumbs in armpits)
I'm Sassy and Fat (point finger and then shape fat figure with both hands)
And I can change my color (shake finger)
Just like that! (Snap fingers)

And what color was he then? He was yellow - yellow like the sun. He was very proud of his new color. He decided that he would take a walk through the jungle.

Whom do you suppose he met in the jungle? He met his cousin Leo, the Lion. Leo the Lion looked at Scat-the-Cat and said, "What are you doing in that yellow coat? I'm the only animal in the jungle that is supposed to wear yellow!" Leo the Lion growled a growl so fiercely that Scat-the-Cat was frightened, so frightened that he ran all the way home.

As soon as he was able to catch his breath, he said,

"I'm Scat-the-Cat (thumbs in armpits)
I'm Sassy and Fat (point finger and then shape fat figure with both hands)
And I can change my color (shake finger)
Just like that! (Snap fingers)

And what color was he then? He was red - red like an apple. He decided he would go out and play with his brothers and sisters and friends.

What do you suppose happened? When his friends and brothers and sisters saw him, they all stopped playing and stared at him. Then they started laughing and making fun of him. "Whoever heard of a red cat?" Do you think they were polite cats? No, they were not. They wouldn't play with him - they just kept laughing.

Scat-the-Cat felt embarrassed and a little sad. Soon he started thinking, and went off by himself. He decided he didn't want to be a red cat anymore, nor a yellow cat. And he didn't want to be a blue cat anymore, because he might not be so lucky next time to have Timothy Turtle help him. He didn't want to be green - because he would be like the grass and trees, and none of his friends would see him.

But do you know what he thought? He thought he would be just himself, a pretty black cat like his brothers and sisters and friends - and he would have lots of friends to play with.

So after that, Scat-the-Cat was always happy being himself - a black cat.

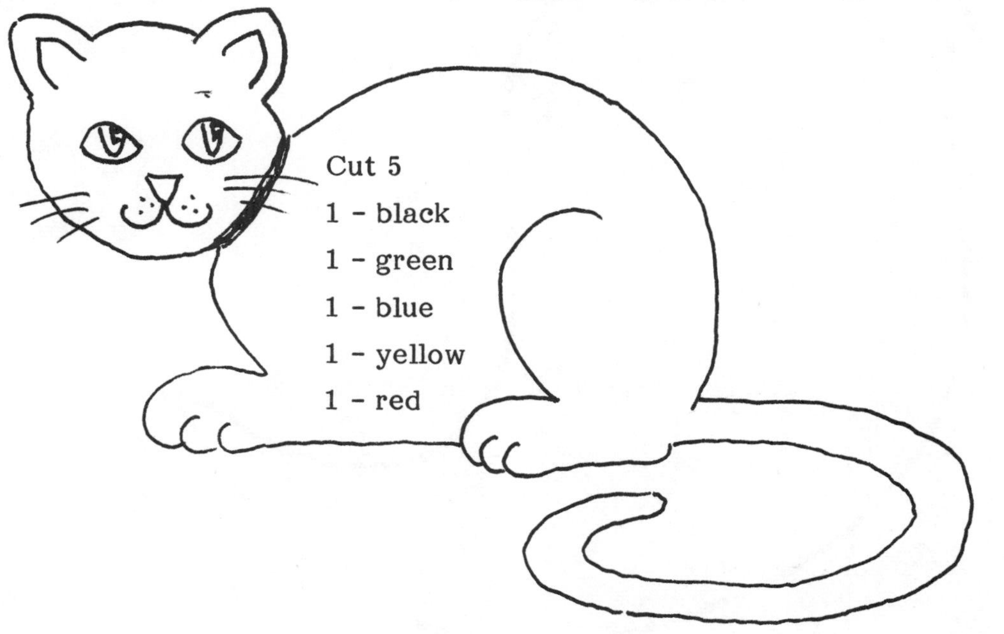

BOO!

IV. COOKING ACTIVITIES

Objective: To improve fine motor coordination through mixing, kneading, carving, decorating, cutting and mixing. Also to develop math skills by counting and measuring ingredients.

Evaluation: The children mixed, kneaded, carved, decorated, cut and mixed using a variety of utensils. They also counted and measured ingredients.

A. Peanut Butter Bugs

4 Tbls. peanut butter
1 Tbls. honey
1 Tbl. wheat germ
2½ Tbls. powdered milk

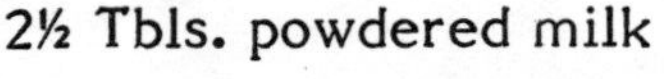

Mix together to form an easy to handle play-dough. Form into oval shapes. Add eyes, legs, wings, etc. Use your imagination! Great!!

B. Toasted Pumpkin Seeds

Carve pumpkin and remove seeds. Clean seeds and let dry on paper towel. Place dry seeds in shallow baking pan, dot with butter, sprinkle with salt. Bake at 350° for 20-30 minutes until brown. Stir occasionally. If an oven is not available, seeds may be fried in an electric fry pan, using oil or oil and butter, add salt. Drain.

C. Jack-O-Lantern Cake

Use small box of cake mix. Prepare as directed and bake in round cake pan. Frost with orange frosting (canned may be used). Add red and yellow food coloring to obtain desired color. Can use licorice, gumdrops, raisins and candy corn for features.

D. Orange Brew

2 6 oz. cans concentrated orange juice
1 C. water
2 C. milk
2 tsp. vanilla
20 ice cubes

Put everything in large blender and whip.

May be served in:

Cut top off orange and scoop out insides. Make face with black magic marker.

E. <u>Pumpkin Sandwiches</u>

Use two pieces of round pumpernickel bread, one piece American cheese. Cut out triangle eyes and nose and smiling mouth out of one piece of bread. Put cheese in middle, will look like light is shining through.

F. <u>Frosting Cookies</u>

Children decorate pumpkin-shaped cookies

<u>Frosting Recipe</u>

1 C. sifted confectioner's sugar

1/4 tsp. salt

1/2 tsp. vanilla

1-1/2 T. cream, milk or water (add or subtract for proper spreading consistency)

Mix well and divide into small individual dishes. Tint each with a few drops of different food colorings. Fill shakers or small dishes with colored sugar sprinkles or jimmies (chocolate sprinkles).

Make sure each child has his own dish of frosting, a spreading knife and choice of sprinkles. Let them spread on frosting and decorate with sprinkles.

G. <u>Peanut Butter Playdough</u>

1 C. peanut butter

1 C. honey

1 C. powdered milk

1 C. oatmeal

(food coloring optional) Make something beautiful and eat it!

H. Witch's Brew

Mix up a "Witch's Brew" with which to concoct a delicious potion to give to a friend or to brew for your group to sip while you tell them a story about witches.

Ingredients:

2/3 cup instant tea

14 ounces Tang (orange flavor)

2 packages dry lemonade mix

2 cups sugar

2 teaspoons cinnamon

2 teaspoons powdered cloves

Mix together and store in jars.

To brew: Add 1-1/2 to 2 teaspoons mix to 1 cup boiling water. Be sure to give directions for brewing on the jar's label if you give some as a gift.

V. MATH

Objective: To identify numbers and count to 20.

Evaluation: The children identified numbers and counted to 20.

A. Apple Tree

Cut out large tree and paste on poster board. Cut out and number 20 apples.

1. Tape apples to tree in numerical order
2. Identify number before placing on tree
3. Place apples on tree. Remove apples by specifying which number to harvest.

B. Mr. Bones

Display a skeleton which may be purchased or drawn. Children can count number of ribs, arm bones and leg bones.

C. Kitty Whiskers

Attach different colored whiskers to cat's face. Have children count them. Also have them count the number of a particular color of whiskers. Can remove the whiskers and repeat using different number of whiskers.

D. Trick or Treat Bag

Place Holloween treats in paper sack. Have children count goodies as they are removed from the bag. Goodies can also be categorized into candy, fruit, cookies, etc.

E. Halloween Shapes

Locate and identify the four basic shapes in the Halloween symbols. Look for circles, rectangles, squares, and triangles.

F. <u>Jack-O-Lantern Dot-to-Dot</u>

Make a large circle by printing the numbers from 1-10 in clockwise order. Draw eyes, nose, mouth, and stem. Connect the dots in numerical order. May be laminated to use again or duplicated.

VI. FINGERPLAYS AND SONGS

Objectives: To improve memory skills and counting skills through repetition.

Evaluation: During the following week we observed that most children remembered the words, numbers, and actions and were able to repeat them.

Peter, Peter

Peter, Peter pumpkin eater
Had a wife and couldn't keep her.
Put her in a pumpkin shell
And there he kept her very well

Five Little Pumpkins (can use felt objects)

Five little pumpkins sitting on a gate
The first one said - My it's getting late
The second one said - Who's there, who's there
The third one said - There are witches in the air
The fourth one said - Let's run, let's run
The fifth one said - It's only Halloween fun
Then Puff went the wind and out went the lights
Away went the pumpkins on Halloween night.

Yellow Pumpkin (Tune of "I'm a Little Teapot")

I'm a yellow pumpkin, fat and round
Growing in a cornfield, on the ground
I'll be a Jack-O-Lantern, wtih two big eyes
Or maybe I'll be baked in two fat pies.

Did You Ever See a Pumpkin? (Tune of Did You Ever See a Lassie?)

(Use felt board with large orange felt pumpkin, black felt eyes, nose, mouth.)

Did you ever see a pumpkin, a pumpkin, a pumpkin
Did you ever see a pumpkin with no face at all?
With no eyes (point) and no nose (point) and no mouth (point) and no teeth (point)
Did you ever see a pumpkin with no face at all?

So I made a Jack-O-Lantern, a Jack-O-Lantern, a Jack-O-Lantern
So I made a Jack-O-Lantern with a big, funny face.
With big eyes and big nose and big mouth and big teeth
So I made a Jack-O-Lantern with a big funny face.

BOO!
See my big and scary eyes
Watch out now, a big surprise. BOO!

Three Little Witches (Tune of Ten Little Indians)

One little, two little, three little witches
Fly over haystacks, Fly over ditches
Slide down the moon without any hitches
Heigh-Ho Halloween's here.

Stand on your head with a lop-sided wiggle
Tickle your black cats till they giggle
Swish through the air with a higgly piggle
Heigh-ho Halloween's here.

TEN LITTLE FINGERS

Suggestion: Count anything as working, playing, driving (flowers, cars, dishes, buildings)

<u>Five Little Fishies</u>

Five little fishies swimming in a pool,
(wiggle five fingers)
First one said, "The pool is cool."
(wrap arms around body)
Second one said, "The pool is deep."
(voice deep)
Third one said, "I want to sleep."
(rest head on hands)
Fourth one said, "Let's dive and dip."
(hand dives and dips)
Fifth one said, "I spy a ship."
(peer out under hand)
Fisherman boat comes,
(fingers form V and move away from body)
Line goes ker-splash,
(pantomime throwing fishing line)
Away the five little fishies dash.
(wiggle five fingers away)

FUNNY LITTLE LADY

A fun-ny lit-tle la-dy with a
(Make pointed hat with hands on top

point-ed hat, on my door went rap, rap, rap
of head) (pantomime Knocking)

When I went to o-pen it, she was not there,
(pantomime opening door) (shake head) but

up on her broomstick high in the air.
(point to sky)

Eentsy Weentsy Spider

The eentsy, weentsy spider went up the water spout.

(make circles out of thumbs and forefingers - put tips together - twist upward)

Down came the rain and washed the spider out;

(wiggle fingers while moving downward - push outward)

Out came the sun and dried up all the rain;

(make a big circle with arms over head)

And the eentsy, weentsy spider went up the spout again.

(make circles out of thumbs and forefingers - put together - twist upward)

VII. SCIENCE

Objective: To discover how red and yellow make orange

Evaluation: The color orange was made from red and yellow

A. Paper Towel Magic

Fold paper towel several times and dip into red colored water and then into yellow colored water. Open the towel carefully and allow it to dry. Orange designs will appear on the paper. May be mounted on construction paper.

Objective: To explore indoor environment

Evaluation: Many interesting things were discovered in the room.

B. A Rainy Day Walk Inside

Take a walk in our schoolroom and see what we can find. Look for things made of wood. Touch them all. Find things made of glass. Hunt for big things, hunt for blue things, etc. Hunt for opposites.

Objective: To observe the different properties of leaves

Evaluation: We collected leaves and observed their differences

C. Take a Fall Walk

On a day when the weather is crisp, dress the children appropriately and take a walk through the neighborhood. Observe the changes that are occurring all around us; the leaves in the trees, the different types of flowers, birds flying south and the different smells in the air.

D. Matching Leaves

On a fall walk, have children collect a variety of leaves in individual paper bags. Back in the classroom, have children sort the leaves into piles. Teacher can have large poster board displaying different types of leaves. Children can match their leaves with teacher's.

E. <u>Science activities with water</u>

Plants actually "drink" water from the ground or soil. Put a piece of celery into a glass of water and a few drops of red food color. Soon the celery will show red streaks as the piece of celery drinks the water.

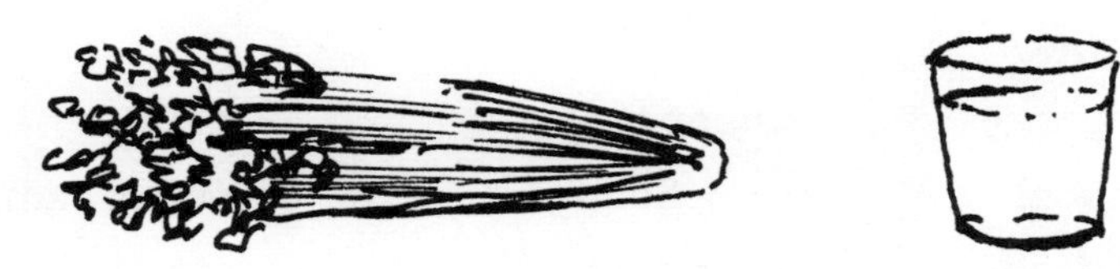

Here are some experiments using zip lock bags.

Fill bag 1/2 way with water and ask the children, "What color is it?"

Fill bag 1/2 way with water, zip shut and turn it all around. Children will see the water keeps level.

Look through the water in the bag and ask the children, "What do things look like when you see them through the water?"

Fill the bag with water and zip it shut. Put two pinholes into bag. One at the top and one near the bottom. Squirt out the water and ask the children, "Through which hole does the water shoot out farther?"

F. Grow your own <u>Witch's Crystal Garden</u>

Materials neded:

Porous bricks or charcoal briquettes	1/4 cup salt
Food coloring	1/4 cup laundry bluing
1 taplespoon of ammonia	1/4 cup water

How to: Put two drops of food coloring on the brick or charcoal. Mix together remaining ingredients and slowly pour onto brick. Enough for 4-6 bricks. The garden will begin to grow into weird and wonderful shapes in a few hours.

G. Sinking and floating

Materials:

- dishpan
- water
- cork
- sponge
- spool
- spoon
- rubber ball
- Ivory Soap
- other soap
- coins
- styrofoam
- stones

Directions:

1. Fill a dishpan about half full of water.
2. Put sinking and floating objects next to dishpan.
3. Let children float and sink the objects.
4. Ask questions:
   Will this sink or float?
   Which one will sink first?
   Is this heavy or light?
5. Use any safe household objects for the children to try out.
6. A good activity for the bathtub too!

Sink and float Jello

In a clear pyrex bowl make a package of fruit flavored Jello following directions on the box.

When slightly cool add different types of fruits or vegetables to see if they sink or float.

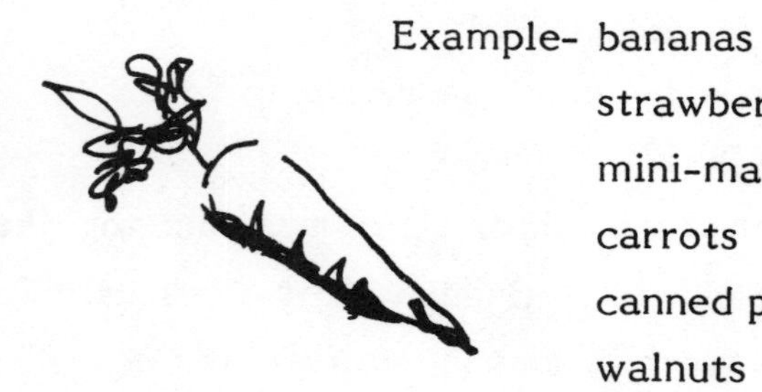

Example- bananas
strawberries
mini-marshmallows
carrots
canned pineapple
walnuts

Some will float, some will sink - talk about why.
Chill and serve -

VIII. PHYSICAL DEVELOPMENT GAMES

Objective: To increase social interaction, improve good sportsmanship and have fun.
Evaluation: The children played well with each other, learned to take turns, be a better loser or winner and had fun.

A. Halloween Walk

Line up on one side of room. Cross room in following ways:
Fly like a bat, gallop like a cowboy on a horse, hop like a bunny, roll like a pumpkin, dance like a princess, creep like a cat, walk like a skeleton, float like a ghost, stomp like a monster.

B. Halloween Chatter

Cackle like a witch, screech like a cat, hoot like an owl, make spooky noises like a ghost.

C. Halloween Treasure Hunt

Give each child a paper bag. Show them some of the Halloween-type things you have hidden in the room such as a skeleton, black cat, apple, pumpkin, etc. Have the children find as many of the things as they can and put them into their bags. Then have each of the children tell a story about one of the things they have found.

D. Filling in the features - What's missing?

Have children look at the two faces and point out how they are alike - ask them, "Is this face the same as the other face? Are both eyes looking in the same direction? Both smiling?", etc.

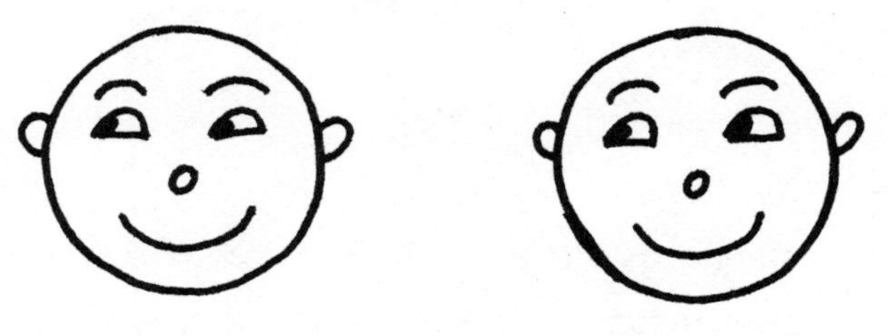

Now look at these faces - one face needs a line drawn in - can you do it? (some children may need help from an adult).

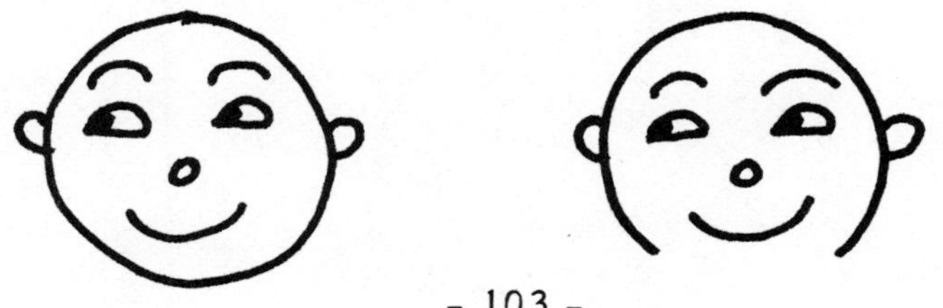

D. Filling in the features - What's missing? (continued)

What is missing in this face? Can you draw it in?

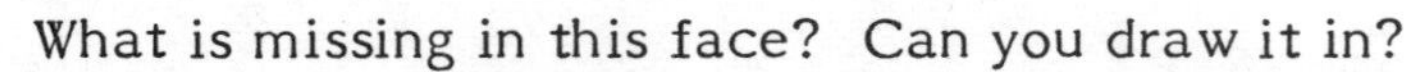

What is missing in this face? Can you draw it in?

What is missing in this face? Can you draw it in?

E. Drop the Witch into a Jar

Decorate clothes pins with a witch's face. Have children drop them into a jar. When jar is filled, have children count them - to improve coordination and counting skills.

F. Pass the Pumpkin

Put on a record. Use small pumpkin. Have children sit in a circle and pass pumpkin until music stops. Child with pumpkin gets pumpkin sticker. Last child without sticker gets to choose another game and gets two stickers.

G. Doggie, Doggie, Where's Your Bone?

Children sit in circle with hands closed in lap. A child selected as "doggie" leaves room or sits in center of circle and covers eyes. A small block (the bone) is placed under chair. A child from circle is selected to tiptoe up, take bone and sit down in same place in circle with bone hidden underneath him. Then all say:

"Doggie, doggie where's your bone
Hurry up and bring it home."

The doggie uncovers eyes and has three guesses to find bone, etc.

H. Halloween

Paper pumpkin hunt: hide paper pumpkins around room and have children search for them.

Blindfold game of pin the nose (or mouth) on the pumpkin.

Blindfold game of put the hat on the witch.

Pin the tail on the cat.

DRAMATIC PLAY

Objective: To express themselves freely and become uninhibited in their actions through role play.

Evaluation: The children used props and expressed themselves freely.

Children love to dramatize. It is an integral part of their learning experience. A box of discarded clothing, shoes and hats is a great source of enjoyment for them.

Dramatic play kits to be made up:

Ice Cream Parlor

- Empty ice cream cartons
- Cones made from paper
- Plastic spoons
- Small empty margarine tubs
- Napkins
- Yarn pom-poms in various colors for ice cream scoops

Grocery Store

- Empty food containers
- Grocery bags
- Play money
- Cash register or muffin tin

Beauty Parlor

- Old hair dryers (cord removed)
- Rollers, hair clips, barrettes
- Combs, brushes
- Unbreakable mirror
- Empty shampoo bottles
- Empty make-up jars
- Powder puffs
- Smock

Hospital

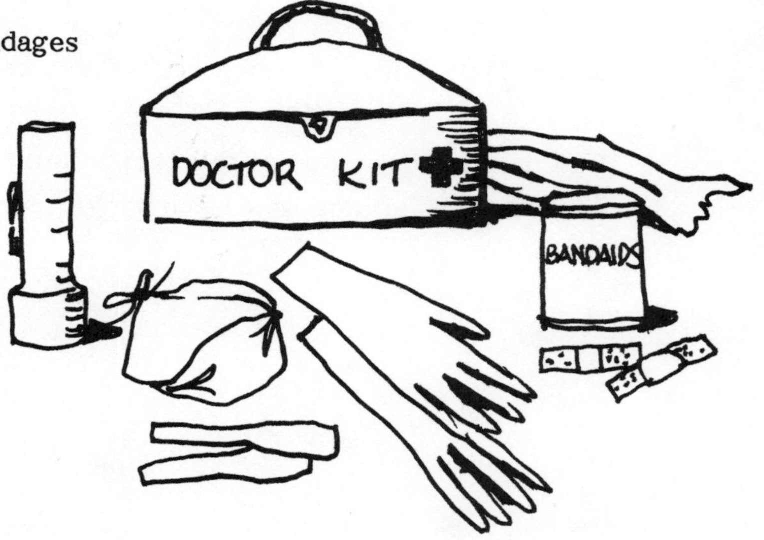

- Torn sheets for slings and bandages
- Doctor and nurse kit
- Band aids
- Tongue depressors
- Small flashlight
- Rubber gloves
- Inexpensive masks
- Simple paper hats

Birthday Party

- Hats
- Balloons
- Wrapping paper, boxes, ribbons
- Blowers
- Pretend cake
- Pin the Tail on the Donkey game
- Clothespins and a container

Picnic

- Basket
- Tablecloth or blanket
- Pitcher
- Plastic silverware
- Paper plates and cups
- Small clean grill

Beach

- Towels
- Beach ball
- Swimsuits
- Sunglasses
- Empty suntan bottles
- Float toys
- Inner tube
- Sand pails and shovels

Baby

- Bottles, pacifiers, bibs, spoons, diapers
- Bathtub, small towel and cloth
- Rattles, blankets, baby dish

IX. FIELD TRIPS

Objectives: To increase an awareness of their surroundings.

Evaluation: Children become more familiar with their surroundings outside their neighborhood.

A. Pumpkin Patch
B. Detroit Zoo
C. Cranbrook - bees
D. Farm trip
E. Cider Mill

X. BOOKS AND RELATED ACTIVITIES

Hunting Witch	Balian, Lorna
The Halloween Party	Andersen, Lenzo
Hester	Barten, Byron
Wabble the Witch Cat	Calhoun, Mary
Georgie	Bright, Robert
Georgie's Halloween	Bright, Robert
Space Witch	Freeman, Don
How Spider Saved Halloween	Kraus, Robert
Trick or Treat	Slobodkin, Lewis
Tillie Witch	Freeman, Don
Millions and Millions of Cats	Gag, Wanda
There's a Nightmare in My Closet	Meyer, Mercer
Where the Wild Things Are	Sendak, Maurice
Mr. and Mrs. Opposite	Tester, Sylvia
Scienceland:	Scienceland Inc. 501 Fifth Avenue New York, NY 10017
What Makes a Shadow?	Bulla
Clifford's Halloween	Bredwell
Good Night Moon	Wise Brown
The Witch Next Door	Bredwell
Record: Witches Brew	Hap Palmer

NOVEMBER

I. ARTS AND CRAFTS

Objective: All these activies are developed to increase small motor coordination.

Evaluation: The children will color, draw, cut, tear, paint, stuff, grate and string to increase small motor coordination.

A. Hand Turkey

Child or teacher draws around child's open hand held palm down on paper. Fingers are the tail and thumb is the head. Child adds feet, wattle and colors.

B. Pine Cone Turkey

Pine cone, cocktail toothpicks, muffin cup paper liner, 4" white or brown pipe cleaner, small piece of red pipe cleaner.

Put pine cone on its side. Fold muffin cup liner in half and insert at large end for a fan of tail feathers. Toothpicks are stuck in for legs. Stick 4" pipe cleaner in small end for neck. Loop end of pipe cleaner into a head. Fasten red pipe cleaner to head for wattle.

C. <u>POTATO TURKEY</u>

Potato, toothpicks with ruffled cellophane ends, colored cocktail toothpicks, 4" white or brown pipe cleaner, small piece of red pipe cleaner, golf tees.

Stick 3 party toothpicks and as many colored ones as desired into one end of potato for feathers. Insert 4" pipe cleaner in other end and loop to make head. Add red pipe cleaner wattle, add legs of golf tees.

D. <u>Thankful Book</u>

Have children do one or more pages each day. Adult can put book together with a cardboard or construction paper cover.

I'm glad for hands that clap for fun
(child's handprints)
I'm glad for feet to jump and run
(draw around feet and color)
I'm glad for my mother who cooks for me
I'm glad for my father who is as tall as can be
(photo of them or magazine pictures)
I'm glad for this baby who sleeps all day
(draw or cut out picture)
I'm glad for the children who laugh and play
(pictures of same)
I'm glad for the trees that stand up tall
(sponge paint or paste on)
That shake their leaves and let them fall
(sponge paint or paste)
I'm glad for the birds that fly up high
Up in the trees and up in the sky
(use bird gummed stickers)

E. <u>Hand Print Turkey</u>

Paint each finger on child's hand a different color. Paint their thumbs and palms brown and press their hands on paper. Add beak, eyes, wattle, etc.

F. Indians - Salt Clay

1. Mix 1 c. flour with 1 c. salt
2. Add a little cool water and mix with hands. If too dry, add a little more water.
3. Mix until you have a ball of clay; firm, not sticky. If too sticky, add more flour. Store in plastic bag.

To make plates:

Take a small piece of clay and press it flat with your hands. Use the round part of a measuring spoon to shape it.

To make saucers and cups:

Use a bottle cap to cut out clay. For cups, make small round ball of clay. Punch your finger into middle and shape clay around it. Pinch clay out a little on one side to make handle.

Let dry 24 hours, paint. Can make designs with thin paint brush.

To make canoe:

Press ball of salt clay into flat rectangle. Fold in half lengthwise. Press each end together to make a point. Press sides slightly rounded and bottom and inside flat.

To make paddle:

Shape clay around one end of toothpick.

Let dry and paint.

F. Indian Headband

Measure around head and cut a 2 inch wide piece of construction paper that length with 2" left over. Paint and decorate it. Staple closed. Draw leaf shapes on 2" x 8" pieces of colored paper and cut out. May cut slits into the paper to make them look like feathers. Staple or paste on feathers.

Have a "feather hunt". Hide feathers around room and have children find them. Put rouge on their faces for war paint. Make chain necklaces or string dyed macaroni, cut straws, cranberries, Fruit Loops or shapes cut out of colored construction paper. Sing "Ten Little Indians."

G. **Sand Painting** use white cornmeal

1. Pour some cornmeal into several small bowls. Sprinkle a few drops of food coloring over meal, using a different color for each dish and mash the mixtures around with a spoon until meal is all colored.
2. Draw a design on a piece of heavy paper.
3. Spread glue on the lines of the design. Sprinkle different colors of cornmeal mixture over glue. Let dry and gently shake off loose cornmeal.

H. Tepee

Decorate 12" circle of brown paper with Indian picture writing. Slit circle from edge to center. Fold and staple. May cut flap.

I. Indian Vest

Cut a large grocery bag along the dotted lines as shown in diagram. Decorate vest with Indian symbols and fringe bottom.

J. Triangle Pilgrims

K. Paper Bag Turkey

Stuff paper bag with paper, twist at tip and put rubber band around. Cut feathers, feet and gobbler and paste on.

L. Paper Bag Pilgrim

Stuff small lunch bag with newspaper, staple shut. Paint bag black. Cut out white figures and paste on dried paint.

M. Cornucopia

Children can cut out cornucopia from piece of brown paper. Paste on large sheet of paper. Children can tear pieces of different color paper up to represent different kinds of harvest foods.

N. Box Turkey

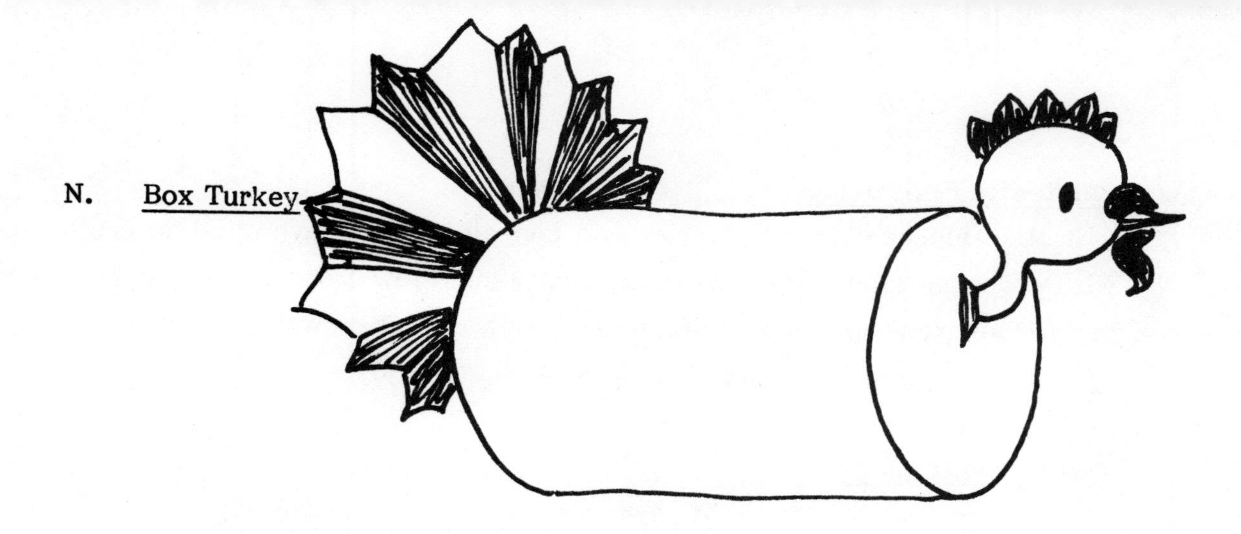

Use either oatmeal or salt box. Wrap brown paper around box and paste. Cut tail feathers from colored paper and paste on one end of box. Cut head from brown paper and paste on other end. Cut into end of neck and fold so it will be easier to paste onto box.

O. Indian Drum

Tape oatmeal box lid on, paint. Decorate with Indian designs.

P. Tie Dye

Make your dyes using natural materials as Indians used to do.
For yellow use saffron, crocuses, daffodils or yellow onionskins.
For green use young grass, broccoli, spinach, escarole.
For blue use blueberries.
For red use beets.
For brown use coffee, tea or walnut shells.

Place in an enamel pot and cover with water. Boil 5 minutes (longer to make colors darker). Strain through a colander. Cool. Cut or tear pieces of white cotton (from an old sheet). Have children dip cloth in colors.

Q. Paint With Fruit Juices

Use blueberries, raspberries and cooked beets. Have children crush them with a wooden spoon in a plastic container (add a few drops of vinegar to prevent mold from growing). Have children use paint brushes on white paper.

Read "Pele's New Suit" by Else Beskaw.

R. Turkey Centerpiece

Materials: 2 lightweight paper plates, glue, and scraps of paper.

Fold one plate in half. Color it to look like a turkey's body and draw wings. The second plate will be used to make a tail. Cut as shown below. Color bright feathers on both sides. Make the inside circle brown. Two inches from the back of the body, cut a slit, slanting it a little toward the front. Cut two heads from colored paper. Glue them together and add eyes, beak, and wattle. Slide the head in place in a 1-inch slit along fold line and glue it. Insert the tail in the slit cut at back of body.

S. Wampum Necklace

Cut a section of yarn about 25" long (or use thin craft wire). Tie a large piece of macaroni to one end and wrap the other end of yarn with tape to make needle. String wagon wheel macaroni, rigatoni, Fruit Loops, cheerios, pieces of colored paper, or 1" pieces of straw. Rigatoni or macaroni can be colored - dip in small bowls of water mixed with food coloring. Dry on paper towels.

Bulletin Boards

Large piece of poster board.

Class Project: Draw big turkey. Cut 3" to 4" squares of colored tissue paper, yellow, brown, orange, etc. Have children cover turkey with paste or Elmer's Glue, crumple up tissue paper in their hands and stick them on.

Barnyard Turkeys

Paint hands using brown, yellow, red, or orange. Have them make prints all over barnyard. Draw on feet and wattle or make thumbprint wattle. Put children's names under their print.

Popcorn Tree: Use air popper. Pop corn with children. Draw tree trunk and branches on large construction paper. Have children paste or glue on popcorn.

Sing "I'm a Little Popcorn" (see songs).

Read Popcorn Book by Tommy de Paola.

Cut out large tepee from brown paper. Paint children's 4 fingers and palm and have them print on Indian faces.

II. COLOR DAY - BROWN

Objective: To recognize color brown.

Evaluation: The following day children were able to find brown in their clothes and around room.

Have children wear something brown. Bring in and hold up bag of different brown objects. Use brown in craft, easel paint, and in snack (make chocolate pudding). Can do finger painting with chocolate pudding for craft.

Read Brown Bear, Brown Bear by Bill Martin Jr., pictures by Eric Carle.

III. STORY

Objective: To develop an appreciation of literature. To improve color recognition.

Evaluation: Children enjoyed story and recognized colors.

Tommy Turkey

Tommy was all brown and didn't like the way he looked. he went for a walk and met a duck who was yellow and orange. The duck said, "Ha, ha, ha, ho, ho, hee. You're the funniest turkey I ever did see." Tommy said, "I want to be yellow and orange like you." So he put on yellow and orange feathers and didn't like them. Then he met a snake who said, "Ha, ha, ha, ho, ho, hee, your're the funniest turkey I ever did see. Tommy said, "I want to be green like you." So he put on the green feathers and didn't like them. Then he met a cardinal who said, "Ha, ha, ha, ho, ho, hee, you're the funniest turkey I ever did see." Tommy said, "I want to be red like you. So he put the red feathers on and didn't like them either.

Then he met the wise old owl. Tommy said, "I don't like the way I look, Mr. Owl." Mr. Owl suggested that the children give him a bath and make all the colors run together. Well, he was the happiest and most beautiful turkey in the world, and this is how the turkey got so many colors.

red
yellow
orange
brown

Mr. Purple's Thanksgiving Dinner

(Author unknown)

Mr. Purple opened his box of holiday decorations. He pushed aside the purple pumpkin. He pulled the cone-shaped horn of plenty from under his purple Christmas wreath.

"I shall fill this horn with purple plums and purple grapes," he said. "Now I shall plan my specialThanksgiving dinner. What shall I cook? Turkey is too ordinary. Ham, the same."

Mr. Purple went to the kitchen cupboard. "I have cans of soup, cartons of crackers, peaches, and potatoes," he said, "but I have nothing special for Thanksgiving dinner."

Mr. Purple put on his purple coat. He went to the bakery. He saw tall wedding cakes and French apple pies. "These are not what I want," he said, "for my Thanksgiving dinner."

He went to the grocery store. He saw cans, boxes, and bags of food. "But there is nothing for a special Thanksgiving dinner," said Mr. Purple.

He felt very sad. His mustache drooped. He walked slowly down the street.

Mr. Purple saw his friend, Mrs. Rainbow, waiting for the bus. She looked very sad, too. "What is wrong?" asked Mr. Purple.

"I want to make a special Thanksgiving dinner," said Mrs. Rainbow, "but I cannot decide what to cook."

"I have the same problem," said Mr. Purple. "In my cupboard I have soup and crackers, peaches and potatoes. But nothing special."

"I have only peas and pork chops in my kitchen," said Mrs. Rainbow. She sighed. "I am going home to read my cookbook. Dinnertime will come soon. I must find a special Thanksgiving meal."

Mr. Purple waved good-bye to Mrs. Rainbow. He went home also. He remembered how sad Mrs. Rainbow had looked. He went to the kitchen. He peeled and boiled potatoes. He simmered soup. He put the hot pots in a big box and added the crackers and peaches. Then he went to Mrs. Rainbow's house.

"Hello again, Mr. Purple." said Mrs. Rainbow when she answered the door. "Come in."

Mr. Purple went right to the kitchen. Mrs. Rainbow followed.

"I have brought soup and crackers, potatoes and peaches," said Mr. Purple. "I will help you prepared the pork chops and peas. If we put our food together, we will have..."

"A whole meal," said Mrs. Rainbow.

"Sharing what we have, we will have a special Thanksgiving dinner," said Mr. Purple.

"Of course!" said Mrs. Rainbow. "Thanksgiving does not come in boxes, cans, or cookbooks."

She began to prepare the pork chops while Mr. Purple put the soup on to simmer.

The Story of the Pilgrims

(Author unknown)

A long time ago, the people of England were ruled by a cruel king named King James. He ordered all of the English people to go to his church. If they refused, he put them in prison.

One group of people did not like the King's church. They wanted to worship in their own way. One night when it was very dark, they got on a big ship and sailed across the waters to find a new home.

(Song - "Sailing")

This group of people were called "Pilgrims." A Pilgrim is one who travels from country to country.

They sailed to Holland, the land of the Dutch people. Holland is a land of windmills and canals. The windmills were used to pump the water off the land and into the canals.

(Song - "Windmills")

In Holland, the Pilgrims were free to worship God the way they thought was right. The Dutch people were very kind to them. The boys and girls played with the Dutch children, and soon learned to wear wooden shoes like their Dutch friends.

(Song - "Wooden Shoes")

The Pilgrim boys and girls also began to learn to speak the Dutch language.

Although the Pilgrim mothers and fathers were very happy in Holland, they did not want their children to grow up to be Dutch people.

They began to talk about America, the new land which Columbus had discovered. They said, "In America, we could have our own church. Our children would speak English and grow up to be English men and women." So they decided to leave Holland and sail to America. This time they sailed across the ocean in a ship called the "Mayflower."

(Sailing)

It was wintertime when the Mayflower reached America. The Pilgrim fathers cut down trees in the forest and made log cabins for their families.

Friendly Indians showed them how to hunt and fish. In the spring they gave them corn and showed them how to plant it.

(Indians)

There were plenty of deer and wild turkeys in the forest. In the fall the Pilgrims had a fine harvest. They said, "Let us have a special day to thank God for our good harvest and all this food."

They decided to have a big feast and invite their Indian friends. The fathers brought wild turkeys, deer meat, and fish. The mothers made puddings, baked bread and pumpkin pies. The Indians brought wild cranberries, nuts and maple sugar.

(Getting Ready)

When the food was all cooked and on the table, the Pilgrims said prayers to thank God for their blessings in the new land.

The Indians had such a good time at this First Thanksgiving that they stayed for three days!

Today we still cerebrate "Thanksgiving Day" with a feast, but each one of us should remember to do as the Pilgrims did, and thank God for all our blessings in America.

This story can lead to a discussion of how our country has grown and changed.

A THANKSGIVING BASKET

(Author unknown)

It was the day before Thanksgiving Day. Little Gray Squirrel was sitting all alone in her house in the hollow oak tree.

Gray Squirrel could not run about like the other squirrels. One day, when she had been out gathering nuts for the wintertime, she had caught her foot in a trap that some bad boys had set in the woods.

She had pulled and pulled, and, at last, she had managed to get her foot out of the trap. But her foot was broken! Poor Gray Squirrel had hopped and jumped on one foot, and, somehow, she had managed to reach home.

That had happened more than a month ago. All that time Gray Squirrel could not move outside the door of her house. Before she had hurt her foot she had gathered a few nuts. She had eaten only a few each day to make them last. Now they were all gone and tomorrow was Thanksgiving Day! Poor little Gray Squirrel! She felt very sad sitting there all alone.

"I wonder how Gray Squirrel is getting along," said Mrs. Red Squirrel to herself. "It's a shame! I haven't been to see her for days and days. I know what I'll do! I'll fix up a basket of good things and take them down to her for her Thanksgiving dinner."

Mrs. Red Squirrel took her biggest basket down from the hook. From the cupboard in her hollow-tree home she filled the basket with as many chestnuts as she thought she could carry. Then she started off for little Gray Squirrel's house.

Soon she cam to Mrs. Brown Squirrel's house. Mrs. Brown Squirrel was out in her garden digging up some of the nuts she had put there for the winter.

"Good Afternoon, Mrs. Red Squirrel," said Mrs. Brown Squirrel. "Where are you going with your basket this lovely day?"

"I'm going down to little Gray Squirrel's house to take her a Thanksgiving dinner," answered Mrs. Red Squirrel.

"Oh, do let me put some of these hickory nuts into your basket," said Mrs. Brown Squirrel. "I have plenty, and I shall feel so happy to think that I can give some of them to little Gray Squirrel."

Mrs. Brown Squirrel put so many hickory nuts into the basket that Mrs. Red Squirrel had all she could do to carry it.

"Thank you kindly, Mrs. Brown Squirrel," said she, and off she started again.

Soon she came to Mr. Rabbit's bramble house. Mrs. Rabbit was standing at the door.

"Good afternoon, Mrs. Red Squirrel," said she. "Where are you going this lovely day?"

"I'm going down to little Gray Squirrel's house to take her a Thanksgiving basket," answered kind Mrs. Red Squirrel.

"Oh, just wait a minute!" said Mrs. Rabbit. I have something that I can send, too. Some boys were having a picnic the other day, in the woods back of my house. When they went away I ran around there and found ever so many good things they had left. Wait just a minute and I will get them from my cupboard."

Mrs. Rabbit ran into her house and opened her cupboard in the dry grass and straw.

"Come in, Mrs. Red Squirel," she called; "come in with your basket." And Mrs. Red Squirrel went into the little bramble house.

"Here are the peanuts I found," said Mrs. Rabbit. "I know Gray Squirrel will like them. I have plenty of cabbage and carrots stored away, and I really don't need the peanuts. You may take this red apple too. Perhaps Gray Squirrel will eat it."

"Thank you," said Mrs. Red Squirrel. "You are very, very kind.

"Oh, no, not at all!" said Mrs. Rabbit. "It makes me feel so happy to think that I can help little Gray Squirrel."

"Thank you, all the same," said Mrs. Red Squirrel. And once more she started off for little Gray Squirrel's house.

The basket was very heavy now, and it was all Mrs. Red Squirrel could do to carry it.

"Why, Mrs. Red Squirrel!" said a voice, "where are you going with that heavy basket?"

Mrs. Red Squirrel looked about and saw Mr. Rabbit sitting among the brambles by the roadside.

"I am going down to little Gray Squirrel's house to take her a Thanksgiving basket," answered Mrs. Red Squirrel.

"Did you stop at our house?" Mr. Rabbit asked. "I think Mrs. Rabbit may have something for your basket."

"Yes, I stopped at the house on my way," said Mrs. Red Squirrel, "and Mrs. Rabbit gave me some peanuts and a red apple for my basket."

"I am very glad she thought of them," said Mr. Rabbit. "Now, you must let me help you carry that heavy basket."

"Oh, thank you," said Mrs. Red Squirrel, "but I think I can manage it the rest of the way. I'm almost there now."

"Never mind," said Mr. Rabbit, "I can help you carry it for even a litte way." And he took hold of the other side of the heavy basket.

Mrs. Red Squirrel was very glad to have Mr. Rabbit's help, for the basket was indeed too much for her to carry along.

They soon reached the hollow oak tree in which little Gray Squirrel lived. Mr. Rabbit knocked at the little door.

"Who's there?" called a sad little voice.

"How do you do, little Gray Squirrel?" answered Mr. Rabbit. "This is Mrs. Red Squirrel. She has brought you a Thanksgiving basket." And they opened the door and went in.

Little Gray Squirrel had been crying because she felt so lonely and hungry.

"Oh, Mrs. Red Squirrel," said she, "how can I thank you!"

Then Mrs. Red Squirrel told little Gray Squirrel about Mrs. Brown Squirrel and Mrs Rabbit. "And Mr. Rabbit helped me carry the basket," said she.

Little Gray Squirrel felt very happy to know that she had so many friends. Tomorrow would be Thanksgiving indeed!

The wonderful Thanksgiving basket lasted little Gray Squirrel all winter long, and that was all she needed, for, when the warm springtime came, her foot was quite well and she could run about again.

THANKSGIVING TURKEY

Hobble goes the turkey,	(Hands on hips, squat down,
See him strut along.	and walk "turkey fashion")
Gobble says the turkey,	(Rise up slightly, stretch neck)
He'll not be here long!	(Run and hide)

Use tom-tom to beat the rhythm.

Hobble goes the turkey

The Old Lady and the Turkey

Once upon a time there lived an old lady who had scrimped and saved all year to buy a turkey for her Thanksgiving dinner. When it was nearly Thanksgiving, she went to the market and bought the plumpest little turkey her money could buy and stuffed it into her shopping basket. Then she set off home thinking of the fine dinner she would have.

By and by, she came to a gate which she could not open, burdened as she was with her basket and her turkey. "Oh, deary me," she sighed,"what am I to do? If I can't open the gate, how am I going to get my turkey home for my Thanksgiving dinner?"

As she said the word "turkey," an elf appeared on the gate. "If you will invite me to share that turkey with you, old lady," he said, "I will open the gate for you."

"Gladly," said the old lady.

In a twinkling of an eye, the elf opened the gate and the old lady went on her way.

By and by, she came to a stile and, try as she might, the old lady could not get the turkey over the stile.

"Oh, my, oh, my!" she cried. "What am I to do? If I can't get the turkey over the stile, I can't get it home to cook for Thanksgiving dinner!"

Up popped a leprechaun. "Turkey!" he said. "My favorite! If you will do me the honor of inviting me to partake of a bit of that delicious-looking bird, old lady, I'll have it over that stile in a jiffy."

"Gladly," said the old lady, "for if I don't, I will never get my turkey home, and I won't have any Thanksgiving dinner, and neither will the elf."

So the leprechaun put his hand on the handle of the basket and said a magic word. The basket (and the turkey and the old lady, too) floated over the stile as easily as if they were feathers. And the old lady was on her way again.

By and by, she came to a rickety old bridge over a rushing stream. The old lady tried with all her might, but she could not carry the heavy basket over the bridge.

"Oh, mercy me, what am I to do?" she cried. "If I can't get the turkey over the bridge, I'll never get it home in time to cook it for Thanksgiving dinner."

"Turkey?" A fierce-looking troll poked his head out from under the bridge. "I love it! If you ask me to dinner, I'll get the turkey across for you, old lady."

"Gladly," said the old lady, "for if I do not, I will never get my turkey home, and I won't have any Thanksgiving dinner, and neither will the elf nor the leprechaun."

The troll jumped from under his bridge, tucked the turkey under his arm, and before the old lady could say, "Jack Robinson," they were all across the stream.

The old lady went on her way, and by and by she came to a farmyard where her way was barred by an angry, barking dog.

"Oh, dear, now what am I to do?" the old lady wailed. "The dog will have my Thanksgiving dinner instead!"

"Oh, no, he won't, old lady!" said a goblin sitting under the hedge. "If you ask me to share your dinner, I'll deal with that old fleabag this minute."

"Gladly," she said, "for if I do not, I will never get my turkey home, and I won't have any Thanksgiving dinner, neither will the elf nor the leprechaun nor the troll."

The goblin jumped astride the dog's back as if he were riding a horse. The startled dog yelped and ran away as fast as ever he could.

The old lady again set off for home but, by and by, she came to a flooded place in the road.

"Oh, mercy, mercy," sobbed the old lady, "now how can I get my turkey home to cook for Thanksgiving dinner?"

"Turkey!" cackled a witch, swooping down on her broomstick. "If you invite me to share your Thanksgiving dinner, I can soon have you over the water."

"Gladly," said the old lady, "for if I do not, I will never get my turkey home, and I won't have any Thanksgiving dinner, neither will the elf nor the leprechaun nor the troll nor the goblin."

So the witch took the old lady and her basket and her turkey on her broomstick, and in two shakes of a lamb's tail they were over the water. Now at last the old lady made her way safely home.

It was with a heavy heart the old lady awoke on Thanksgiving Day. Her turkey, which had seemed too big and plump at the market, now looked very small for six to share. She had no money left and the cupboard was nearly bare. She stuffed the turkey the best she could and put it in the oven at one o'clock. At two o'clock the leprechaun arrived, bringing six beautiful potatoes, which the old lady put in the oven to bake with the turkey.

At three o'clock the elf arrived with a basket full of wild blackberries, which the old lady made into a pie and put in the oven with the turkey and the potatoes.

At four o'clock the troll arrived with peas and carrots fresh from his garden, which the old lady put on the stove to cook.

At half past four the goblin arrived with two hot crusty loaves of bread, which the old lady put on the table.

And at five o'clock when the witched swooped in with a big jug of apple juice, they all sat down to have thanks for their best Thanksgiving dinner ever.

(And the next week, they came for turkey soup.)

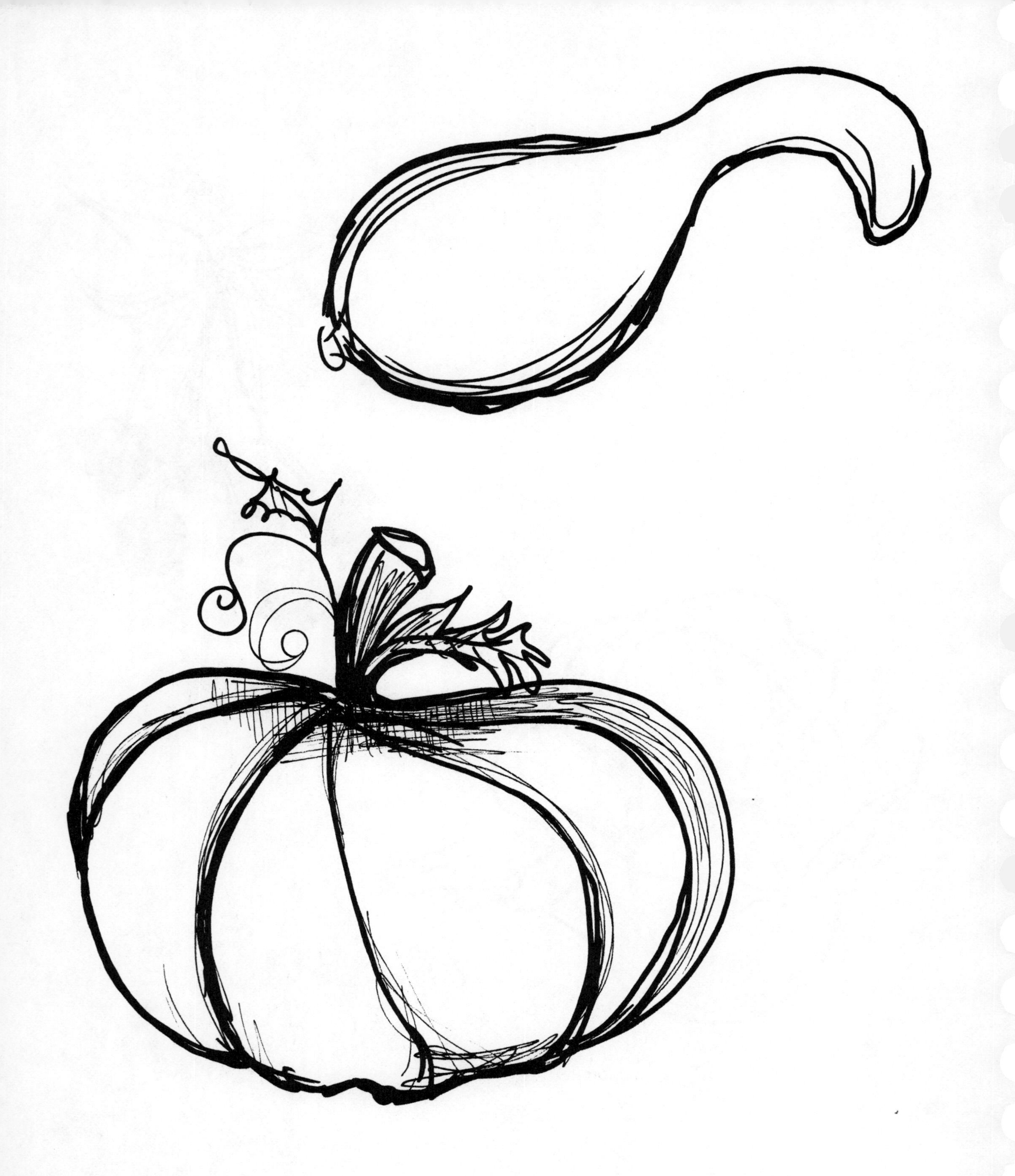

IV. COOKING

Objective: To improve fine motor coordination through mixing, kneading, powdering, decorating. Also to increase math skills by counting and measuring ingredients.
Evaluation: The children mixed, kneaded, carved and decorated using a variety of utensils. They also counted and measured ingredients.

Cranberry Sauce

2 cups water
2 cups sugar
1 pound package of cranberries
Boil water, sugar and cranberries until cranberries pop. Chill and serve.

Popcorn Balls

In electric skillet melt 6 T. butter. Add 3 c. miniature marshmallows and stir until melted. Blend in 3 T. orange Jello. Pour over popcorn and mix well. Butter hands and form into balls.

Snuffles Truffles

1 8 oz. package cream cheese
1 T. honey
1/3 c. chopped raisins
2 T. chopped nuts
Graham cracker crumbs
Combine ingredients one through four. Roll into balls. Then roll in crumbs and chill.

Cranberry Relish

Put through food grinder:
2 cups sugar
2 oranges (peeled)
1 qt. cranberries
1/2 C. crushed pineapple
Have children take turns putting cranberries and oranges into grinder and adding sugar. Put in small containers to take home.

Crazy Peanut Butter

Mix: 1 c. peanut butter
1/4 c. honey
1/2 c. powdered milk

Roll into balls in wheat germ. Chill

Banana Bobs

Cut bananas into chunks
Dip into honey
Roll in wheat germ
Use toothpicks for serving.

Thanksgiving Feast: For a special treat on Thanksgiving, we recommend the following menu:

1 turkey leg or chicken drumstick per child (small)
Cornmeal muffins made by children
Cranberry sauce made by children
Jello made by children
Carrot sticks grated, washed and cut by children
Popcorn made in class - empty margarine tubs can be used and decorated by kids to look like an Indian.

On empty margarine tub children use permanent magic marker to paint on face. It takes two pieces of colored paper cut into the shape of feathers, glued together with a toothpick in center and then slipped under the rubber band. Children can make as many feather as they like. Children can make pilgrim and Indian hats to wear at the feast.

Cornmeal Muffins

1 c. yellow cornmeal
1 c. all purpose flour
1/4 c. sugar
4 t. baking powder
1/2 t. salt
1 c. milk
1 egg
1/4 c. vegetable oil

Combine cornmeal, flour, sugar, baking powder and salt. Add milk, egg, and shortening. Mix until fairly smooth, about 1 minute. Bake in greased baking tins at 425° for 20 to 25 minutes. Makes 12 muffins.

Children can pour, mix, and measure with help of teacher.

Orange-cup "Turkeys"

1. Cut oranges in half, scoop out the pulp and mix with cranberry sauce. Then fill each orange cup for turkey body with cranberry sauce.
2. For the turkey's head use toothpicks to attach a radish, spiced apple, cherry tomato or kumquat. Raisins can be added for the features and carrot sticks or celery tops for the tail.

Cranberry "Mayflower" Boats

1. Fill a peach or pear half with cranberry sauce, one for each child.
2. For a sail, poke a toothpick through a carrot shaving or a lemon or orange peel and stick in the peach.

Yams and Pineapple

1 lg. can yams

1 sm. can crushed pineapple

12 large marshmallows

Drain yams and put in casserole. Add pineapple and juice and add to yams. With a potato masher, mash yams and pineapple together gently. Cover with marshmallows. Bake uncovered for 20 minutes at 350 °.

Navajo Fry Bread

Sift together:

1 c. flour

1 tsp. baking powder

1/2 tsp. salt

Blend in about:

1/2 c. lukewarm water

Stir with a fork or fingers until you have dough which you can handle. Roll out 1/4" thick and cut into 2" squares. You may poke a hole in the middle if you wish. Fry in hot fat (1/2") until puffed--then turn and brown other side. Drain on paper towel. Serve hot and dip in honey, jam, fruit yogurt, gravy, etc.

This is an excellent kids' project for home or school while studying about Indians and Pilgrims, since fry bread is a universal Indian food.

Pumpkin Bread

1 c. oil
2 c. sugar
2-1/2 c. flour
1 tsp. vanilla
1 c. raisins
2 eggs
2 c. canned pumpkin
1 tsp. cinnamon
1 tsp. salt
2 tsp. baking soda
1 c. chopped nuts

Sift all dry ingredients. Add oil, eggs, pumpkin, and vanilla. Beat well. Add raisins and nuts. Bake at 350° for 1 hour and 15 minutes. Bake in greased loaf pans. Makes 2 loaves.

V. MATH

Objectives: To improve counting skills

Evaluation: The following day we repeated activities and observed that most were counting.

Setting Thanksgiving Table

Count how many people will be at the Thanksgiving dinner. Set table while counting number of napkins, glasses, silver and dishes needed. Have too many of one item and count number of extra items. Have too few of another item. Then ask, "How many additional items are needed?"

Popcorn Number Chart

Make a number chart and glue corresponding number of popcorn pieces beside each number.

VI. FINGERPLAYS (can use felt objects for excellent math experience)

Objective: To improve memory and counting skills through repetition.
Evaluation: During the following week, we observed that most children remembered the words, actions, and numbers and were able to repeat them.

Five little Pilgrims on Thanksgiving Day
(hold up 5 fingers)
The first one said, "I'll have cake if I may."
(lower 5 fingers, then raise respective finger)
The second one said, "I'll have turkey roasted."
The third one said, "I'll have chestnuts toasted."
The fourth one said, "I'll have pumpkin pie."
The fifth one said, "Oh, cranberries I spy."
But before they ate any turkey or dressing,
All of the pilgrims said a Thanksgiving blessing.
(fold hands)

Five little Indians running through a door
(raise 5 fingers)
One fell down and then there were 4
(lower 1 digit)
Four little Indians in an apple tree
One climbed down and then there were three
(lower 1 finger)
Three little Indians stirring a pot of stew
One went to play and then there were two
(lower 1 finger)
Two little Indians playing in the sun
One went in and then there was one
(lower finger)
One little Indian left all alone
He went home and then were was none.
(lower finger and shake head sideways)

Five little turkeys sitting in a tree
Said the first little turkey, "What do I see?"
Said the second little turkey, "A man with a gun!"
Said the third little turkey, "Away let's run!"
Said the fourth little turkey, "I'm not afraid!"
Said the fifth little turkey, "Let's hide in the shade!"
Then BANG! BANG! BANG! went the gun, and away they did run.

Five little turkeys by the barn door
One saw some corn and then there were 4.
4 little turkeys flew up in a tree
One fell down and then there were 3.
3 little turkeys gobbled as they do
A dog chased one and then there were 2.
2 little turkeys strutting in the sun
The wind came along and then there was 1.
1 little turkey began to run
For he saw a farmer--and then there was none!

The Brave Little Indian

The brave little Indian went looking for a bear.
He looked in the woods and everywhere.
The brave little Indian found a big bear--
He ran like a rabbit! Oh, what a scare!

5 plump turkeys are we
We sat all night in a tree
But when the cook came around
We couldn't be found
That's why we are here you see!

Every day when we eat our dinner
Our table is very small
(palms of hands close together)
There's room for father, mother, sister, brother,
and me--that's all
(point to each finger)
But when it's Thanksgiving Day
and the company comes
You'd scarcely believe your eyes
(rub eyes)
For that same table stretches
Until it is just this size.
(spread hands wide)

Thanksgiving Turkey

Hobble goes the turkey
See him strut along
"Gobble," says the turkey
"You'll not be here long!"

A turkey is a funny bird
His head goes wobble, wobble
And all he says is just one word
Gobble, Gobble, Gobble.

Turkey in the barnyard
What does he say?
Gobble, gobble, gobble, gobble all day

Turkey on the table
What do you say?
Yummy, yummy, yummy, yummy all day

Turkey in my tummy
What do you say?
I ate too much turkey
On Thanksgiving Day!

THANKSGIVING SONGS

A Funny Bird
(make up your own tune)
The turkey is a funny bird
His head goes wobble, wobble
And all he says is just one word
Gobble, gobble, gobble

"I'm a Little Popcorn"
(tune of a Little Teapot)
I'm a little popcorn in a pot
Heat me up and watch me pop
When I get all fat and while I'm done
Popping corn is lots of fun!

"Gobble, Gobble, Gobble"
(tune of "Ever See a Lassie")
Gobble, gobble, gobble, fat turkey, fat turkey am I
I'm not here for living
I'm here for Thanksgiving
Gobble, gobble, gobble, fat turkey am I

VII. SCIENCE

Objective: To be aware of the different types of clothing and fabrics that are worn through the year.
Evaluation: Children were able to arrange clothes according to the season.

A. Dressing for the seasons.

This is a good time in the year to become aware of different weight and textured materials worn throughout the different seasons. Arrange clothes in housekeeping center. Have children observe different textures and weights of clothes.

Objective To discover which objects float and why.
Evaluation: Children experimented with floating objects.

B. Floating objects.

Fill a shallow pan with water. Spread different objects that you've collected in the table near pan of water. Encourage children to experiment to see which objects float and which will not. (See page 102)

Objective: To understand condensation.
Evaluation: Through experiment children understood condensation.

C. Making steam - how does water change to steam.

You will need a hotplate, pan, a glass lid that will fit completely over the top of the pan, and water. Explain to children about safety rules. Help children to fill pan one-half full of water and bring to a boil on the hotplate. Be sure glass is on pan. When water begins to boil, droplets of water will form on inside of glass lid. The lid may be lifted so the children can see steam. Children must not attempt to touch steam. Discuss the fact that water turns into steam when it boils.

Objective: Children will learn how to assemble and care for a terrarium.

Evaluation: Children made their own terrariums.

D. Baby Terrarium

Materials: baby food jars or aluminum foil pan, trowel, 1 pail per child, five pieces of charcoal from fireplace, extra soil and pebbles.

Take a walk and gather mosses, pebbles, acorns, twigs, etc. Children can pick up these items in their pails. At home have a good supply of soil, some charcoal and an extra supply of pebbles. Have children place at bottom of their terrarium a layer of pebbles, then charcoal, and then soil. Now arrange woodland treasures. Water and cover with saran wrap. Plants will survive indefinitely if kept moist.

Objective: To print beautiful and interesting leaves.

Evaluation: The children enjoyed printing the leaves.

E. Print Leaves

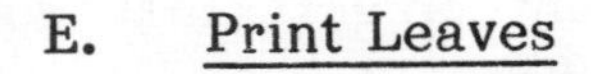

Lay leaves in newspaper with vein side up. Paint the upper side of the leaf with a tempra paint that has been thinned with water.

Transfer the leaves carefully to a clean sheet of paper, keeping the painted side up. Lay another sheet of paper on top of leaves, press, lift up top sheet and see what a beautiful and interesting print.

Objective: To recognize various objects through feel.
Evaluation: Children became more aware of the shape of objects and began to identify them.

F. Feeling bag.

Place various fruits and vegetables in a bag or old pillowcase after children have examined items. Then let a child reach into bag and see if he can identify the first item he touches by its feel. When he guesses, he takes item out to see if he is right. The same game can be played to teach such textures as sticky, slippery, rough, smooth, etc. Very good for Thanksgiving foods.

Objective: To observe corn growing.
Evaluation: Children watched new corn grow.

G. Indian Corn

You will need: An ear of Indian corn and a long shallow dish (example: ice cube tray).

Lay the corn in the dish and add about one inch of water. Change the water every day and watch what grows.

Objective: To sort animals, birds, and fish into the proper categories.
Evaluation: The children sorted the pictures well.

H. Animal, Bird, or Fish

Mount 3 envelopes on a large piece of cardboard. Glue picture on each envelope to designate category. Provide pictures of animals, birds, or fish and sort into proper categories.

Objective: To observe the difference in trees by their bark.
Evaluation: The children observed the different barks through their rubbings.

I. Bark on Trees

Some Indians use bark for their homes. Bark is the outer covering of the trunk and stems of trees. Different trees can be distinguished by their bark. Go outside, use large white paper and peeled crayons. Rub bark and observe different patterns.

VIII. PHYSICAL DEVELOPMENT & GAMES

Objective: To increase social interactions, develop good sportsmanship, and have fun.
Evaluation: The children palyed well with each other, learned to take turns, be a better loser or winner and had fun.

A. Statue

Play the piano or a record while the children go through free motions. When music stops, children must freeze.

B. Hot Potato

Children sit in a circle and keep the "hot potato" ball rolling by pushing with hands or feet.

C. Dramatic Play - Cookie Jar

I looked in the cookie jar and what did I see?
A big round turkey mother put there for me.
Mother looked in the cookie jar but she did not see
The big round cookie that she put there for me.

D. Guessing Games

What's Missing?

Use any 4 or 5 familiar objects or toys that can be easily handled. Spread them out on floor or table and ask child to name each item. Then ask a child (or whole group) to close eyes. Remove one item. When he opens his eyes, ask him to tell which item is missing. Gradually add more items. Two or three items may be removed at a time.

Exercises - Heads, Shoulders, Knees, and Toes

Children form circle and do exercises in rhythm as they sing to tune of Mulberry Bush.
Heads, shoulders, knees and toes
Heads, shoulders, knees and toes
Heads, shoulders, knees and toes
Clap, clap, clap.

E. Action Rhymes

Flopsy Flora

I'm just like Flopsy Flora
My doll that's made of rags
My arms go flop--my feet go plop
My head just wigs and wags

F. Wooden William

I am just like wooden William
Who stands up straight and tall.
My arms and legs are wooden
They just don't move at all.

Games

G. "Pin the Feathers on the Turkey"

Draw large turkey. Blindfold children. Have them each pin on a feather. Take off blindfold and tell what color it is.

H. "Turkey, Turkey, Indian"

Children stand in circle. One child holds felt turkey and walks around outer edge of circle saying, "Turkey, turkey, turkey, turkey...Indian." When he says Indian, he drops the turkey behind a child and taps child. Child chases him around circle back to original spot...then that child walks round outside with turkey.

I. Animal Guess

Each child takes a turn imitating an animal. The group guesses what animal it is.

IX. FIELD TRIPS

Objectives: To increase an awareness of their surroundings.

Evaluation: Children become more familiar with their surroundings outside their neighborhood.

A. Turkey Farm
B. Dunkin Donuts
C. Bagel Factory
D. Pottery Studio
E. Museum with Indian Artifacts

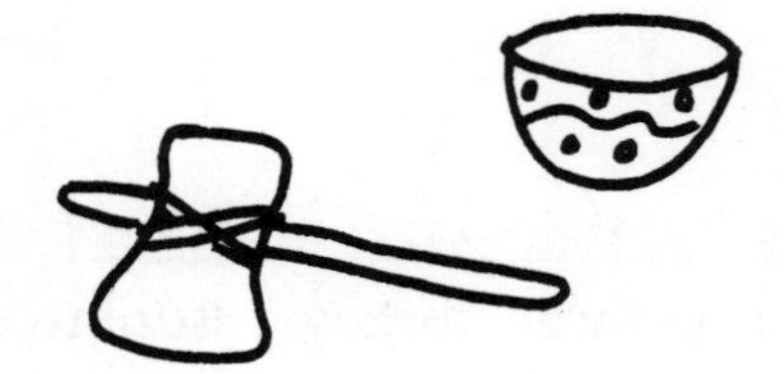

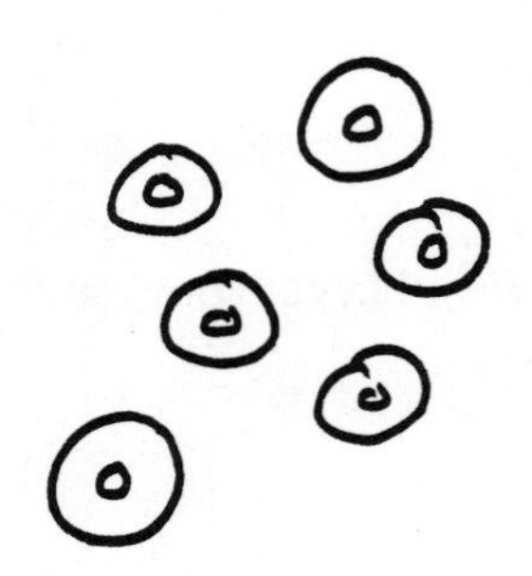

X. BOOKS

Granny and the Indians	Peggy Paris
The Fox	Peter Spier
Pelle's New Suit	Else Beskaw
Indian Bunny	Bornstein
Red Fox and His Cane	Benchley
Henny Penny	Hutchinson
Throw a Kiss, Mary	Mary Chalmers
The Surprise Party	Pat Hutchins
The Rooster Crows	Petersham
The Magic Blanket	Stella Farris
It is Red, It is Yellow, It is Blue	Habern
The Tale of Squirrel Nutkin	Potter
The Little Witches Thanksgiving Book	Linda Glevach
The Meanest Squirrel I Ever Met	Gene Zion

RECORDS

"Ella Jenkins Nursery Rhymes"
"Let's Sing Fingerplays" - Tom Gleezer

"A Pumkin in a Pear Tree" (creative ideas for twelve months of the year)
by Ann Cole, Carolyn Haas, Elizabeth Hilber, Betty Weinberger

DECEMBER

I. ARTS AND CRAFTS

Objective: To increase small motor coordination through cutting, pasting, printing, decorating and painting.

Evaluation: The children will cut, paste, print, decorate and paint

A. Paper Chains

Good practice for cutting; draw lines on red and green paper and have children cut them out. Glue or staple together; one red, one green, etc.

B. Make Wrapping Paper

Use large white easel paper. Cut Christmas trees and candy canes out of sponges. Dip in paint and print on paper. Or may use potatoes, carrots, etc., to print.

C. Paper Cup Santa

Paint eyes and nose on cup. Paint tip of cup red for cap. Paint on a red mouth. Paste on cotton for hat, brim and beard. Add string.

D. Egg Cup Ornaments

Use empty egg carton. Cut into 12 sections. Paint on glue, sprinkle with sparkles. Punch hole in top and insert pipe cleaner, fasten inside.

E. Christmas Tree Ornament

Make a Christmas tree out of green construction paper glued on to tag board. Decorate with colored popcorn (shake in tempera), glue on Fruit Loops, macaroni, sprinkles. Punch hole in top for string.

F. Christmas Stocking

Cut out large red stocking from construction paper. To decorate: use cotton balls, colored popcorn, cereal, glitter.

G. Macaroni Wreath

Cut a hole in the middle of a paper plate. Glue different shapes of macaroni onto ring. Spray with gold or green spray paint and hang.

H. Tube Santa

Use toilet paper roll. Cover with paper that has been cut to size and glue in place. Have children draw on eyes, nose and mouth. Cut triangle hat, glue on, glue cotton on hat and beard. Punch hole in top of hat.

I. Paper Plate Santa

Use large paper plate. Have children cut out triangle eyes, nose, half-moon mouth and paste on. Use cotton for beard and hat decoration.

J. Paper Plate Wreath

Cut out center of large paper plate: Give each child several squares of green tissue paper. Paint glue all over plate. Wrinkle up squares and cover whole plate. Glue on red crepe paper bow. Very attractive! (or may use red ribbon)

K. Meat Tray Ornament

Draw tree on meat tray. Have children decorate it with cereal, sprinkles, etc. Punch hole on top.

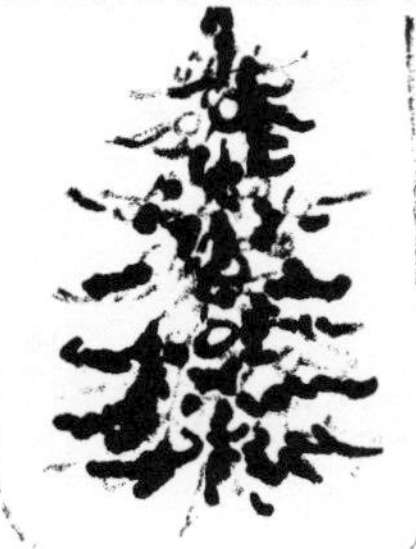

L. <u>Ornaments</u>

A triangle of green construction paper, punched with a paper punch and backed with red tissue paper, simple and attractive. Hang with string, yarn, or wire.

Cut a diamond shape from heavy paper on cardboard. Children can glue on macaroni or shells. Spray with gold paint - while wet, sprinkle with glitter. Punch hole when dry.

M. <u>Cozy Cup Ornaments</u>

Can decorate with tissue paper. Punch hole on top and string bell with wire through.

N. <u>Triangle Santa</u>

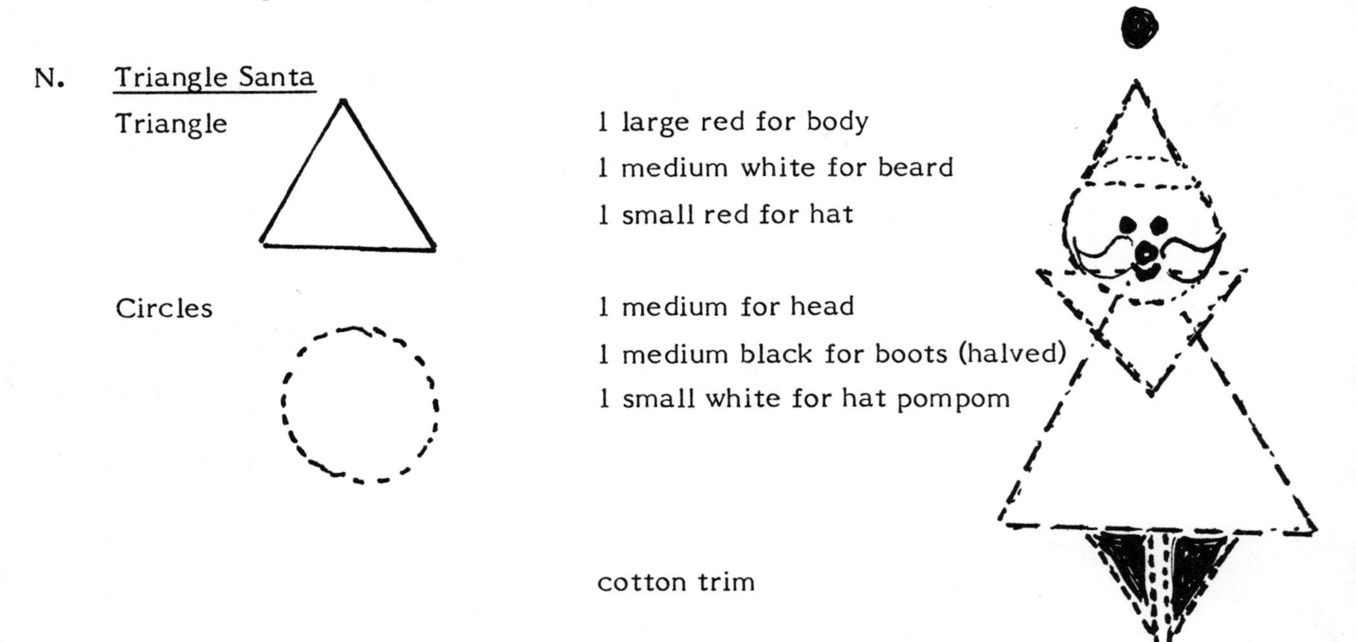

Triangle

1 large red for body
1 medium white for beard
1 small red for hat

Circles

1 medium for head
1 medium black for boots (halved)
1 small white for hat pompom

cotton trim

O. <u>Make a Chanukah Dredyle</u>

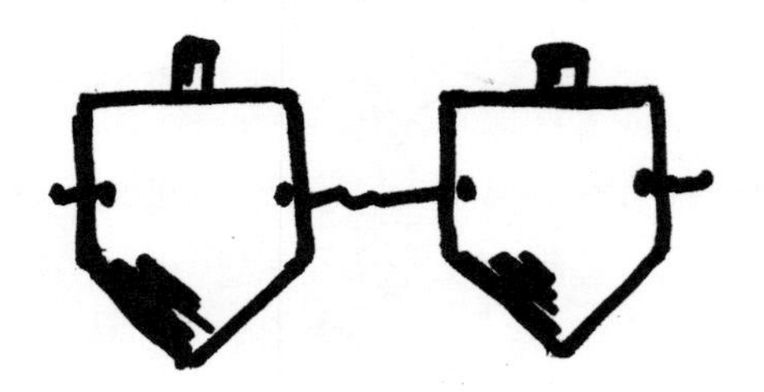

Have children trace and cut out dredyles. Can make several, paint them, punch holes in sides, and string together.

P. Cottage Cheese or Yogurt Lid Ornament

Paste a variety of dry cereals to both sides of a cottage cheese or yogurt lid. Punch a hole, use string or wire and use as an ornament on tree.

Q. Star-Shaped Santa

Cut a large 5-pointed star from red poster board. Cut out circle of pink paper for face, paste on. Draw in face. Use black felt marker, draw belt and buckle and complete with other details.

R. Paste Christmas paper back to back, trace patterns around cookie cutters and cut into holiday shapes. String and use for ornaments.

S. Make a Christmas angel of a pine cone, a small styrofoam ball, and wallpaper wings. Spray and hang with string.

T. Paint spools and apply glitter. String them together and hang them up.

U. Menorah

Ahead of time, cut out menorahs (cut three or four at once by holding your drawing on top of several sheets of paper). Glue to oaktag sheets. Give each child scissors, paste and brush the menorah with yellow paper. Cut out a sample flame to show how. The children cut out flames and glue atop candles. You may wrap picture in colored plastic wrap, and punch for hanging.

The flames cut will be different sizes, the creativity lies in how different each one looks. Read The Story of Chanukah for Children by Beverly Rae Charette and make potato latkes.

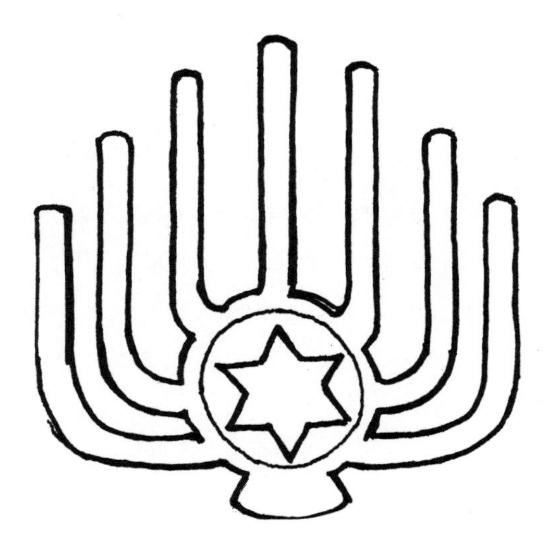

V. Santa Mouse

Read book and make craft

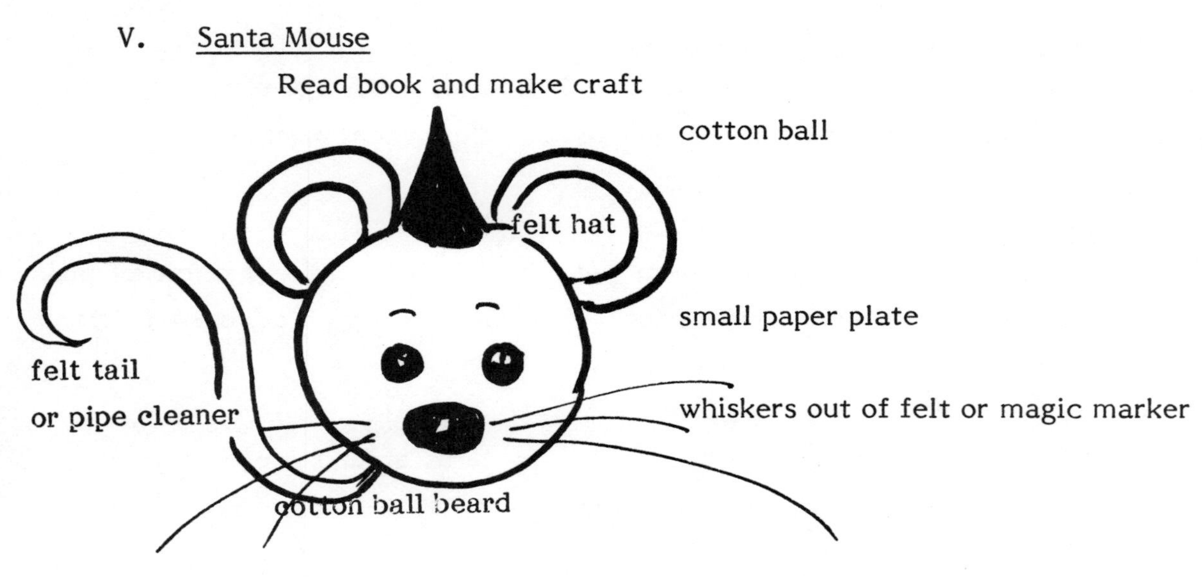

Can use walnut instead of paper plate for older children.

W. Paint on easel with evergreen bough, use Christmas colors.

X. Pine Cone Christmas Tree

Paint pine cone with glue. Then decorate with sequins, cereals, sprinkles, etc. Make a stand from a piece of clay.

Y. Handprint Wreath

A lovely gift for children to bring home -- Parents love it!

Measure and cut a piece of muslin to a 12" x 12" size. Cover child's hand with green paint and print hand randomly around in a circle to resemble a wreath. Use the child's thumb in the red paint to stamp "holly berries" around the wreath or may use a Q-tip dipped in red paint. Glue the top to a dowel and string with yarn or glue on heavy paper. We love this gift!

II. COLOR DAYS / RED - GREEN

Objective: To recognize colors red and green
Evaluation: The following day, children were able to find red and green in their clothes and around room

Have children wear something red on one day, green on another. Bring in and hold up bag of different red or green objects. Use color in craft, easel paint, and in snack.

Read I Like Red by Marie Norkin Warach

Rectangle Santa Claus
(Good Bulletin Board)

Cut two large and two small rectangles from red paper. Glue or staple these together so that the two larger rectangles hang down for Santa's legs and the smaller rectangles stick out on each side for his arms. (See illustration.)

Cut a head and hands from pink paper and attach them as shown. Give Santa a red hat and black boots and belt. Draw his face, then give him a cotton beard. Trim his suit and hat with cotton.

Have children paint all parts. Cut out large bag and have children find toys from magazines and cut out to paste on board.

III. STORY

Objective: To appreciate the joy of literature

Evaluation: The children listened to the story and enjoyed it very much

PETER AND THE WOLF

Early one morning Peter opened the gate and went out into the big green meadow. On a branch of a big tree sat a little bird, Peter's friend. "All is quiet," chirped the bird gaily. Soon a duck came waddling around. She was glad that Peter had not closed the gate and decided to take a swim in the deep pond in the meadow. Seeing the duck, the little bird flew down upon the grass.

"What kind of bird are you if can't fly?" said he. To this the duck replied, "What kind of bird are you if you can't swim?" and dived into the pond. They argued and argued, the duck swimming in the pond, the little bird hopping along the shore.

Suddenly, something caught Peter's eye, he saw a cat crawling through the grass. The cat thought, "The bird is busy arguing. I'll just grab him." Stealthily she crept towards him on her velvet paws.

"Look out!" shouted Peter and the bird flew up into the tree.

The duck quacked angrily at the cat from the middle of the pond.

The cat thought, "Is it worth climbing up so high? By the time I get there, the bird will have flown away."

Grandfather came out. He was angry because Peter had gone to the meadow.

"It is a dangerous place. If a wolf should come out of the forest then what would you do?"

Peter paid no attention to his grandfather's words. But Grandfather took Peter by the hand, led him home, and locked the gate.

No sooner had Peter gone then a big gray wolf came out of the forest. In a twinkling the cat climbed up the tree.

The duck in her excitement jumped into the pond. But no matter how hard the duck tried to run, she couldn't escape the wolf. He was getting nearer and nearer - catching up with her . . . and then he got her, gulp and swallowed her.

So this is how things stood: the cat on a branch, the bird another, not too close to the cat, and the wolf walked around and around the tree.

In the meantime, Peter stood behind the closed gate watching it all.

He ran home, took a strong rope and climbed up the high stone wall. One of the branches of the tree around which the wolf was walking stretched out over the wall. Grabbing hold of the branch, Peter lightly climbed over onto the tree.

Peter said to the bird, "Fly down and circle around the wolf's head, but take care that he doesn't catch you."

The bird almost touched the wolf's head, while the wolf snapped angrily at him.

Meanwhile Peter made a lasso and, letting it down, caught the wolf by the tail.

Just then hunters came out of the woods. But Peter, sitting in the tree, said, "Don't shoot! The bird and I have already caught the wolf. Help us take him to the zoo."

Now just imagine the triumphant procession: Peter at the head, followed by the hunters leading the wolf. And winding up the procession came Grandfather and the cat.

Patterns appropriate for puppets or flannel board can be used with "Walt Disney" recording.

Sonya
Ivan

Gate

Wolf

Sasha
Grandpa

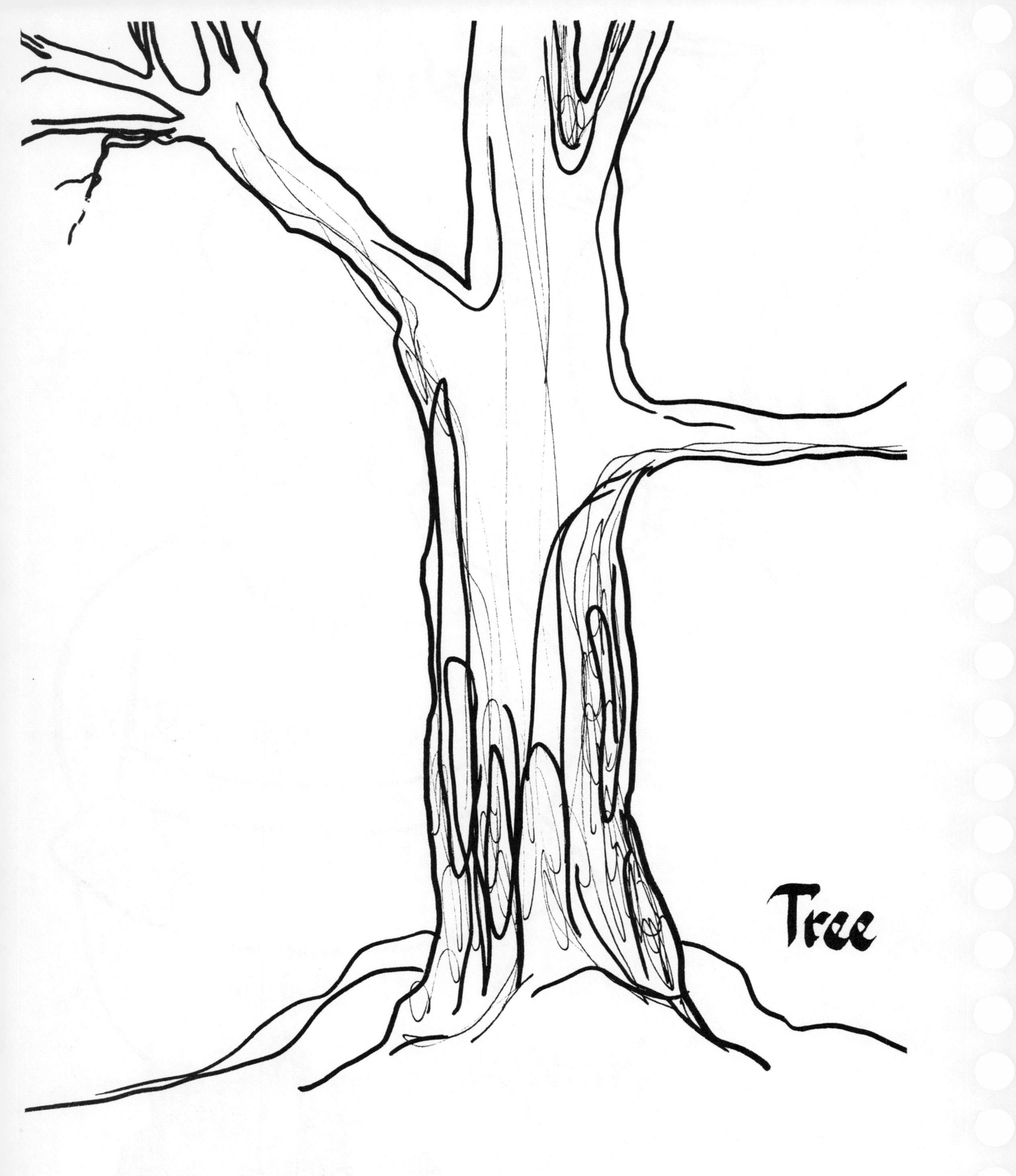
Tree

Vladimir
Pond

Yasha

Misha

Celebrating Hannukah

Each year, around mid-December, Jewish people celebrate the holiday of Hannukah, which recalls a heroic victory and re-dedication of the temple in Jerusalem. A very special part of this celebration is the lighting of candles placed in a holder called a menorah.

Over 2000 years ago Judah Maccabee led Jewish soldiers to victory over the Syrians. In celebration of this victory, Judah directed the purification of the temple and the renewal of its services. Thus Hannukah, being an abbreviation of the words "Hannukat ha-Mizbe'ah' (the consecration of the altar) was marked out for future generations as an annually recurring festival. Today Hannukah commemorates the heroic acts of Jews throughout the ages.

When it was time to rekindle the eternal light in the Holy Temple, Judah could find only enough oil for one day. But " . . . a miracle occurred and it lasted for eight days." The Menorah, then, is lit each of the eight nights during the Hannukah Festival to commemorate those important days.

Celebrating Hannukah in the Home

Ceremony: A menorah, a special candlelabrum, is placed in a central location in the home. The menorah has eight candles at the same level, and one place for the Shamash candle that is either higher than the others, or that is somehow set off from the others. The Shamash is lit first, and it is used to light all of the other candles as a b'raha (a blessing) is recited. All males wear a yarmalke or hat during the ceremony.

This holiday lasts for eight days. On the evening prior to the first day the the holiday, the Shamash and one candle are lit. On the evening of the second day the Shamash and two candles are lit. Each evening one additional candle is lit until on the evening of the eighth day the Shamash and eight candles are lit.

Gifts: It has been customary for many families to give small gifts to their children on this holiday. Some families give their children one gift each evening of the holiday and others give just one gift on the first evening.

Games: The most prominent game of the Hannukah holiday is called dreydle. A dreydle is a small four-sided wooden or metal top that is spun by hand. Each side has a Hebrew letter on it, --nun, gimmel, heh and shin. The children play the dreydle game with each participant contributing gelt (candy, marbles, raisins, etc.) to the pot. The children spin the dreydle in turn. If it stops with the nun showing, the spinner gets nothing; gimmel, the spinner gets the pot; heh, the spinner gets half; shin, the spinner has to add two items to the pot.

Songs: The entire family sings together many songs of the holiday after the Menorah is lit. The Ma'oz Tsur (Rock of Ages) is a favorite.

Foods: It is traditional to serve a kind of potato pancake called Latkes during Hannukah. These are easy to prepare in child care centers:

Ingredients: (Onion, a traditional ingredient has been left out--kids don't seem to like it!)

12 large potatoes
3 tsp. salt
3 beaten eggs
9 tbsp. flour
1½ tsp. baking powder
veg. oil for frying

Wash and peel the potatoes. Cut in half and grate. Put grated potatoes into a mixing bowl. Add flour, baking powder, salt and eggs. Mix until smooth and thin. The teacher should drop the mixture by spoonfuls into a frying pan with about 1/4" of hot oil. Turn when brown. Dry on paper towels. Serve plain or with applesauce, sour cream or jam.

IV. COOKING

Objective: To improve small motor coordination through decorating, mixing, rolling, grating. To improve math skills through measuring and counting ingredients.
Evaluation: The children decorated, mixed, rolled, grated and measured ingredients.

A. Apple Santa

large, polished red apple
5 marshmallows
2 cotton balls
5 cranberries
5 toothpicks
cloves

Place apple stem side down. Insert toothpicks; one at each side for arms, and two in front for feet (Santa is sitting). Push a marshmallow on arm toothpick, followed by cranberry for hand. Do same for other arm and legs. Push a toothpick in on top for head. Then push into toothpick in this order, flattened cotton ball for beard, marshmallow for head, flattened cotton ball for hat, cranberries for top. Stick cloves in for eyes and use clove buttons for trim on apple.

B. Church Window Candy

1 6 oz. pkg. semisweet chocolate pieces (1 cup)
1/4 C. butter or margarine
3 C. multicolored tiny marshmallows
3/4 C. chopped nuts

In large saucepan over low heat melt chocolate pieces and butter. Remove from heat and cool. Stir in the marshmallows and 1/4 cup nuts. Divide mixture in half. Shape each half into a log about 1-1/2 inches in diameter and 6 inches long. Roll logs in remaining 1/2 cup nuts. Chill. Cut into 1/2" slices. Makes about 2 doz. pieces.

C. <u>No Cook Mint Patties</u>

1/3 C. light corn syrup

1/4 C. butter

1 tsp. peppermint extract

1/2 tsp. salt

1 lb. confectioner's sugar

1 drop red and green food coloring

Blend corn syrup, butter, and peppermint. Divide mixture into three parts. Make one part red, one part green, and leave one part white. Shape into balls and flatten with fork (on waxed paper). Let dry.

D. <u>Peanut Butter and Jelly Bars</u>

3 C. unsifted flour

1 C. sugar

1 C. butter or margarine (softened)

2 eggs, beaten

1 C. grape jelly

2 C. (12 oz. pkg.) Reese's Peanut Butter Chips

Combine flour, sugar and baking powder. Cut in butter or margarine until mixture resembles coarse crumbs. Stir in beaten eggs, stir until mixture is smooth. Reserve one half of mixture, press remaining half of mixture onto bottom of greased 13 x 9 pan. Spread grape jelly over crust in pan. Sprinkle 1 cup Reese's Peanut Butter Chips over jelly. Crumble remaining dough over chips. Bake at 375° for 30-35 minutes or until lightly browned. Remove from oven. Immediately sprinkle with remaining 1 cup chips. Cool, cut into squares.

E. <u>Toffee</u>

1 C. butter	1 tsp. vanilla
1 C. sugar	3 milk choc. bars (1.2 ozs)
3 T. water	1/2 C. nuts

Boil butter, sugar and water until mixture browns and pulls away from side of pan (about 10 minutes). Then add vanilla. Pour onto buttered cookie sheet and place chocolate bars on top of hot sugar mixture. Spread chocolate evenly as it melts. Sprinkle nuts over chocolate. Cool and break into pieces.

F. No Bake Cookies

1 C. sugar
1/2 C. milk
3 C. oatmeal
1 C. coconut
1/2 tsp. salt
1/2 C. butter
1/2 tsp. vanilla
1/2 C. chopped walnuts
6 Tbsp. cocoa

Cook sugar, butter, milk and vanilla until it comes to a full rolling boil in electric fry pan or in pot on hot plate. Boil for 5 minutes. Combine the dry ingredients with liquid mixture and mix thoroughly. Drop by teaspoons on wax paper and let set until cooled. Can decorate with M&M's, raisins, chocolate chips, etc.

G. Gingerbread Men

1 C. sugar
1 C. shortening
1 C molasses
1 egg
2 Tbsp. vinegar
5 C. flour
1-1/2 tsp. soda
1/2 tsp. salt
1 tsp. cinnamon
2-3 tsp. ginger
1 tsp. cloves

Cream sugar with shortening. Stir in molasses, egg, and vinegar and beat well. Sift dry ingredients and mix with liquid ingredients. Chill about three hours. Roll dough to 1/8" thickness on lightly floured surface and cut with gingerbread cookie cutter. Place on greased cookie sheet and bake at 375° for 5-6 minutes. Cool and decorate with icing, red hots, raisins and chocolate chips. (Can use Gingerbread Box Mix.)

H. Cereal Christmas Tree or Wreath

3 Tbsp. margarine
3 C. miniature marshmallows
1/2 tsp. vanilla
1/2 tsp. green food coloring
4 C. Cheerios or Rice Krispies

Place margarine and marshmallows in a saucepan over low heat stirring until melted. Remove from heat and stir in vanilla and food coloring. Fold in cereal until evenly coated. Quickly shape warm mixture on wax paper with buttered hands. Use about 1/2 C. mixture per tree or wreath. Gumdrops, red hots, raisins, or chocolate chips can be used for decoration.

I. <u>A holiday treat</u>

A nice centerpiece for the holiday table.

cone shaped ice cream cones
2 C confectioner's sugar
1/4 C margarine
2 Tbsp. milk
green food color
red hots, marshmallows, chocolate chips, raisins for decoration

Combine confectioner's sugar and margarine. Add milk and food coloring and frost cones. Decorate.

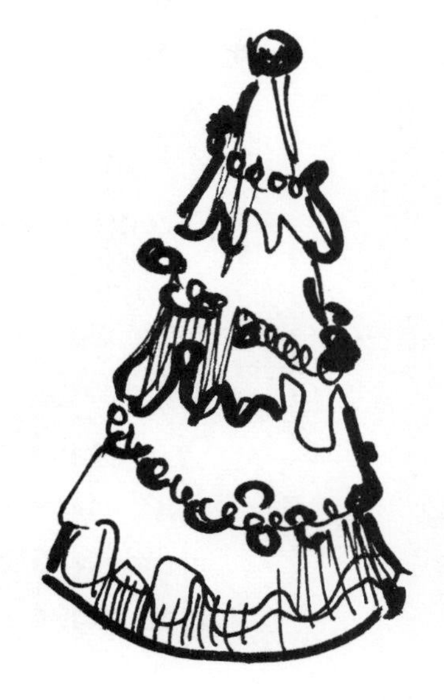

J. <u>Graham Cracker House</u>

1 pkg. graham crackers
Royal Frosting (3 egg whites, 1 lb. confectioner's sugar)
trims - raisins, nuts, candies
1/2 pint-sized and pint-sized paper milk containers

1. Make royal frosting by beating egg whites to a frothy foam and then, beating in confectioner's sugar.
2. Use milk cartons as the base, royal frosting as glue and graham crackers as the walls, stuck to cartons.
3. Place two graham crackers on top for roof.
4. Frost crackers and decorate with trims.

K. Gum Ball Christmas Tree

Ingredients:

2 bags jelly bean candy

Equipment:

1 box toothpicks

styrofoam cone

1 round base (optional)

Directions:

Place toothpicks on cone. Put candy on picks. Trim base with ribbon or felt. Can be used as centerpiece.

L. Orange and Cranberry Relish

Have children put cranberries and oranges through a food chopper or grinder. Store in boiled baby food jars or plastic cups only for a few days. Can give as a gift to parents or grandparents.

Have children peel and divide oranges into quarters, remove seeds. Then put orange sections and cranberries through the coarse blade of a food chopper or grinder. Add sugar, to taste. Store in clean baby food jars or plastic cups - cover tightly with plastic wrap.

M. Potato Pancakes (Latkes) for Hannukah

4 medium potatoes	2 Tbsp. sour cream
1 small onion	2 eggs
1/2 C. pancake mix (can use Bisquick)	
1 tsp. salt	1/2 tsp. pepper
1/2 C. oil	

You'll need:

vegetable peeler	grater
large mixing bowl	measuring cup
measuring spoons	tablespoon
frying pan	metal spatula
large plate or platter	paper towels

Here's what you do:

1. Peel potatoes and grate them into the bowl. Pour off the extra liquid into the sink.
2. Peel onion and grate it into the bowl.
3. Add eggs, pancake mix, sour cream, salt and pepper and mix well.
4. Heat oil until it sizzles.
5. Carefully drop the batter into the hot oil by tablespoonfuls. Flatten each pancake with the spatula.
6. When pancakes are golden brown, carefully turn them over with spatula.
7. Put 3 or 4 paper towels on platter. When pancakes are done, remove with spatula and let drain on towels.
8. Six people can enjoy them with applesauce, sour cream, or just plain.

N. Modeling Dough Ornaments

1-1/2 C. water

2 C. salt

1 C. cornstarch

Mix salt, cornstarch together. Bring water to a boil; remove from heat. Add salt and cornstarch slowly while stirring. Continue to cook over low heat until the dough is hard to stir. Remove from pan. Let cool. Knead. Store in an air-tight container.

Then, model ornaments and paint. Take home. Makes a wonderful present.

O. <u>Bread Dough Recipe</u>

8 C. flour

3 C. water

2 C. salt

Mix flour and salt, add water, mix and knead. Soft shape. Roll dough. Put hole for string. Place on wax paper and dry overnight or bake 1 hour on ungreased cookie sheet at 300o. When dry, paint. (Thick shapes - bake one hour, thin shapes, bake 1/2 hour)

Make excellent Christmas gifts for parents or grandparents. To preserve, paint on shellac.

V. MATH

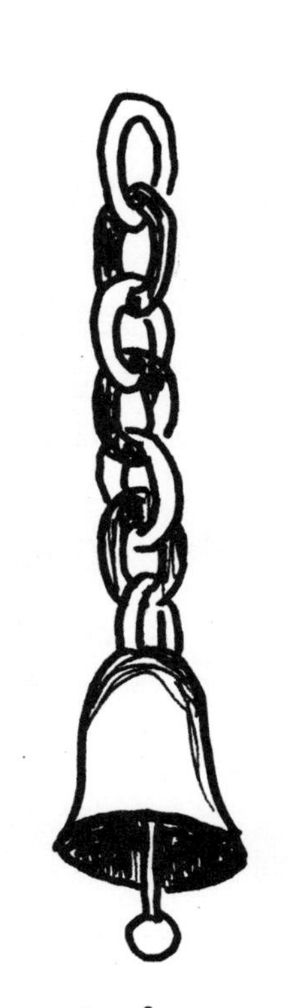

Objective: To improve counting skills.

Evaluation: Children improved counting skills through these activities.

A. Christmas Bell

How many days till Christmas
It's mighty hard to tell
Take off a link every night
When Sandman casts his spell
And Christmas Eve will be here
By the time you reach the bell.

Glue together 1" strips of red and green construction paper to form a chain. Add a loop for each day until Christmas. Attach a bell to the end of chain. Can write poem on bell. Remove one loop each day until Christmas.

B. Paper Chain Patterns

When making paper chains begin a pattern. Example: 3 green loops followed by one red loop, etc. Complete the chain with the same pattern.

C. Count the Reindeer

Make felt reindeer for flannelboard.

1, 2, 3, 4, 5 little reindeer stand beside the gate
"Hurry Santa," said the five, "so we will not be late!"
"1, 2, 3, 4, 5 little reindeer," Santa said, "please wait."
Wait for 3 more little reindeer and then that will make 8

Have children tell how many reindeer it will take to make 8. Can change number of reindeer waiting. Example: "1, 2, 3 little reindeer . . . " and "Wait for five."

D. Star

Make two equilateral triangles and glue them together to form a star. Discuss that the sides of the triangle are the same.

VI. FINGERPLAYS

Objective: To increase memory and counting skills through repetition.

Evaluation: The children remembered the words and actions, and numbers through repetition.

A. Santa's Workshop

Here is Santa's workshop (form peak with both hands)
Here is Santa Claus (hold up thumbs)
Here are Santa's little elves (wiggle fingers)
Putting toys upon the shelves.

B. Here is the Chimney

Here is the chimney (make fist and tuck in thumb)
Here is the top (cover with other hand)
Open it up quick (lift hand up)
And out Santa will pop! (pop out thumb)

C. Song (Tune of "London Bridge")

Guess whose beard is long and white, long and white, long and white
Guess whose beard is long and white
Dear old Santa

Guess who comes on Christmas Day, Christmas Day, Christmas Day
Guess who comes on Christmas Day
Dear old Santa

Guess whose boots are shiny and black, shiny and black, shiny and black
Guess whose boots are shiny and black
Dear old Santa

Guess who's got a twinkle in his eye, in his eye, in his eye
Guess who's got a twinkle in his eye
Dear old Santa

D. <u>Ring the Bells</u> (Tune of "Row Your Boat", give children bells)

Ring, ring, ring the bells
Ring them loud and clear
To tell the children everywhere
That Christmas time is here.

Shake, shake, shake your head . . . .

Clap, clap, clap your hands . . . . . .

Stamp, stamp, stamp your feet . . . . . .

E. <u>The Little Boy</u>

Here is a little boy just ready for bed (point finger up)
Down on the pillows he puts his head (place finger in palm of other hand)
He wraps himself in the cover so tight (curl fingers around pointer)
And dreams of his Christmas tree
With all its bright lights (rest head on hands)

F. <u>Twinkle, Twinkle, Little Star</u>

Twinkle, Twinkle, Little Star, (open and close fingers above heads)
How I wonder what you are. (point to head)
Up above the world so high (point to sky)
Like a diamond in the sky. (touch pointers and thumbs to make a diamond)
Twinkle, Twinkle, Little Star (blink fingers)
How I wonder what you are. (point to head)

HORA

There are four counts to each measure and a step for each count. Begin with feet together and head lowered. On count 1, step to the side with the left foot. On count 2, tap the right foot behind the left. On count 3, raise head, hop on left foot and kick right foot forward. On count 4, hop on right foot and kick left foot forward. The dance may be done in one large circle or in two smaller circles, one inside the other. For variation, have the inner circle begin on the right foot.

Come Light the Menorah

O Hanukkah, O Hanukkah, come light the menorah!
Let's have a party, we'll all dance the hora.
Gather 'round the table, we'll give you a treat,
Dreydles small to play with, levivot to eat.
And while we are playing, the candles are burning low.
One for each night, they shed a sweet light.
To remind us of days long ago.

Hora

Briskly

G. Christmas Bells

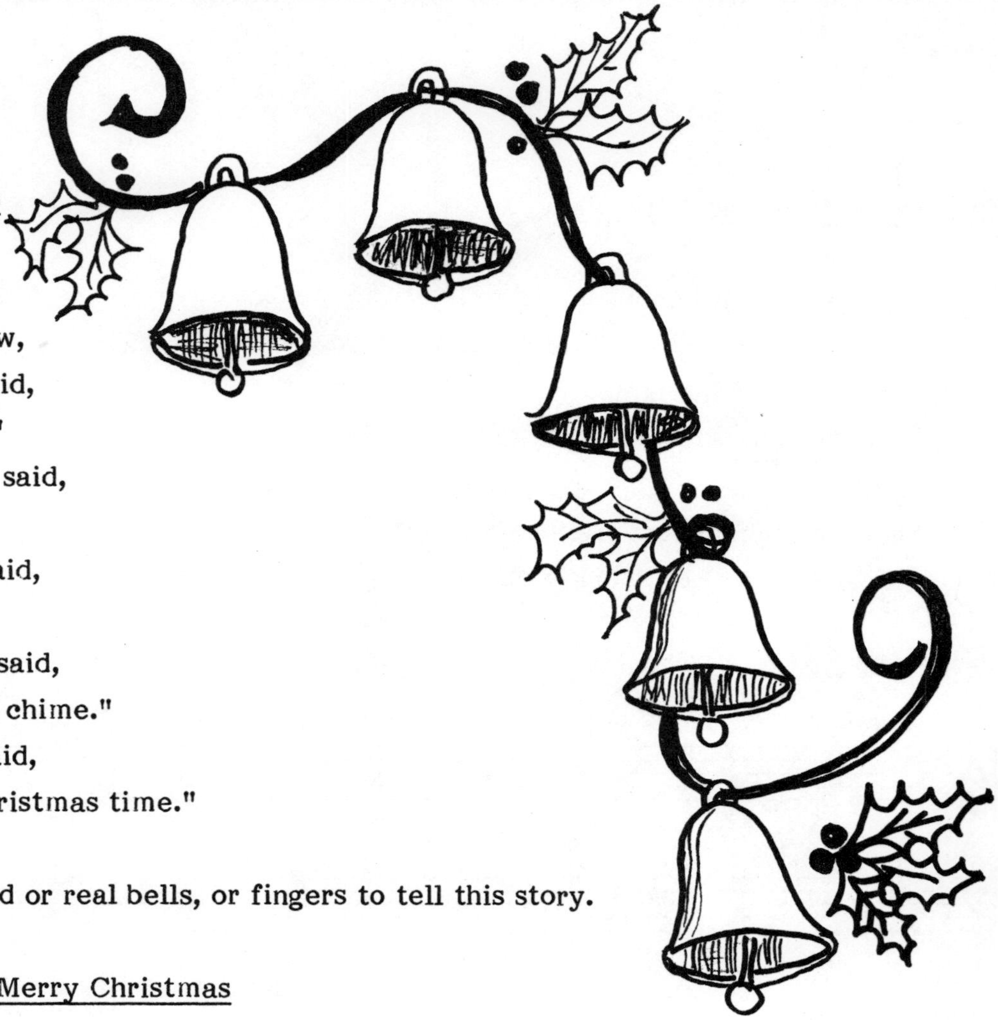

Five little bells
Hanging in a row,
The first one said,
"Ring me slow."
The second one said,
"Ring me fast."
The third one said,
"Ring me last."
The fourth one said,
"Ring me like a chime."
The fifth one said,
"Ring me at Christmas time."

Use flannelboard or real bells, or fingers to tell this story.

H. We Wish You a Merry Christmas

(Chorus)
We wish you a merry Christmas,
We wish you a merry Christmas,
We wish you a merry Christmas
And a happy New Year.

(Verse 1)
Let's all do a little clapping,
Let's all do a little clapping,
Let's all do a little clapping
And spread Christmas cheer.

(2) Jumping
(3) Twirling
Suggestion: On chorus, join hands and ring around circle. On verses, stand still and do motions. Repeat chorus after each verse. Add your own verses.

I. My Dreydle

I have a little dreydle, A pretty little top;
Around and round it's spinning, I'll never let it stop!
Oh, dreydle, dreydle, dreydle, Oh, little top that spins!
The children all are happy When Hanukkah begins.

J. Christmas is Coming

(Chorus)

Clap, clap your hands
(clap hands)
And sing out with glee,
(hands by mouth as if calling)
For Christmas is coming
(clap hands)
And happy are we.
(draw smile on face)
Our stockings we'll hang
(pantomime words)
And while we're asleep
(pantomime sleeping)
Down the chimney will Santa Claus creep.
(creep fingers downward)

2. He'll empty his pack
(pantomime emptying pack)
And up he will go
(fingers creep up)
Calling his reindeer
(hands by mouth, calling)
Will dash away home.
(fingers dash away)

(Chorus)

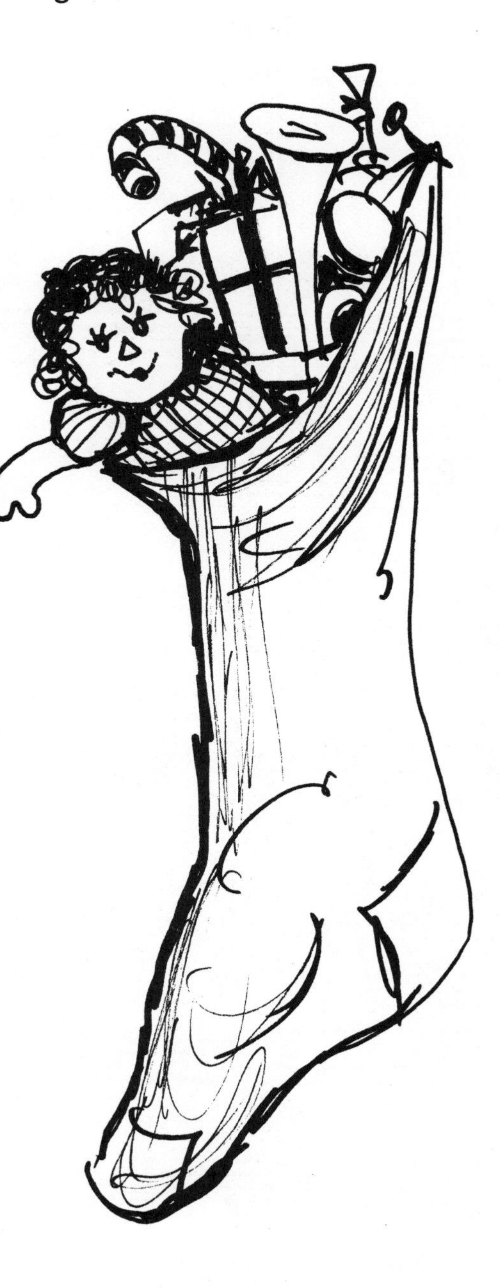

Songs

- Jingle Bells
- Up on the House Top
- Here Comes Santa Claus
- Santa Claus is Coming to Town
- We Wish You a Merry Christmas
- Rudolph the Red-Nosed Reindeer
- Dreydl Song

My Dreydle

Clearly

C G7 C G7 C

I have a lit - tle drey-dle, A pret - ty lit - tle top; A-
round and round it's spin-ning, I'll nev - er let it stop! Oh,
drey-dle, drey-dle, drey - dle, Oh, lit - tle top that spins! The
chil-dren all are hap - py When Ha - nuk-kah be - gins.

VII. SCIENCE

Objective: To compare the different sounds of bells.
Evaluation: The children experimented with different types of bells.

A. Bells

Discuss the many uses for bells. Example: Doorbells, fire alarms, telephone, church bells. Use several different sizes and kinds of bells. Discuss why the sounds are different.

Objective: To observe variation of tones in glasses of water
Evaluation: Children experimented with a variety of tones

B. Glass and Water - Music

Fill several glasses with different levels of water. Have the children tap the glasses carefully with a spoon and listen to the variation in sounds. The glass with the smallest amount of water will have the highest pitched sound, etc.

Objective: To teach properties of light and shadow
Evaluation: Children observed their shadows and had fun with them

C. Silhouettes (Excellent Christmas gifts for parents)

Need: Dark construction paper, thumbtacks, glue scissors

Thumbtack a sheet of paper to the wall. Place a lamp on the table in front of the paper. Place a chair sideways between the lamp and the paper and have the child sit in the chair looking forward. Trace the outlines of the child's silhouette on the paper. Ask the child to cut out and mount the silhouette on dark-colored construction paper. What made the shadow?

Discuss how the shadow is made. Have the children ask other children if the silhouette looks like them.

D. <u>Make a cement block</u>

Bricks are man-made rocks. The earth gives us the materials to make these simulated rocks.

You will need:

Sand, dry cement, water and pebbles

Mix 1/4 C. dry cement with 1/2 C. sand. Wet the pebbles with water and mix them with the sand-cement mixture. Add water slowly until a thick mush is formed. Pour mixture into a cardboard box to harden. Wet the top of the concrete each day. Allow block to harden for several days. When hard, remove from box.

E. <u>Making Soil</u>

It takes hundreds of years to make soil. Water and wind blow or wash sand and rocks against other rocks which slowly break into smaller pieces and mix with shells, insects, animals, leaves, etc.

Try to make your own soil.

You will need:

small rocks, decaying leaves and insects, large coffee can

Rub rocks together over the coffee can. Sand-like material will fall off to form a base for a soil-mixture. Then add small pieces of decaying leaves and insects.

VIII. PHYSICAL DEVELOPMENT / GAMES

Objective: To increase social interactions, develop good sportsmanship and have fun.
Evaluation: The children played well with each other, learned to take turns, be a better winner or loser, etc.

A. Santa Claus Cootie

Materials: Make enough parts for four people to play (and extras in case some get lost). Need one die.

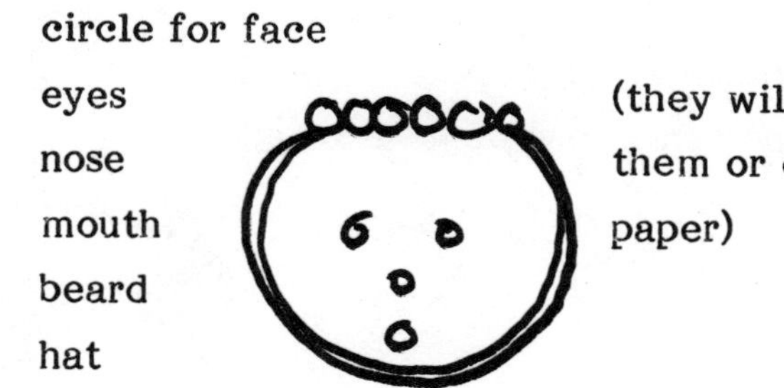

(they will last longer if you laminate them or cover them with clear contact paper)

Procedure:

1. The object of the game is to put together Santa's face, parts are obtained by rolling the die.
2. Each number on the die corresponds to a part of Santa's face:
   #1 face
   #2 one eye
   #3 nose
   #4 mouth
   #5 beard
   #6 hat
3. Children take turns rolling the die. They must get a face (#1) before they can get other parts.
4. The first child to complete his face says, "Santa Claus!"

B. Dog and Bone

Quiet game. One child is chosen to be the dog. He sits in a chair or stool at a distance in front of the other children. The dog closes his eyes. His back is toward the other players. The dog's bone, whatever you wish, book eraser, etc., is placed behind his chair. Choose one child who tries to sneak up to the dog and touch his bone without the dog hearing him. If the dog hears someone coming, he turns around and says "Bow-wow!" Then the player goes back to the group and another child has a chance to outsmart the dog and touch his bone. If successful, he is the next dog.

D. Dreydl Game

A dreydl is a four-sided wooden or plastic spinning top. There is a Hebrew letter on each side. Children can spin and chant song:

I have a little dreydl
I made it out of clay
And when it's dry and ready
Then dreydl I shall play

E. Santa's in this Shop

This game is played like Farmer-in-the-Dell.

The children all walk around in a circle with one child, Santa, in the center. Sing the song to the tune of "Farmer-in-the-Dell". On the second verse, "Santa" chooses another child, and that child chooses another on the third verse, etc. All children chosen remain in the center of the circle until the last verse. On the last verse, all the children except the "top" return to the circle. The top stands in the center alone.

Verse 1 Santa's in his shop
Santa's in his shop
What a scene for Christmas
Santa's in his shop

2 Santa takes a drum
3 The drum takes a doll
4 The doll takes a train
5 The train takes a ball
6 The ball takes a top
7 They're all in the shop
8 The top stays in the shop

IX. FIELD TRIPS

Objective: To increase awareness of their surrounding.

Evaluation: The children were more aware of their surroundings.

A. Toy Store - visit Santa Claus.

B. Visit Nursing Home - have children bring a piece of fruit or individually wrapped cakes. Bring bells and sing carols.

C. Go to a nursery, look at different types of wreaths, Christmas trees, pointsetta plants, etc.

D. Go to a bakery - see different types of holiday baked goods.

CHRISTMAS IS COMING

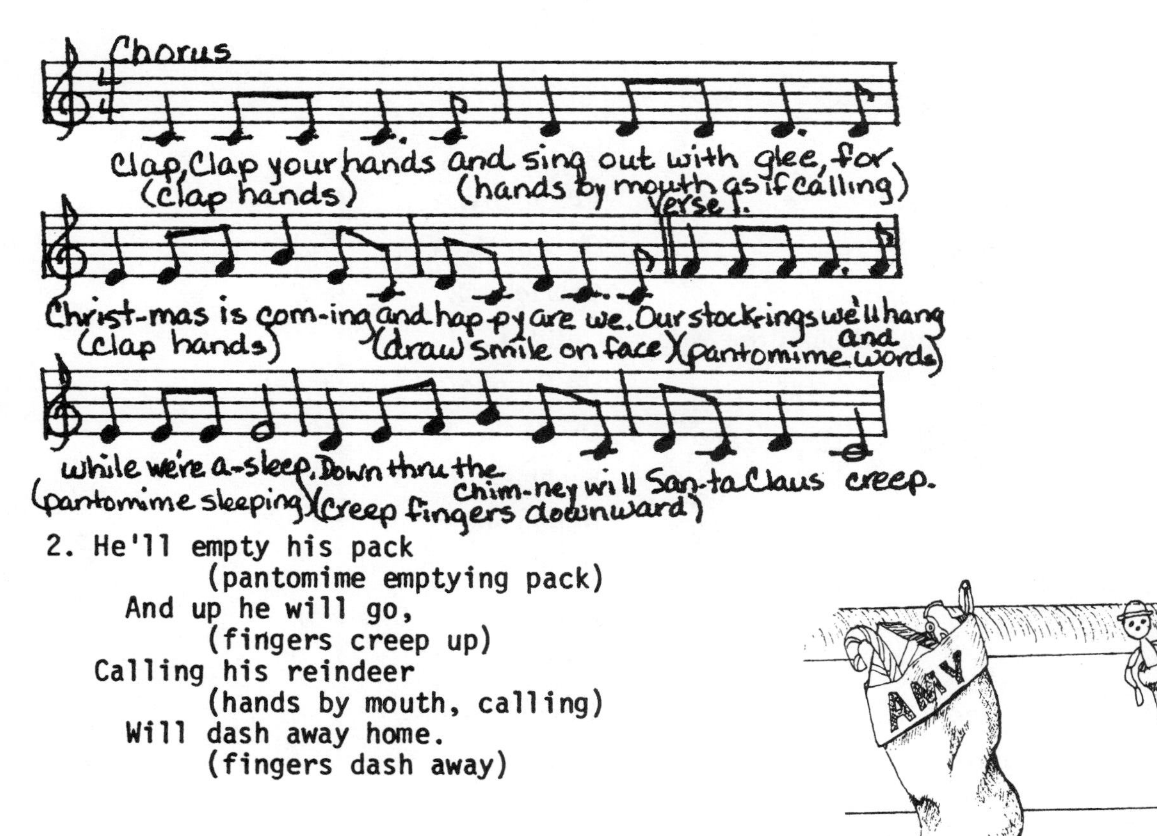

2. He'll empty his pack
(pantomime emptying pack)
And up he will go,
(fingers creep up)
Calling his reindeer
(hands by mouth, calling)
Will dash away home.
(fingers dash away)

X. BOOKS AND RELATED ACTIVITIES

Christmas is a Time for Giving	Anglund
On Christmas Eve	Brown
A Christmas Story	Chalmers
Nine Days to Christmas	Ets
How the Grinch Stole Christmas	Geisel
The Little Drummer Boy	Keats
How Spider Saved Christmas	Kraus
The Night Before Christmas	Moore
The First Christmas	Trent
Where's Spot?	Hill
Spot Goes for a Walk	Hill
Santa Mouse	
Hanukah Money	Shalom Aleichem
Potato Pancakes All Around	Marilyn Hirsch

PICTURE BOOKS

The Christmas Party	Adams, A.
The Steamroller	Brown, M. W.
Paul's Christmas Birthday	Carrick, C.
Over the River and Through the Woods	Child, L. M.
* Babar and Father Christmas	De Brunhoff, J. (France)
The Family Christmas Tree Book	De Paola, T.
Corduroy	Freeman, D.
* Emmet Otter's Jug-Band Christmas	Hoban, R.
The Twelve Days of Christmas	Kent, J.
The Tomten	Lindgren, A. (Sweden)
The Elves and the Shoemaker	Littledale, F.
The Year Without a Santa Claus	McGinley, P.
The Little Engine That Could	Piper, W.
* Rosa	Politi, L (Mexico)
The Christmas Tomten	Rydberg, V. (Sweden)
The Best Christmas Book Ever	Scarry, R.
A Charlie Brown Christmas	Schulz, C. M.

	Title	Author
	Noel for Jeanne-Marie	Seignobosc, F. (France)
	The Thank-You Book	Seignobosc, F.
*	The Littlest Angel	Tazewell, C.
*	The Littlest Snowman	Tazewell, C.
*	The Mitten	Tresselt, A. (Ukrain)
*	The Doll's Christmas	Tudor, T.
	The Twelve Days of Christmas	Wildsmith, B.
	The Story of Chanukah for Children	Charette, B.

* books for older preschoolers

NON FICTION / TEACHER RESOURCES

Many seasonal books are available inexpensively in grocery and discount stores:

Frosty the Snowman

The Gingerbread Boy

The Night Before Christmas

Rudolph the Red-Nosed Reindeer

The Twelve Days of Christmas

and many more!

RECORDS

How the Grinch Stole Christmas/Christmas Songs From Many Lands. Random House

Learning Basic Skills Through Music, Vol. I. Hap Palmer. Educational Acitivities, Inc., Freeport, N.Y. 11520. "Birds."

JANUARY

I. ARTS AND CRAFTS

Objective: All these activities are developed to increase small motor coordination.
Evaluation: The children increased their small motor coordination.

A. Snowman

Stand a toilet tissue roll on end and paste cotton around roll. Stuff ball of cotton in one end for head. Dab on features with magic marker.

B. Snowflakes

Use white napkin or light white paper in square shape. Fold square in half, then fold in three parts radiating from center-point on fold

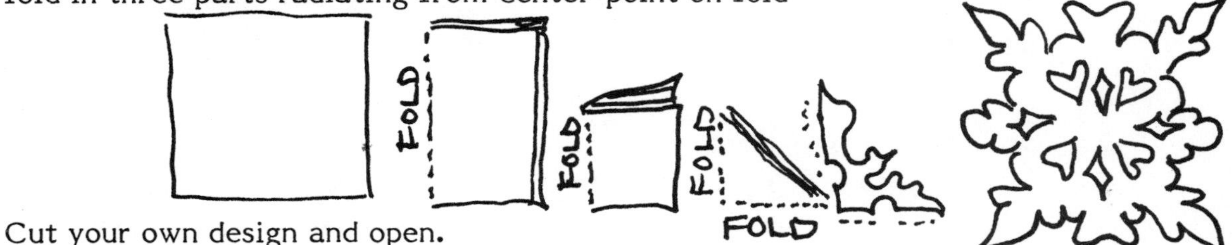

Cut your own design and open.

C. Use a rectangular piece of paper that children can cut out for tree trunk. Paste on dark blue construction paper for the backing. Dip a small sponge into white paint and dab on paper to show snow on the tree.

D. Whipped Soap Painting

Mix 1 C. Ivory Snow powder with 1/2 C. warm water in bowl. Have children beat with eggbeater until mixture is frothy but not stiff. Then apply mixture to dark construction paper with either easel brushes or tongue depressors to create a design. Can add food coloring to whipped flakes.

E. Cotton Ball Snowman

By gluing cotton balls and scraps of yarn and fabric on dark construction paper, the children can create their own snowman.

F. Using large paper plate, glue buttons. seeds, beans, bits of paper, fabric, etc. to make face. Glue on construction paper for hat.

G. Frost on Windowpane

On construction paper, draw outline of a window. Spread glue on frame and sprinkle with glitter or use water sprinkled with sugar.

H. Doily Snowman

Paste doily on dark construction paper. Make face out of markers or scraps.

I. Mittens

Read book The Mitten - Tresselt, or One Mitten Lewis - Kay. Have children cut mittens out of colored construction paper, punch holes and string yarn through holes. Wear mittens around neck. Can decorate mittens.

J. Honeycomb Snowflakes

To make a snowflake design, glue Honeycomb cereal on dark construction paper or glue edges of Honeycomb cereal together to make snowflake design.

K. Spatter Paint Snowflake

Cut a large circle from black or blue construction paper. Fold in half and open. Dip brush into white tempera paint that is thinner than normal. Hold brush over paper, being careful not to touch brush to paper. Shake brush, allowing paint to fall randomly. Fold on original crease and press. Open and symmetrical design appears.

L. Winter Scene

Draw winter scene on brightly colored construction paper using crayons. When finished, cover entire piece of paper by rubbing with side of white chalk.

M. Tempera Snow Painting

Mix primary colors, red, blue and yellow in unbreakable containers to light cream consistency. Use large brushes; go outside and paint on snow.

N. Coconut Snowman

Draw outline of a snowman on black paper with chalk. Spread paste all over snowman. Sprinkle shredded coconut all over paste. Use raisins for eyes.

O. Paper Clip Fun

Have someone bring in a bunch of paper clips. Try making designs and pictures with them by linking them together. You can also make bracelets and chains from paper clips.

P. Art Toothpick Drawing

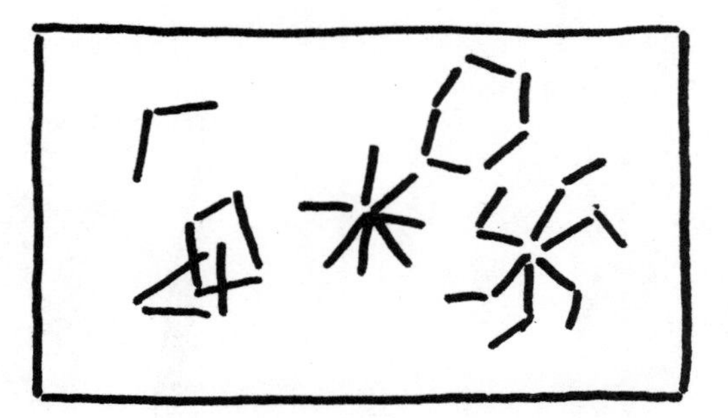

Materials:

colored construction paper
colored or natural toothpicks
paste or glue

Directions:

1. Put paste or glue on a scrap piece of paper or jar top (for 3 - 4-1/2 year olds).
2. Younger children - have them cover the colored sheet of paper with glue or paste all over.
3. Have them place the toothpicks to make an abstract design.
4. For older children (5 - 12 years), have them dip the toothpicks in the glue or paste and then make a picture design.

II. COLOR DAY - WHITE

Objective: To recognize and identify the color white.
Evaluation: The following day children were able to find white in their clothes, outside, and inside the room.

Identify various white objects in room and outside (snow). Have children wear something white. Use white paint at the easel (on dark paper), white in the craft and snack.

III. STORY

Objective: To improve memory skills through repetition and enjoy story.
Evaluation: The children improved memory skills and enjoyed story.

"I Know an Old Lady"

I know an old lady who swallowed a fly,
I don't know why she swallowed a fly,
I guess she'll die!

I know an old lady who swallowed a spider,
That wriggled and wriggled and tickled inside her.
She swallowed the spider to catch the fly.
But I don't know why she swallowed the fly!
I guess she'll die.

I know an old lady who swallowed a bird,
Now how absurd, to swallow a bird!
She swallowed the bird to catch the spider
That wriggled and wriggled and tickled inside her.
She swallowed the spider to catch the fly,
But I don't know why she swallowed the fly!
I guess she'll die!

I know an old lady who swallowed a cat.
Now fancy that, to swallow a cat!
She swallowed the cat to catch the bird.
She swallowed the bird to catch the spider
That wriggled and wriggled and tickled inside her.
She swallowed the spider to catch the fly,
But I don't know why she swallowed the fly!
I guess she'll die!

I know an old lady who swallowed a dog.
My, what a hog to swallow a dog!
She swallowed the dog to catch the cat.
She swallowed the cat to catch the bird.
She swallowed the bird to catch the spider
That wriggled and wriggled and tickled inside her.
She swallowed the spider to catch the fly,
But I don't know why she swallowed the fly!
I guess she'll die!

I know an old lady who swallowed a goat
Just opened her throat, and in walked the goat?
She swallowed the goat to catch the dog.
She swallowed the dog to catch the cat.
She swallowed the cat to catch the bird.
She swallowed the bird to catch the spider
That wriggled and wriggled and tickled inside her.
She swallowed the spider to catch the fly,
But I don't know why she swallowed the fly!
I guess she'll die!

I know an old lady who swallowed a cow.
I don't know how she swallowed a cow.
She swallowed the cow to catch the goat.
She swallowed the goat to catch the dog.
She swallowed the dog to catch the cat.
She swallowed the cat to catch the bird.
She swallowed the bird to catch the spider
That wriggled and wriggled and tickled inside her.
She swallowed the spider to catch the fly,
But I don't know why she swallowed the fly!
I guess she'll die!

I know an old lady who swallowed a HORSE!
She's dead, OF COURSE!

Title: I Know an Old Lady who Swallowed a Fly

Figures can be made out of felt for telling or re-telling of the story

Title: I Know an Old Lady (continued)

Title: I Know an Old Lady (continued)

I'm a Little Snowman (Tune: I'm a Little Teapot)

I'm a little snowman, short and fat,
Here is my broomstick, here is my hat.
When the sun comes out, I melt away,
Down, down, down, down, whoops . . .
I'm a puddle!

I'm a Little Teapot

I'm a little teapot, short and stout,
(act very stout)
Here is my handle,
(place one hand on hip)
Here is my spout.
(extend other arm, elbow and wrist bent)
When I get all steamed up, then I shout,
(nod head vigorously)
"Tip me over and pour me out."
(tip sideward in direction of extended arm)

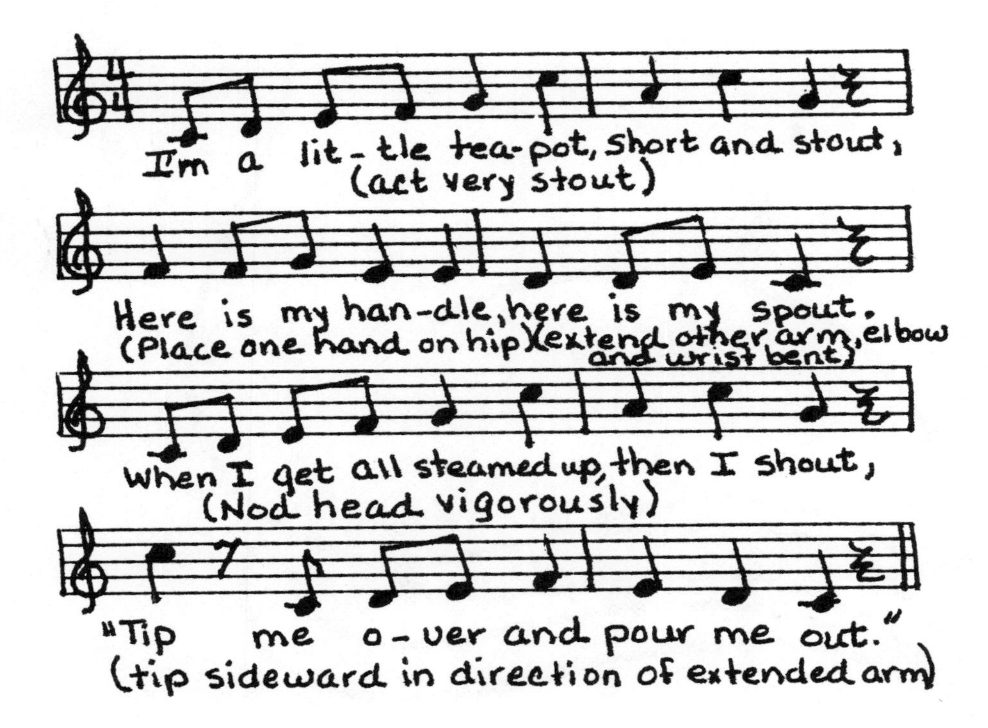

IV. COOKING

Objective: To improve fine motor coordination through mixing, pouring and measuring.

Evaluation: Small motor coordination was improved through mixing, pouring and measuring.

A. Snow Cones

Put crushed ice into paper cups. Pour concentrated fruit punch or 6 ozs. concentrated orange juice mixed with 3/4 C. water over ice.

B. Snow Balls

3/4 C. marshmallow creme

3 oz. semi-sweet chocolate chips

2 C. peanut butter

Shredded coconut

Mix first 3 ingredients and roll into small balls. Then roll in coconut - refrigerate.

C. Hot Chocolate

Add milk or water to Instant Hot Chocolate mix. Heat. Wonderful to serve after playing in the snow.

D. Banana Snowmen

2 C. raisins

2 bananas

shredded coconut

Chop bananas and raisins in blender. Put in bowl and refrigerate until mixture can be handled. Roll into balls and into shredded coconut. Stack 3 balls and fasten with toothpick.

E. Snow Ice Cream

Snow

1/2 C. sugar

1 C. milk

1 egg

1 tsp. vanilla

Put a clean container outside to catch the new snow. Then mix the remaining ingredients together. Add snow mixture until it is the consistency of sherbet. Put in paper cups. Delicious!

F. White Chocolate Pretzels

Melt: 1 lb. white chocolate

Add: 1-3/4 C. Spanish peanuts

Dip in: 1-3/4 C. thin pretzel sticks, broken

Drop on waxed paper (makes about 50).

G. Popcorn Snowballs

Use air popper - children watch corn pop. Mix with melted margarine and marshmallow whip or marshmallows. Form into large snowballs.

H. Maple Syrup Candy

Make by boiling 1 cup of maple blend syrup for 7 minutes. Pour over flat sheet of ice. It will turn hard. Eat!

I. Make coffee Sand

(don't eat)

4 C. dried, used coffee grounds

2 C. cornmeal

1 C. flour

1/2 C. salt

Mix in large plastic dishpan - use:

scoops, spoons, sifters, plastic cups, funnels, etc.

V. MATH

Objectives: To improve counting skills, recognize largest and smallest shapes, and matching.

Evaluation: The children counted, recognized largest, smallest, shapes and matched mittens.

A. Give each child a dark piece of construction paper and 3 white circles of different sizes.
Ask which circle is the largest?
Smallest? What are the shapes of the snowballs? How many do you have?
Have them build a snowman by gluing the circles from largest to smallest - discuss bottom, middle and top. Have them cut out squares for eyes, triangle for nose and oval for mouth and glue on.

B. Matching Mittens
Draw several mittens and have children draw lines to match them.

Or, cut out pairs of mittens from construction paper or wallpaper and put them in box. Have them find the pairs.

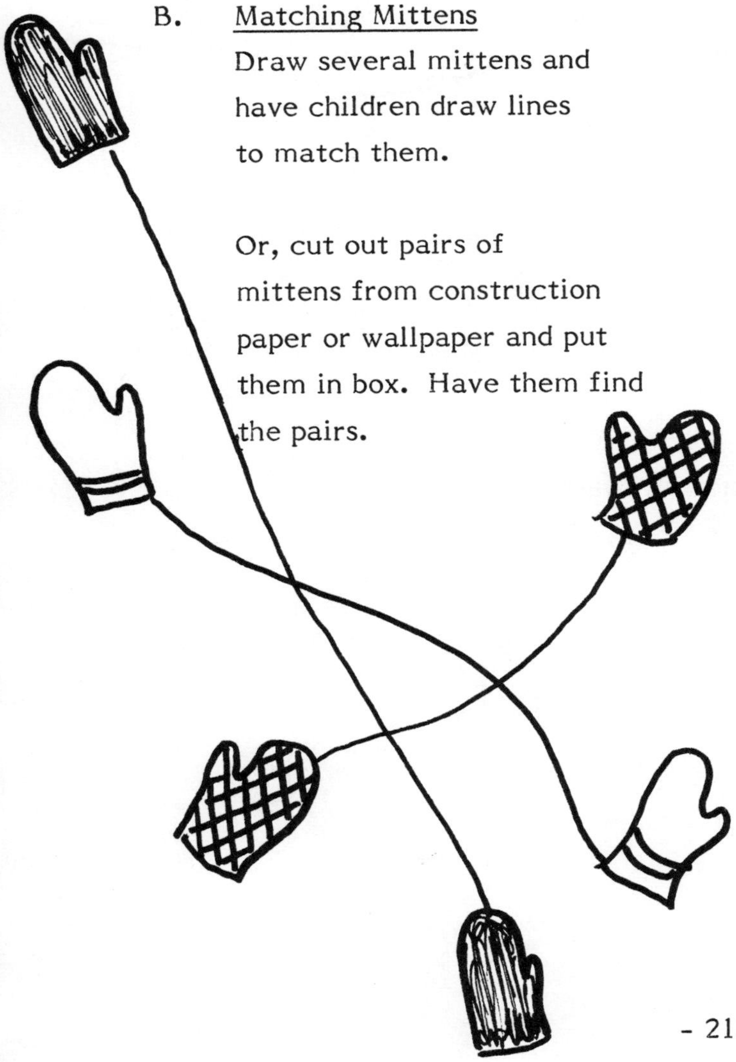

VI. FINGERPLAYS - SONGS

Objectives: To develop memory and counting skills through repetition.

Evaluation: During the following week, we observed that most children remembered the words, actions and numbers and were able to repeat them.

Five Little Snowmen

Five little snowmen all in a row
Each with a big tall hat and a big red bow
Now they are ready but where will they go?
Down through the fields with the melting snow.

Five little snowmen fat
Each had a pointed hat
Out came the sun
And melted one
What a sad thing was that

Four little snowmen fat
Etc.
(Can make felt snowmen for math experiences)

Here's a Hill

Here's a hill (make hill with left arm)
All covered with snow
We'll get on our sled
And ZOOM! Down we'll go (Swoop right hand downward)

Here's a Chimney

Here is a chimney (tuck thumb in fist)
Here is the top (other hand on top of fist)
Take off the lid (remove hand)
Out smoke pops! (pop up thumb)

Songs

Tune: "Did You Ever See a Lassie"
Children put your coats on, your coats on, your coats on,
Children put your coats on, one, two and three.
(Boots, gloves, scarves, etc.)

Tune: "The More We Get Together"
Come sing a song of winter, of winter, of winter,
Come sing a song of winter, the cold days are here.
With winter winds blowing and rosy cheeks glowing,
Come sing a song of winter, the cold days are here.

The Snowman

Roll him and roll him until he is big (roll hands into big ball)
Roll him until he's as fat as a pig (arms in large circle)
He has 2 big black eyes and a hat on his head (point to eyes and hat)
And he stands there all night (stand erect)
While we go to bed (head to side)

Mitten Song

"Thumb in the thumb place,
Fingers all together!"
This is the song we sing in mitten weather.
When it's cold
It doesn't matter whether
Mittens are wool
Or made of finest leather.
This is the song we sing in mitten weather;
"Thumb in the thumb place,
Fingers all together!"

This song is fun to sing while dressing to go outside (the first four lines) or use as a starting point when discussing what materials clothes are made of.

Red Mittens

Ten red mittens, hanging on the line,
This one blew away, and then there were nine.
Nine red mittens, each one had a mate,
This one fell down, and then there were eight.
Eight red mittens, one belonged to Evan,
This one found its boy, and then there were seven.
Seven red mittens, doing fancy tricks,
This one found a girl, and then there were six.
Six red mittens, looking so alive,
This one found the baby, then there were five.
Five red mittens, as pretty as before,
This one floated off, and then there were four.
Four red mittens, waving wild and free,
This one lost a clothespin, then there were three.
Three red mittens, looking very new,
This one fell in the mud, then there were two.
Two red mittens, left in the sun,
This one faded away, and then there was one.
One red mitten, left all alone,
It blew up in the air, and then there were none.

Use flannelboard mittens, real ones, or fingers to tell this story. This is a nice variation from the usual "Five little . . .

Jack Frost

The temp'rature is freezing. It's less than thirty-two.
Cause look who's on my window. It's Jack Frost, that's who!

Zippers

Three little zippers on my snow suit, Fasten up as snug as snug can be,
It's a very easy thing, as you can see, Just zip! zip! zip!

I work the zippers on my snow suit, Zippers really do save time for me.
I can fasten them myself, with one, two, three, Just zip! zip! zip!

Making a Snow Man

Roll it, roll it, get a pile of snow,
Rolling, rolling, rolling, rolling, rolling, here we go.
Pat it, pat it, face it to the south.
Now my little snow man's done, eyes and nose and mouth.

Snow Balls

The snow is soft for the snow ball fight.
Roll it round and ready to throw.
Roll it round and hard, roll it round and hard,
Roll it round and ready to throw.

We'll build a fort where we hide from sight.
Roll it round and ready to throw.
Roll it round and hard, roll it round and hard,
Roll it round and ready to throw.

Whirling Snowflakes

Snowflakes falling everywhere,
Whirling, whirling, in the air,
Whirling round and round,
Falling on the ground

Fun in the Snow

It's fun to play in the snow.
Bundled warm as toast.

It's fun to play in the snow.
Take your sled and coast.

The North Wind Doth Blow

The north wind doth blow, We soon shall have snow,
And what will poor robin do then, poor thing?
He'll sit in the barn to keep himself warm,
And hide his head under his wing, poor thing.

Ice Skating

Ice skating is nice skating, But here's some advice about ice skating:
Never skate where the ice is thin, Thin ice will crack and you'll fall right in,
And come up with icicles under your chin, If you skate where the ice is thin.

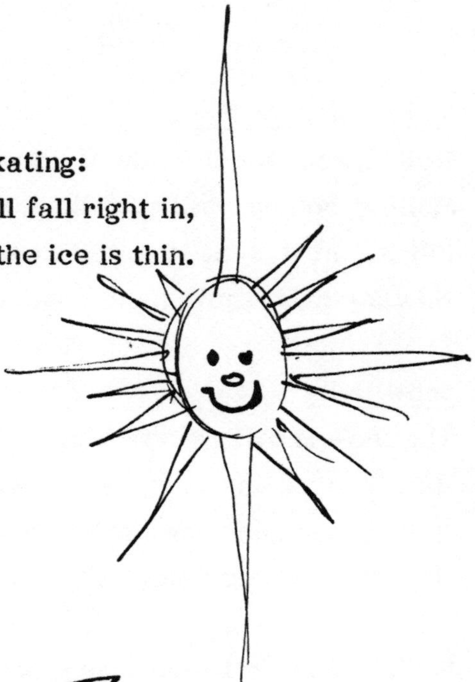

The Snowman and the Bunny

A chubby little snowman (make a fist)
Had a carrot nose (poke thumb out)
Along came a bunny
And what do you suppose? (other hand - make rabbit ears)
That hungry little bunny,
Looking for his lunch (bunny hops around)
Ate that snowman's carrot nose (bunny nibbles at thumb)
Crunch, crunch, crunch.

Snowman Countdown

Three little men made of snow
Out came the sun and stayed all day
One little snowman melted away.

Use the appropriate number of fingers for each verse and continue until none are left. You may want to substitute children, people, girls, etc., for "men" or even the names of specific children. Or, have the children act it out using as many actors as you'd like.

Build a Snowman

First you make a snowball
Big and fat and round.
Then you roll the snowball,
All along the ground.
Then you build the snowman -
One - two - three!
Then you have a snowman,
Don't you see?
Then the sun shines all around and
melts the snowman to the ground.

This is a scale song. Start at middle C (low) and say each line at a different tone working up to high C (high). Come down the scale from high to low for each word in the last line. Make appropriate motions with the song.

Five Little Snowmen

Five little snowmen knocking at the door,
One melts away and then there were four.
Four little snowmen climbing a tree,
One melts away and then there were three.
Three little snowmen looking for something to do.
One melts away and then there were two.
Two little snowmen are now having fun,
One melts away and then there was one.
One little snowman all by himself,
He melts away, now there are none.

Use stick puppets, flannelboard snowmen or fingers to tell this story.

BINGO

There was a farmer had a dog and Bingo was his name-o.
B-I-N-G-O, B-I-N-G-O, B-I-N-G-O,
and Bingo was his name-o.

2. ...(Clap)-I-N-G-O...
3. ...(X)-(X)-N-G-O...
4. ...(X)-(X)-(X)-G-O...
5. ...(X)-(X)-(X)-(X)-O...
6. ...(X)-(X)-(X)-(X)-(X)...

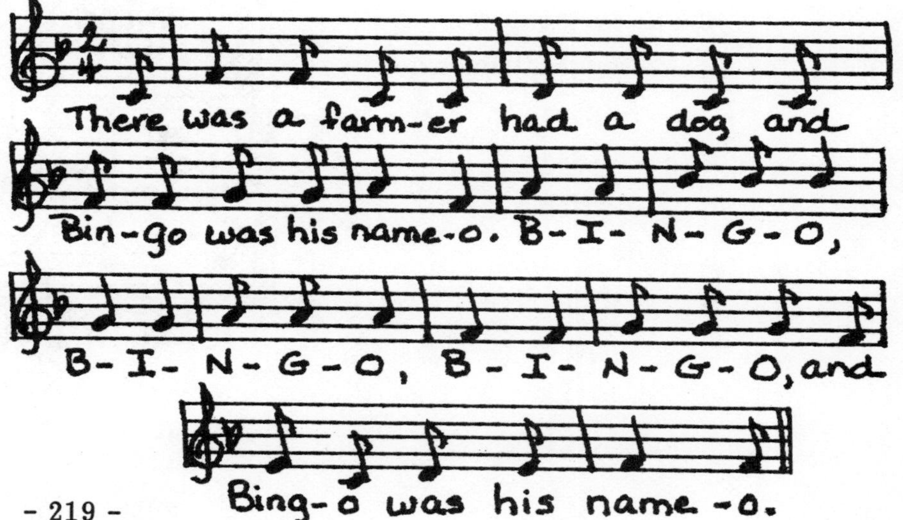

John Jacob Jingleheimer Schmidt

John Jacob Jingleheimer Schmidt,
that's my name too!
Whenever I go out,
the people always shout,
"John Jacob Jingleheimer Schmidt."
da da da da da da da da!

Repeat four times, each time softer, except loudly on the "da da."

Bumblebee

Bumblebee was in the barn,
(circle finger in air)
Carrying his dinner under his arm.
(closer to child)
Bzzzzzz........
(poke child)

Where is Thumbkin? (Tune: Are you Sleeping?)

Where is Thumbkin? Where is Thumbkin?
(Place hands behind back)
Here I am, here I am;
(show one thumb, then other)
How are you today sir?
(Bend one thumb)
Very well I thank you,
(Bend other thumb)
Run away, run a way.
(Wiggle thumbs away)

2. Pointer
3. Tall Man
4. Ring Man
5. Baby
6. All the Men

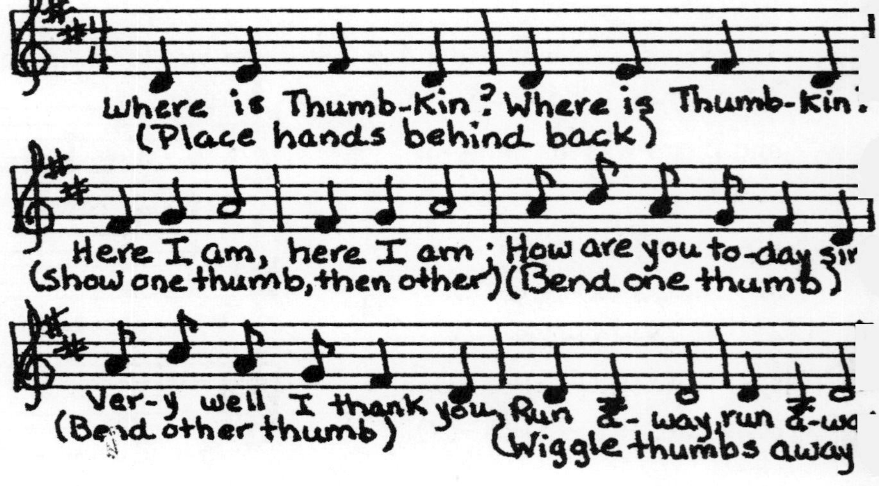

Here is the Church

Here is the church,

(fold hands, fingers inside)

And here is the steeple.

(index fingers up)

Open the doors,

(thumbs apart)

And see all the people.

(wiggle inside fingers)

Close the doors,

(thumbs together)

And hear them pray.

(hands to ear)

Open the doors,

(thumbs apart)

And they all walk away.

(fingers walk away)

Mitten Song

1. "Thumbs in the thumbplace, Fingers all together!"
   This is the song, We sing in mitten weather.
2. When it is cold, It doesn't matter whether
   Mittens are wool, Or made of finest leather.
3. This is the song, We sing in mitten weather:
   "Thumbs in the thumbplace, Fingers all together!"

VII. SCIENCE

Objectives: To have children observe effects of temperature changes.

Evaluation: Children observed effects of temperature changes.

A. Ice Cream

1 qt. half & half

2 C. sugar

Vanilla

Kosher salt, lots of

Crushed ice

tin small tomato paste cans

plastic container

Layer ice, salt, ice, salt, ice, salt, etc. into tin juice cans. Fill half full with half & half mixture. Stir, cover with foil, stir again until mixture hardens and eat. Yum!

Good for winter and summer alike.

B. Make a felt weather doll so preschool children can dress and undress dolls to correspond to the weather.

C. Snow is fun - One day when fresh snow falls, go outside and observe surroundings. See what snow does to trees, houses, etc. Take a piece of black paper or cloth outside. Catch some snowflakes on it. Look at snow, if magnifying glass is available, use. Have children blow on with hot breath. What happens? Why?

D. Making Frost

Changes in temperature cause dew. Frost is really frozen dew. We will need tin can with lid removed, rock salt, crushed ice.

Have children put two cups of crushed ice and one-half cup of rock salt in a can. Have the children stir mixture rapidly. Go on to another activity and tell the children they will return in 30 minutes. When we return, the outside of the can will have dew on it. If we wait a while longer, this dew will change to frost.

E. Frost

On a very cold morning go outside with kids and investigate why everything is white. The moisture in the air freezes on the cold grass. When you walk, notice how the ground crackles. Explain that the water in the ground freezes and rises. It sticks up from the ground. The crunch feeling is frost.

F. Bird Feeders

Bird feeders can be made from a variety of scrap material; then filled with bird treats.

1. Cut a hole in the lower part of a plastic bleach bottle. Then glue the bottle onto an aluminum pie tin.
2. Scoop out an orange or a grapefruit.
3. Hang up a plastic berry basket.
4. Roll a pinecone in peanut butter and seeds.
5. Remove the cardboard tube from a coat hanger and insert the open ends of the wire into a corn cob.
6. Hang a mesh bag from potatoes or oranges. Fill with large bread crumbs or bird seed.
7. Cut a large square in opposite sides of a milk carton, leaving an opening. Put a towel across the botton and secure with string.
8. Remove both ends from a large tin can, be sure there are no sharp edges.

Fill your completed feeders with seeds, suet, raisins, crumbs, etc., and hang them from a tree or on a post. You can find a tree nearby your classroom and hang up feeders. This is a wonderful way to observe birds, talk about different kinds of birds and their habits.

G. Snow, water and ice

What is snow made of? Experiment in the following ways.

1. Give each child a paper cup to fill with snow. Bring cups inside and discuss changes as snow melts. What is happening to the snow?
2. Put a cup of water outside on a window ledge. Put a mark where water line fills, watch snow expand and contract.

H. Ice

Experiment with an ice cube. Place an ice cube beside another ice cube; place on floor; lay it on open hand, hold it in closed hand; place in mouth, chew, place it on plate and sprinkle salt over it, place it in a cup of hot water.

Discuss:

1. The solid form of water is ice
2. Which ice cube melted first?
3. How do we melt ice when it forms on windows, street, etc.?

I. Put a mitten on one hand. Hold ice cube in each hand. Which is colder? This is why mittens are worn.

VIII. PHYSICAL DEVELOPMENT - GAMES

Objectives: To develop large motor coordination. To increase social interaction, develop good sportsmanship and have fun.

Evaluation: The children experienced and played well with each other, took turns and learned how to be a better winner or loser.

Freeze

Children march in time to the music. When music stops, children "freeze" or stand perfectly still.

Snowman Follow the Leader

Play follow the leader in the snow. When new snow has fallen, teacher can go first and make footprints. Children follow the footprints.

Who has the Ice Cube?

Make a circle. Enclose an ice cube in a small plastic bag. One child is "it". "It" hides eyes in center of circle. Play music and pass bag around circle. When music stops, child in center guesses who has the ice, etc.

Punching Bag

An old pillow case or laundry bag can be stuffed with rags. Tie or sew ends together. Children can release energy by punching, kicking and slapping the bag.

Snowman Melt

Ask the children if they ever saw a snowman melt in the sun. Discuss the process. Where does the sun first start melting the snowman? How does the snowman change shape?

Have each child stand like an upright snowman.

Have children close their eyes and go from a standing snowman to a puddle of water by verbalizing these directions slowly:

a. You are a beautiful, glistening snowman.
b. The sun shines on your head and you feel the warmth.
c. The sun gets hotter and the top of your head starts to water and slip.
d. The sun bathes your shoulders in warmth, they start to lose their shape and slump over.

e. Now your body starts to slump over.

f. Your feet and legs begin to shrink. The sun is hot. You fall into your own clump of watery snow on the ground.

g. The clump slowly dissolves with the heat into a pool of warm water. It is all warm and comfortable and your shape has totally disappeared.

IX. FIELD TRIPS

Objectives: To increase awareness of their surroundings.

Evaluation: The children were more aware of their environment.

1. Go for a Winter Walk and try to identify animal tracks in the snow.
2. Visit a car wash.
3. Visit a Burger King - arrange to take a tour of the kitchen.
4. Visit an airport - some airlines will give a tour of an airplane.

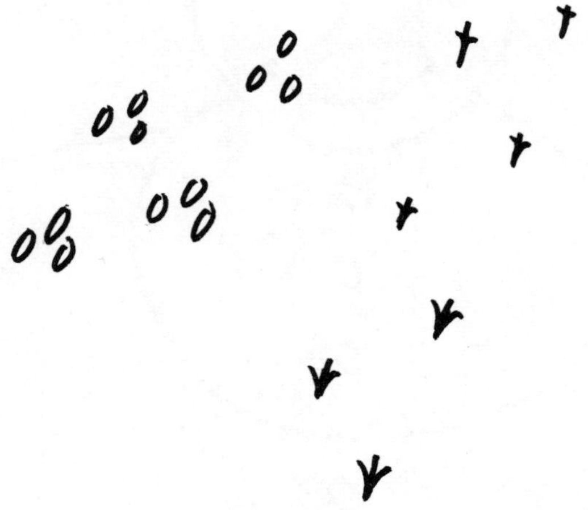

X. BOOKS AND RELATED ACTIVITIES

The Big Snow	Hader
The Winter Picnic	Welber
The Day My Daddy Stayed Home	Kessler
Katy and the Big Snow	Burton
The Snowy Day	Keats
The Mitten	Tresselt
Hamilton Duck	Getz
White Snow, Bright Snow	Tresselt
Marmalade's Snowy Day	Wheeler
Oh Lewis	Rice
My Mother Hates Me in January	Balton
One Mitten Lewis	Kay

FEBRUARY

I. ARTS AND CRAFTS

Objective: All these activities are developed to enhance small motor coordination through cutting, gluing, shaving, stringing, printing and painting.

Evaluation: Children will develop small motor coordination through cutting, gluing, shaving, stringing, printing and painting.

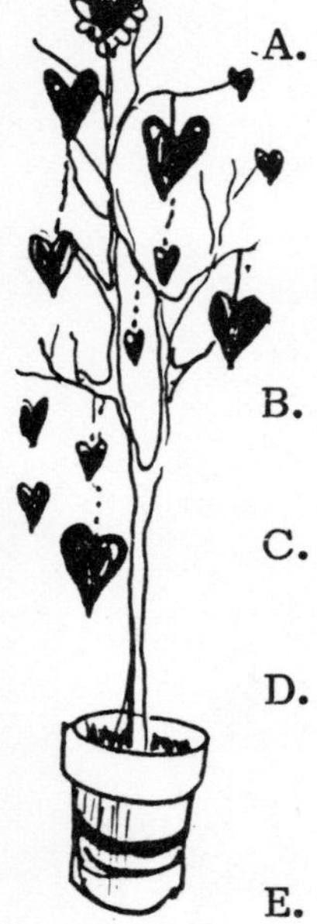

A. Valentine Tree

Stick a small, bare branch into a flower pot weighted with sand, pebbles, or play-dough. Trim the tree with tiny hearts the children have cut out and decorated and hang them on strings or thread.

B. Sew around a red heart with white yarn.

C. Cut out old Valentine cards and make a collage on shirtboard or on meat tray.

D. Make a red finger painting. Adult or child may cut it in shape of heart. Paste on black paper. Can do in a metal tray, use freezer wrap paper to make prints.

E. Draw bare branches on red paper. Have popcorn and small candy hearts to glue on branches.

F. Have children cut out large red or white hearts. Dribble on contrasting paint (blue and white on red, or red and pink on white). Fold and rub. Open to find lacy design.

G. Stained Glass Heart

Have children grate red, pink, and white crayons onto waxed paper. Adult presses waxed paper with warm iron to melt crayon shavings. Allow to cool. Cut out a heart shape from center of construction paper. Tape the waxed paper behind the heart-shaped hole. Or, cut the waxed paper in the shape of a heart, punch a hole on top, put string through hole and hang as a mobile.

H. Tissue Paper Heart

Have children cut out heart from construction paper. Crumple small squares of red and pink tissue paper and glue to heart. Or, draw large heart on poster board and have children do same.

I. Love Beads

Cut piece of yarn 25" in length and tie a small piece of straw to one end. Wrap other end of yarn tightly with tape to make needle. Thread half of yarn with 1" pieces of straw (that children can cut) or macaroni or Fruit Loops. Then thread with paper heart that has hole punched in top center. Continue adding pieces of straw, etc. Tie ends of yarn together to make necklace.

J. Jello Design

Drip glue on paper to make a design or put glue on paper in a heart shape with a Q-tip. Sprinkle flavored jello powder or Kool-Aid over glue and shake off excess.

K. Potato Prints

Cut a potato in half. Carve a heart out of each end. Dip in red paint and print on white paper.

L. George Washington's Hat

Have children cut 8-1/2" x 11" piece of construction paper crosswise to form three equal rectangles. Staple narrow ends of strips together to form triangular hat. Attach cherry sprig for decoration.

M. Log Cabin (Lincoln's Birthday)

Cover an eight ounce milk carton with ready-to-spread frosting. Place pretzel sticks on the frosting to make log cabin; or, instead of frosting, use glue.

N. Post office

Use large cardboard carton from an appliance store. Carton from refrigerator or freezer is best. Cut hole for window and door. Use large paint brushes and have child paint entire carton to be used as a post office.

O. Sponge Prints

Cut sponges in the shape of hearts of varying sizes; dip in paint and print.

P. Valentine Mail Box

Have each child bring in a shoe box to paint. Have them cut heart shapes from folded colored paper. Glue onto box. Or, decorate small paper bags. Can use doilies, hearts, Valentine candies.

Q. Valentine Cards

Use 9" x 12" paper, scissors, glue, small pieces of red, pink, and white construction paper, paper doilies, foil paper, tissue paper, bits of lace and ribbon, pictures from magazines or old Valentine cards. Fold paper in half to form card. Allow children to create their own Valentine using the materials available. Write message dictated by the child on inside of card.

R. Heart Collage

Have children cut out hearts of varying sizes and colors. Glue hearts on paper to form objects or designs.

S. Sparkle Paint

Cut out a jumbo heart from easel paper. Mix kosher salt into red, white and pink paint. Paint heart.

II. COLOR DAY - RED

Objective: To recognize color red.
Evaluation: The children recognized color red.

Have children wear something red. Point out different red objects in room. Use red easel paint. Red jello hearts for snack (see Cooking section).

Can have Clifford Day

Read Clifford the Big Red Dog (filmstrips are also available)

Craft: make Clifford

Have children cut two ovals out of red construction paper. Use small paper plate for face. Put ears on with brads so they will move. Draw on face. Can also glue on tongue depressor to make puppet.

COLOR DAYS - PINK DAY

Objective: To be familiar with color pink
Evaluation: Children recognized color pink

Have children wear something pink. Find pink around room. At easel, have children mix red and white paints to get pink. Make these two wonderful recipes.

Think Pink: Make pink applesauce

Make your own applesauce using 12 apples, cored and peeled. Steam with 1/3 cup of water. Near the end of cooking time, add two tablespoons of cinnamon red-hots.

Quick Pink Potato Bread

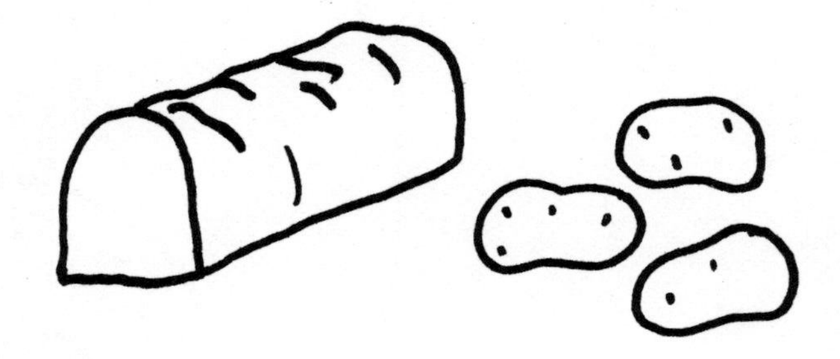

1 package-active dry yeast
4 - 4-1/2 C. flour
2 tsp. salt
Instant mash potatoes
3/4 C. milk
1/4 C. butter
2 eggs

In large bowl of an electric mixer stir together yeast, 1-1/2 cups of flour, sugar and salt. In a pan, prepare 2 servings of instant mashed potatoes, use the amounts of water, milk, butter and salt called for on package. Then stir in milk, butter and eggs; stir until well blended.

Add potato mixture to dry ingredients and beat for 2 minutes at medium speed. Add 1 more cup of the flour and beat at medium speed. With spoon, stir in 1 more cup of flour - form stiff dough. Use red food coloring to make dough pink. Knead until smooth and satiny (children love to knead).

Turn dough over in greased bowl; cover and let rise (1-1/2 to 2 hours). Punch dough down, knead briefly to release air. Place each in a well-greased 9 x 5 inch loaf pan. Cover and rise 45 minutes.

Bake in a 350° oven for 35 minutes.

III. STORY

Objective: To enjoy story.
Evaluation: The story was enjoyed by all.

Tell the following story while making a heart from a folded piece of paper. Draw items on paper according to diagram.

Sally and Jim lived at A (make A). Grandma lived at B (make B). They decided to make a map of the path to Grandma's around the lake (draw lake). They walked around the lake (draw half heart starting at A and ending at B). When they arrived at Grandma's they took scissors and cut along the path they had walked (cut along line). They opened it and gave the Valentine to Grandma!

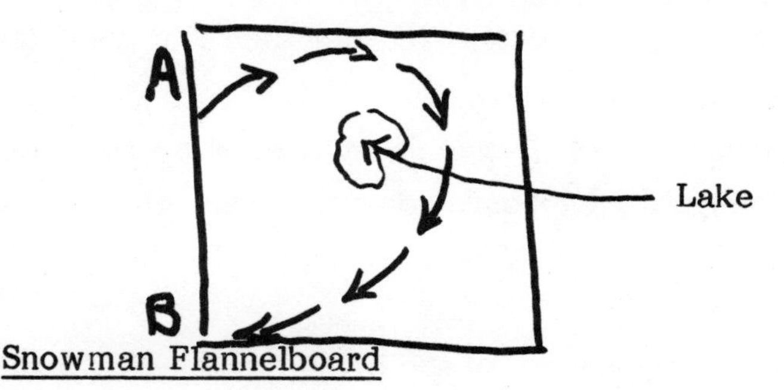

Snowman Flannelboard

Roll a snowman large
Then one of middle size - small -
Use lump of coal for eyes
Place a carrot for a nose,
an old hat on his head
A corncob pipe goes in his mouth,
some buttons on his vest,
And he stands there so round and fat,
Of snowmen he's the best.

Teeny-Tiny

There was once a teeny-tiny woman who lived in a teeny-tiny house in a teeny-tiny town. One day this teeny-tiny woman put on her teeny-tiny hat and went out of her teeny-tiny house to take a teeny-tiny walk. When the teeny-tiny woman had gone a teeny-tiny way, she came to a teeny-tiny gate. Then the teeny-tiny woman opened the teeny-tiny gate and went into a teeny-tiny churchyard. In the teeny-tiny churchyard she saw a teeny-tiny bone upon a teeny-tiny grave, and the teeny-tiny woman said, "This teeny-tiny bone will make some teeny-tiny soup for my teeny-tiny supper." And the teeny-tiny woman took the teeny-tiny bone from the teeny-tiny grave and put it in her teeny-tiny pocket and went back to her teeny-tiny house.

When the teeny-tiny woman got inside her teeny-tiny house, she was a teeny-tiny bit sleepy, so she put the teeny-tiny bone into her teeny-tiny cupboard, and then she went up her teeny-tiny stairs and climbed into her teeny-tiny bed.

After the teeny-tiny woman had closed her teeny-tiny eyes for a teeny-tiny nap, she was awakened by a teeny-tiny voice from the teeny-tiny cupboard down the teeny-tiny stairs that said:

"Give me my bone!"

When she heard this she was a teeny-tiny bit frightened, so she hid her teeny-tiny head under her teeny-tiny blanket and went to sleep again. And when she had a slept a teeny-tiny time, the teeny-tiny voice cried out again a teeny-tiny bit louder:

"Give me my bone!"

This made the teeny-tiny woman a teeny-tiny bit more frightened, so she hid her teeny-tiny head a teeny-tiny bit farther under her teeny-tiny blanket. And when the teeny-tiny woman had gone to sleep again for a teeny-tiny time, the teeny-tiny voice from the teeny-tiny cupboard down the teeny-tiny stairs said a teeny-tiny bit louder:

"Give me my bone!"

By now the teeny-tiny woman was a teeny-tiny bit more frightened, but she lifted up her teeny-tiny head from under her teeny-tiny blanket and said in her loudest teeny-tiny voice:

"TAKE IT!"

IV. COOKING

Objective: To develop fine motor coordination through mixing, cutting and pouring. Also, to develop math skills by counting and measuring ingredients.
Evaluation: The children mixed, cut and poured, counted and measured ingredients, thus improving their math skills and fine motor coordination.

A. Red Jello Hearts

4 envelopes unflavored gelatin
9 ozs. cherry gelatin
4 C. boiling water

Dissolve gelatin in boiling water and pour into shallow baking pan. Chill. When gelatin is set, cut with metal heart-shaped cookie cutter. Hearts are eaten with hands.

B. Strawberry Milk Shake

10 ozs. frozen strawberries, with juice
4 C. cold milk

Combine fruit and milk in blender. May add a little red food coloring. Blend until smooth and frothy.

C. Love Juice

1 pkg. frozen strawberries, with juice
2 C. pineapple or orange juice
2/3 C. nonfat dry milk powder
8 ice cubes
2 tsp. sugar

Put all ingredients in blender and mix until all ice cubes are crushed.

D. Stone Soup

Read Stone Soup by Marcia Brown. Make soup. Have children bring in carrots, potatoes, cabbage, meat, barley. May add more vegetables, macaroni, etc. Put several large, clean stones in the bottom of the pot, may also add Soup Starter for a better soup. Boil, cover and simmer for 2 hours. Add salt and pepper. Serve with bread and cider.

E. Lentil Soup

Read Lentil Soup by Joe Lasker. Make soup. Have children bring in meat, bones, vegetables, package of lentils, etc. Season, bring to boil, cover and simmer about 2 hours.

F. Chicken Soup with Rice

Read Chicken Soup with Rice by M. Sendak. Have children bring in and cut up vegetables. Add to chicken stock or Soup Starter. Add raw rice. Simmer 1-1/2 hours. For craft, children can dip raw rice in vegetable coloring, let dry, and paste on cardboard or meat trays.

G. Quick Homemade Pizzas

2 lbs. ground beef

2 - 8 oz. cans refrigerated biscuits (20 biscuits)

Salt

Whatever "fixings" you like, or have on hand: pizza sauce, grated mozzarella, etc.

Sprinkle salt in skillet. Brown meat and add remaining salt. Roll biscuits into circles of 4 or 5 inches. Place on greased cookie sheet. Top each biscuit with pizza sauce, beef, or pepperoni sliced thin. Children can make their own creations. Bake at 400° for 10 to 12 minutes. Makes 20 small pizzas.

Use for valentine's party. Children can help make entire recipe themselves.

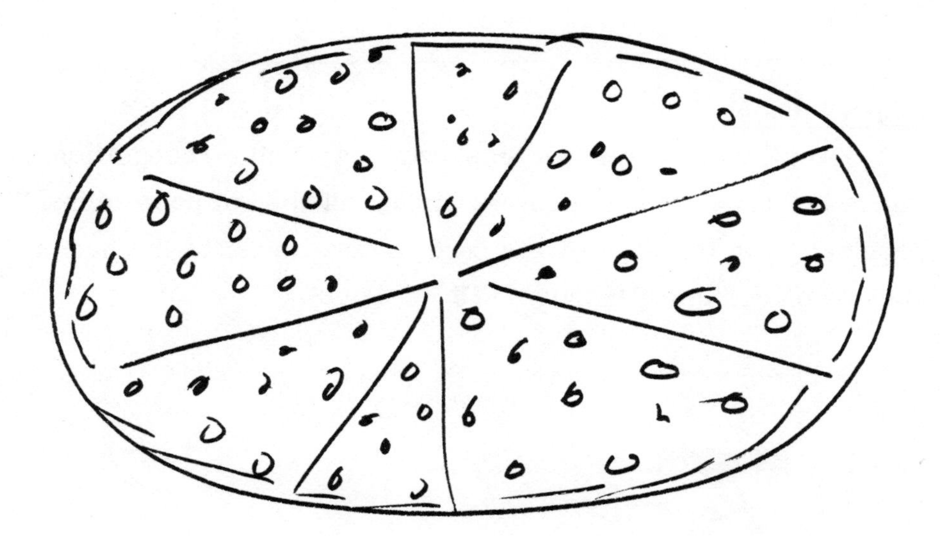

V. MATH

<u>Objectives</u>: To improve counting skills.
<u>Evaluation</u>: Counting skills were improved.

A. Show children Lincoln's face on penny. Sit in a circle on sheet or blanket. Each child is given 5 pennies. Adult instructs children to:

1. Stack pennies on top of each other.
2. Place pennies in a straight line, in a circle.
3. Place one penny in center of circle, "How many do you have?"
4. Pass around bank and put all pennies in. Count as they deposit them.

B. To provide practice in counting and the meaning of numbers. At the top of a piece of posterboard or paper, print the numerals 1-5 for younger children or 6-10 for older children. The child then places the correct number of counters below the printed numerals.

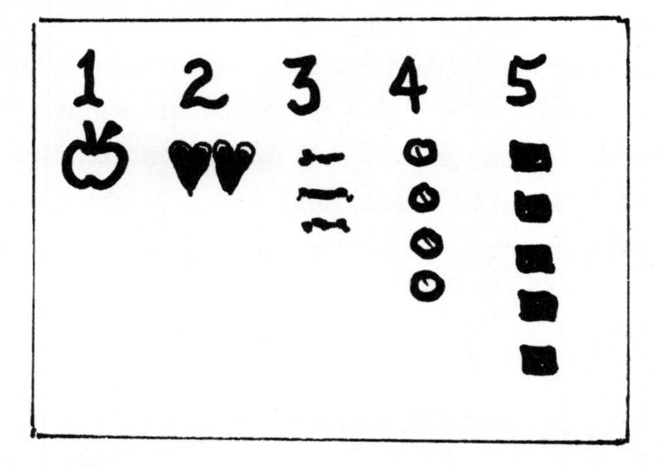

C. <u>Clip a Number</u>

To provide practice in counting and number recognition. Use cards with a numeral from 1-10 and a corresponding number of paper clips. The child places paper clips on the edge of the card to correspond to the numeral. The cards can then be placed in order from 1-10.

VI. FINGERPLAYS

<u>Objective</u>: To develop memory and counting skills through repetition.

<u>Evaluation</u>: Children remembered the words, actions, and numbers, and were able to repeat them.

My Valentine is red (form heart with hands)
My Valentine is blue
I drop it in the letter box
And mail it to you (point to friend)

Listen, Mother, you know what?
On Valentines' Day, I love you a lot (open arms wide)
So I'll throw you a kiss, Mother mine
I want you for my Valentine (form heart)

Valentines, valentines, red, white, and blue (form heart)
I'll find a nice one and give it to you (point to friend)

I love you, I love you
I love you divine
Please give me your bubble gum
You're sitting on mine!

I love you, I love you
I love you so well
If I had a peanut
I'd give you the shell

Pigs love pumpkins
Cows love squash
I love you
I do, by gosh!

I love you, I love you,
With my heart and soul
If I had a doughnut,
I'd give you the hole!

Roses are red
Violets are blue
Sugar is sweet
And so are you

I climbed up the door
And shut the stairs
I said my shoes
And took off my prayers.

I shut off the bed
And climbed into the light
And all because
You kissed me goodnight!

Me 4 U

Roses are red
Violets are blue
R U 4 me?
I am 4 U

I feel flippy,
I feel fizzy,
I feel whoopy
I feel whizzy.

I'm feeling wonderful
I'm feeling just fine.
Because you just gave me
A valentine.

If I were a mailman
Know what I'd do?
I'd always bring mail
With letters for you!

And on Valentine's Day
I'd bring you plenty
I might even bring you
Three hundred and twenty!

George Washington

1. Many, many years ago when our country was still young,
There lived a man so strong and brave, his name was Washington.

On his birthday let's sing in celebration;
We remember Washington, the father of our nation.

2. He became a general, our armies to command,
Then he was made the President, the first one in the land.

My Hat It Has Three Corners

My hat	*Touch head on the word "hat."*
it has three corners,	*Touch each elbow on the word "corners."*
Three corners	*Touch each elbow on the word "corners."*
has my hat,	*Touch head on the word "hat."*
And if it hadn't	
three corners,	*Touch each elbow on the word "corners."*
it wouldn't be my hat.	*Touch head on the word "hat."*

Continue the action through verses 2 and 3

Valentine Song

Oh, Valentine, Oh, Valentine, Oh, will you be my Valentine?
Oh, Valentine, Oh, Valentine, Oh, will you be my Valentine?

Love Me - Love Me Not

They say that daisies will not tell
(shake head for "no")
Of course they never do.
But when you pick their petals,
(pretend to pick petals)
They tell if one you love, loves you.
(place hand over heart)

Roses are Red

Roses are red, violets are blue,
Are you for me? I am for you.

I Will Give You My Heart

I will give you my heart, and you give yours to me
We'll lock them up together and throw away the key.

Five Gay Valentines (Hold up five fingers and bend them down one at a time as verse progresses.

Five gay valentines from the ten-cent store.
I sent one to mother, now there are four.
Four gay valentines, pretty ones to see.
I gave one to brother, now there are three.
Three gay valentines, yellow, red and blue.
I gave one to sister, now there are two.
Two gay valentines, my we have fun.
I gave one to daddy, now there is one.
One gay valentine, the story is almost done.
I gave it to baby, now there are none.

Roses Love Sunshine

Roses love sunshine, violets love dew,
Angels love heaven, and I love you.

Love is a Peculiar Thing

Love is a peculiar thing
It's sometimes like a lizard,
It wraps its tail around your heart
And crawls into your gizzard!

Children love tongue twisters

Have fun with some of these:

1. Lemon liniment
2. Double bubble gum gives double bubble trouble
3. Six, slick, slim saplings
4. Sallow Sally
5. Unique New York

I'm Yours till...

Yours till cement walks.
Yours till ice screams.
Yours till the banana splits
Yours till the bees get the hives.
Yours till the trees pack their trunks.

VII. SCIENCE

Objective: To improve understanding of hibernation.
Evaluation: Children discussed and were interested in hibernation.

A. February is a good month to have a unit in hibernation. Hibernation, a mysterious cycle of life, a way of survival while the world is cold and harsh. A book that is a must for a well developed unit is Winter - Sleeping Wildlife by Will Barker (Harper & Row, Publishers, New York and Evanston, 1958). Some good animals to describe are bears, squirrels, raccoons, bats, snakes, turtles and spiders.

B. An excellent book for pre-schoolers is All Ready for Winter by Leone Adelson.

Objective: To understand crystals.
Evaluation: Children enjoyed watching crystals grow.

C. Crystal Garden

Place piece of charcoal in a shallow bowl or 9" x 9" aluminum pan. Mix together 1/4 cup ammonia, 1/4 cup noniodized salt, and 1/4 cup liquid bluing. Pour this solution slowly over pieces of charcoal. Almost immediately, the crystals will start forming. Do not move container or shake it because the crystals are very fragile and will crumble. If some spots seem bare, drop a little more ammonia. Look at crystals with magnifying glass. Compare to snowflake.

Objective: To understand metamorphosis of a frog.
Evaluation: Children enjoyed watching the eggs turn into tadpoles, etc.

D. From a Tadpole to a Frog

Not all babies look like their parents. You will need: a water tank (one gallon), some frog eggs, pond water and plants, green, leafy vegetables.

Put the frog eggs, pond water and plants in your container. Watch daily for eggs to hatch. After the eggs begin to hatch, supply green vegetables for food for tadpoles. Let the children observe that tadpoles do not look like frogs. Let children continue to watch as the hind legs and front legs begin to grow and tail grows smaller.

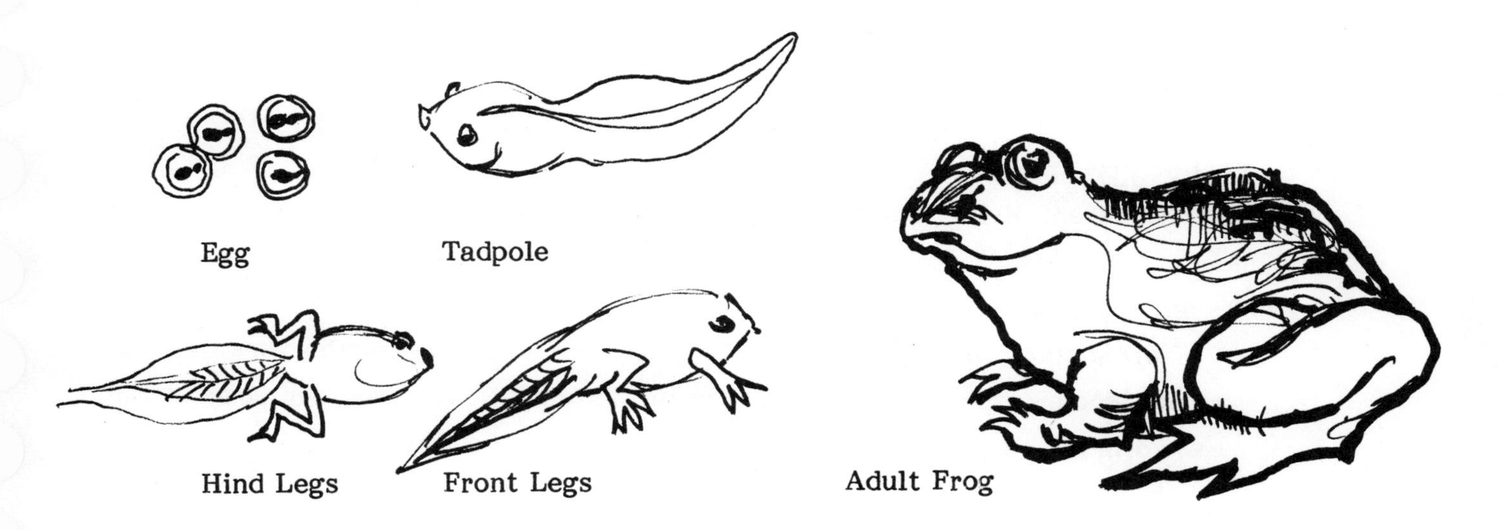

To accompany this project, read Olly's Polliwogs by Anne Rockwell.

Objective: To appreciate the different homes animals have.
Evaluation: The children were able to match the animals to their homes after class discussion.

E. Animal Homes

Animals have homes, different kinds of animals have different homes. Have pictures of animals, pictures of animals' homes, yarn, glue, posterboard.

From magazines, allow the children to cut pictures of animals and homes where they live. Divide posterboard in half. On 1/2 glue the pictures of the animals, on the other half, glue the pictures of the animals' homes. Cut yarn into two-foot lengths. With a hole punch, punch a hole beside each picture. Attach one end of string to a picture of an animal. Encourage children to find the home that belongs to that animal and attach the other end of string to the correct hole, i.e., bird and nest.

Objective: To understand the earthworm's environment.

Evaluation: Through observation, children were able to understand earthworm's environment.

F. Earthworms

Different living things need different environments for living. You will need: large (one to two gallon) glass jar with large mouth, soil, earthworms, gravel, food: cornmeal, cereals.

Mix a small amount of gravel in good, rich soil. Put earthworms into the jar, add food on top of the dirt and keep the soil moist. Children can observe the earthworm in an environment much like the one in which they live.

Objective: To match baby animals with the proper mothers.

Evaluation: Through working with puzzles, children matched baby animals with their parents.

G. Animal Baby Puzzles

Animal babies look much like their parents. Find pictures of animals and babies. Cut these pictures out. Select pictures of animals and of corresponding animal baby. Glue picture of adult animal on one end of strip of cardboard and baby animal on the other end of cardboard. Cut the strips in half in different ways to produce puzzles. Mix several strips together and let the children match the correct animal with the correct baby.

VIII. PHYSICAL DEVELOPMENT - GAMES

Objectives: To improve large muscle coordination, creativity and memory skills.
Evaluation: The children improved large muscle coordination, creativity and memory skills through games.

A. A Tisket, A Tasket

A tisket, a tasket
A red and yellow basket
Sent a valentine to my friend
And on the way I dropped it
One of you has picked it up
And put it in your pocket.

Have children form a circle and sing song. One child (A) walks around outside of circle and drops a bean bag or felt bag (can be heart-shaped) behind another child (B). (B) child picks up bag and chases (A) child around circle to empty space. Repeat.

B. Animal Guess

Each child takes a turn imitating an animal. The group guesses what animal it is.

C. Fast Artist or Chalk Talk

Teacher uses blackboard and chalk to sketch pictures. Children try to guess what it is as the drawing progresses.

D. What's Missing?

Use any 4 or 5 familiar toys or objects that can be easily handled. Spread them out on the floor or table and ask child to name each item. Then ask a child (or whole group) to close eyes. Remove one item. When he opens his eyes, ask him to tell which item is missing. Gradually add more items. Two or three items may be removed at one time.

E. Name Ball

Children stand in circle, one child in center. Center child says name of any circle child and bounces ball to him. Circle child says center child's name and bounces ball back to center. Center child may have one or several turns.

F. Elephant in Spider's Web

"One little elephant went out to play,
in a spider's web one day.
He had such enormous fun,
that he asked someone else to come."

The children form a circle with the "elephant" in the center. He then asks another child to join him. Children sing "1 little elephant . . ." Next verse is "2 little elephants . . ." until all children are in spider's web.

G. Candy Shop Game

The children sit in a circle. Have available four or five different colored cardboard or real lollipops.

One child, holding the lollipops, walks around the outside of the circle while everyone sings (to the tune of "Mulberry Bush"):

Come with me to the candy shop, candy shop, candy shop,
Come with me to the candy shop,
And I'll buy you a lollipop.

When the song ends, the child with the lollipops holds them up to the child nearest him, and says, "Would you like a lollipop?" If that child says, "Yes," the first child then asks him, "What color would you like?"

After the second child chooses a lollipop and names its color, it is then his turn to walk around the circle, carrying the lollipops. When possible, let the children eat the lollipops they identify.

IX. FIELD TRIPS

A. Visit a post office

B. Visit a bakery

C. Visit a candy factory

D. Visit a pet shop

X. BOOKS AND RELATED ACTIVITIES

George and the Cherry Tree	Brandenburg
Things to Make and Do for Valentine's Day	de Paolo
Good Morning to You, Valentine	Hopkins
All Ready for Winter	Adelson
Winter - Sleeping Wildlife	Barker
A Friend is Someone Who Likes You	Anglund
Love is a Special Way of Feeling	Anglund
Let's Be Friends	Bryano
Play With Me	Eets
George and Martha	Marshall
I Learn About Sharing	Roorback
One is Good, Two Are Better	Slobodkin
Do You Know What I'll Do	Zolotow
Stone Soup	Marcia Brown
Lentil Soup	Joe Lasker
Chicken Soup with Rice	M. Sendak

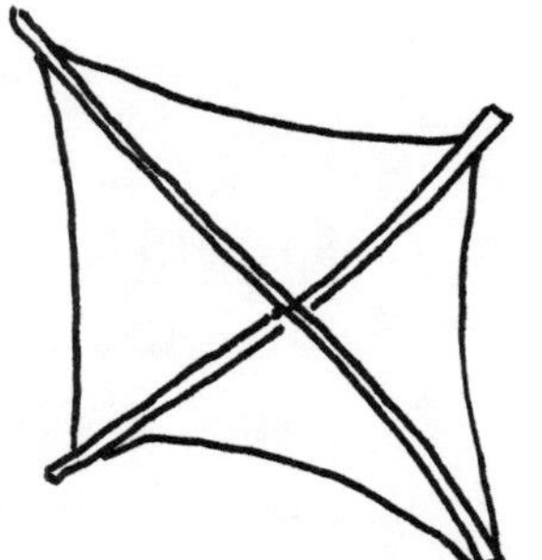

MARCH

I. ARTS AND CRAFTS

<u>Objective</u>: To improve small motor coordination through cutting, pasting, painting, printing and tearing.
<u>Evaluation</u>: Small motor coordination was improved through cutting, pasting, painting and tearing.

A. <u>Kite</u>

Three sheets of clear plastic from the hardware store make about 25 kites. (Plastic doesn't tear as children run). Paint kites with mixture of soap and coloring. Staple on tail. Glue paper bows to tail. Staple string to corners as for regular kite.

B. <u>Kite</u>

Tag board with colored tissue bows for a string tail.

C. <u>Paper bag kite</u>

This type of kite can be made by decorating a bag and attaching a string. When the child runs, air goes into the bag and holds it aloft.

D. <u>Pastel soap painting</u>

Color Ivory detergent flakes with tempera to make pastel shades for painting. A little liquid starch added to the stiff mixture makes it less fragile when dry.

E. Draw two posts on paper and paste a piece of string or yarn across. Children like to paste pieces of cloth on this line to look like clothes hanging on a clothesline, blowing in the wind.

F. <u>Pussywillow Creatures</u>

Individual pussywillows make tiny animals. Let children design their own pussywillow creatures, using either collage materials, crayons or paint. Can paste on construction paper. Can draw on arms, legs, etc.

G. <u>Butterflies</u>

Materials: old crayons, vegetable peeler, waxed paper, newspaper, iron, scissors.

Procedure: shave old crayons into bits using vegetable peeler. Place a sheet of waxed paper on newspaper. Sprinkle waxed paper with crayon bits. Cover with another piece of waxed paper. Press with iron for a few seconds. Cut into butterfly shape. Hang in a window.

H. <u>Clothespin Butterfly</u>

Materials: clothespins, coffee filters, pipe cleaners, food coloring (dye).

Procedure: take coffee filter and dip in several different food coloring dishes. Paper will absorb colors, push onto clothespin. Wrap around pipe cleaner for antennae. Be prepared for children to do several, they simply love the effect.

I. <u>Ink Blot Butterfly</u>

Using precut butterfly shapes that are folded in the center, have the children paint one side. Fold and rub lightly, then unfold. There will be two sides that are identical.

J. Make a butterfly from cylindrical clothespin. Use precut rectangles of tissue paper for wings. Children may decorate with bits of gummed paper or other collage items.

K. <u>Blow Painting</u>

(To illustrate wind). Use straws to blow paint around on a piece of paper. Make sure your children can blow <u>out</u> by practicing first (older children do best at this activity).

L. Cloud Collages

Color a picture on blue paper and glue on cotton balls for clouds. Also, add rick-rack for lightning or cut paper with pinking shears.

M. Pussywillow Prints

Make pussywillow thumbprint pictures. Have the children draw a crayon stem, then put pointer or thumb into gray, silver, or black and white paint and press along the side of the stem. Or, glue cotton balls or puffed cereal on stems. Children can cut out a vase from a wallpaper book and glue it on. If you use yellow paint you will have forsythia. Try to bring in a branch of each. Use your imagination!

N. Clouds

Tear free-form shapes from white construction paper, pieces as large as possible. Paste on blue paper. Just for fun, suggest children tell you what they look like. After finished, make up their own It Looked Like Spilt Milk. Read book by Charles Shaw.

O. Caterpillars

Trace circles on different colored construction paper. Have children cut them out. Past circles on large construction paper side-by-side or overlapping and color on features. Or, cut egg carton in half lengthwise. Have children paint it green. Can add legs and feelers from pipe cleaners. Draw on face. Read The Very Hungry Caterpillar by Carle.

P. Nutty Characters

Bits of wood or broken-off chunks of bark form bases for these mini-sculptures made from a variety of unshelled nuts.

Wash and dry pits from fruit such as peaches, nectarines and cherries.

Arrange to form nutty characters. Join with white glue. Use apple seeds or peppercorns for eyes and dried beans for legs.

Q. Andy and the Lion

This is a terrific book by Daugherty. March is a good month to read it. Accompany with a paper plate lion.

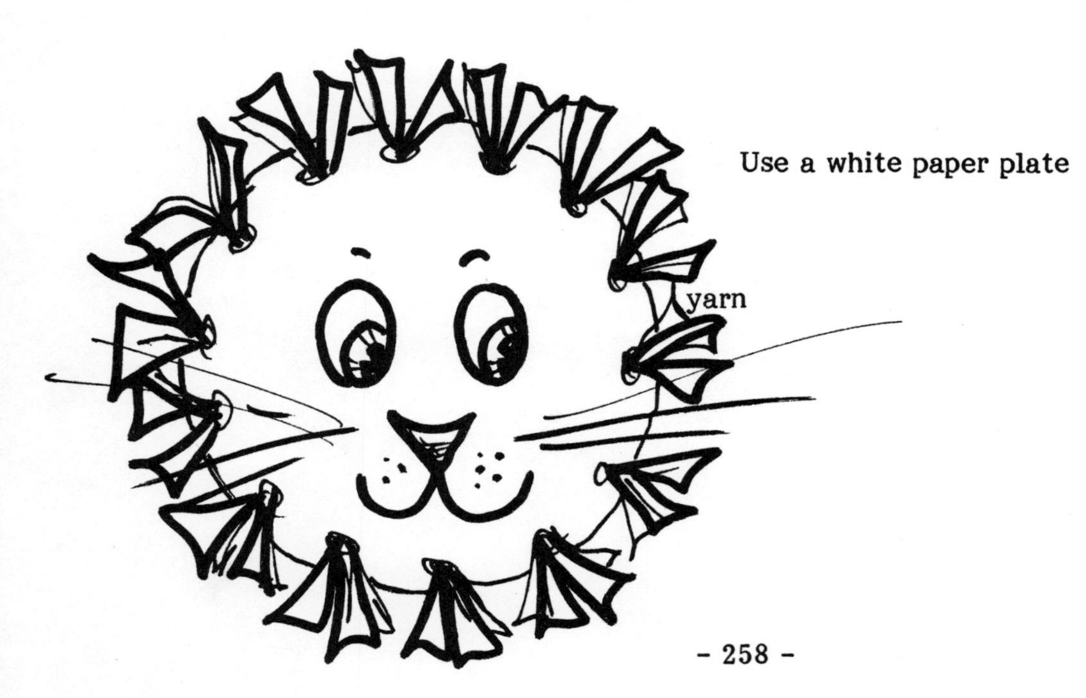

Use a white paper plate

II. COLOR DAY - GREEN

Objective: To recognize color green and to learn how to make green from yellow and blue.

Evaluation: Children recognized color green and learned how to make it using blue and yellow.

Have children wear something green. Point out green objects around room. Have green in snack - raw vegetables, lettuce, green beans, broccoli, avocado. Can make green dip using mayonnaise and green onions in blender or processor. Can plant avocado seed.

Use yellow and blue paints only at easel. Have children discover how mixing yellow and blue will make green. Read Little Yellow and Little Blue.

Use egg carton, fill with water. Have children drop in yellow and blue food coloring with eye droppers to make green.

III. STORY

<u>Objective</u>: To recognize different sounds, to enjoy story.

<u>Evaluation</u>: The various sounds were recognized and the story was enjoyed by all.

The Princess (High note), The Frog (Low ribbit sound) And The Little Bird (Tweet)

Storyteller says the title.

Intro music; then storyteller begins (storyteller should be quite familiar with story).

Once upon a time there was a little princess (high note) who lived in a beautiful castle. Her room was on the top floor. One day there was a knock on her door (pound).

She ran down the stairs (descending notes on string instrument) and opened the door (creak sound on instrument).

At the door there was a little bird (tweet). The little princess (high note) and the little bird (tweet) decided to go for a walk. They hopped (clap hands in rhythm) and skipped (clap hands in rhythm) until they came to a brook (bubble straw in water).

In the middle of the brook (bubble straw in water) sat a frog on a log (low ribbit).

So the little princess (high note), the little bird (tweet) and the frog (low ribbit) had a picnic.

Soon it began to thunder (cymbals) and rain (tap on cup). The wind blew (blow through straw into air) and the brook (bubble straw in water) became a raging torrent (blow through straw).

The little princess (high note) was swept into the brook (straw in water).

The little bird (tweet) could not swim, so he could not help her.

The frog (low ribbit) jumped into the water (straw in water) and brought the little princess (high note) out to dry.

The thunder (cymbals) and rain (tap on cup) stopped; the wind became very gentle (softly blow). The little princess (high note) kissed (smack!) the frog (low ribbit). Then the little princess (high note), the little bird (tweet) and the frog (low ribbit sound) hopped (clap hands in rhythm) and skipped (clap hands in rhythm) back to the castle.

They opened the door (creak on instrument), and ran up the stairs (ascending notes on instrument) to the little princess' room (high note). The little princess (high note), the little bird (tweet) and the frog (low ribbit) lived happily ever after.

(Closing music)
Use whistle for high note, bird caller for tweet, metal snapper for ribbit

Brown Bear

Brown Bear, brown bear
What do you see?
I see a red bird
looking at me

Red bird, red bird
What do you see?
I see a yellow duck
looking at me

Yellow duck, yellow duck
What do you see?
I see a blue horse
looking at me

Blue horse, blue horse
What do you see?
I see a green frog
looking at me

Green frog, green frog
What do you see?
I see a purple cat
looking at me

Purple cat, purple cat
What do you see?
I see a white dog
looking at me

White dog, white dog
What do you see?
I see a black sheep
looking at me

Black sheep, black sheep
    What do you see?
I see a gold fish
    looking at me

Gold fish, gold fish
    What do I see?
I see a teacher
    looking at me

Teacher, teacher
    What do you see?
I see children
    looking at me.

(Make figures on following pages out of felt or laminated tag board, use magnetic strips on back)

Brown Bea

Red Bird

Yellow Duck

Blue Horse

Green Frog

Purple
Cat

White Dog

Black Sheep

Orange Fish

IV. COOKING

Objective: To improve fine motor coordination through mixing and pouring. To improve math skills by measuring ingredients.

Evaluation: Fine motor coordination was improved.

A. Popsicles

Mix and pour into popsicle mold or ice cube trays:

1 cup hot water

2 cups lemonade

1 pkg. green jello

Can be used for St. Patrick's Day lunch. Enjoy when frozen. You can experiment with different flavored ingredients. (The jello slows down the melting process).

B. Green Eggs and Ham

A wonderful cooking experience. First read book Green Eggs and Ham by Dr. Seuss. Then, with green dye, make green scrambled eggs and green ham. Can be done on St. Patrick's Day.

Always stress safety rules when doing any cooking.

C. No Bake Peanut Butter Candy

1 C. peanut butter

1 C. corn syrup

1 C. dry milk

Mix corn syrup and milk. Let sit for 20 minutes. Add peanut butter. Roll into ropes on waxed paper and slice. May add raisins, Rice Krispies, coconut, and chocolate chips.

D. Bubble Solution

1 C. water

1/3 C. liquid soap

1 T. sugar

Make wand by bending end of 8" pipe cleaner to form hook.

Experiment with blowing. Blow into hand like a strong wind or gentle breeze. Feel the difference. To form bubble, blow like a gentle breeze. Can use juice cans with both ends removed, funnel, or circular ends of scissors.

E. Marshmallow Treats

1/4 C. butter
1 lg. pkg. regular marshmallows
5 C. Rice Krispies
1/4 C. peanut butter (optional)
Extra butter for bottom of pan

Melt butter in a large saucepan over low heat. Add marshmallows and peanut butter and stir until completely melted, stirring constantly. Remove from heat. Add Rice Krispies and stir. Press mixture into buttered 9 x 13 inch pan and cut into squares when cool.

Makes 24 squares, 2 inches x 2 inches.

V. MATH

Objective: To improve counting skills, to understand sequential order and concept of more or less.

Evaluation: Children counted, knew their numbers in the proper order, and understood more or less.

A. Counting

Count the buttons on your coat, shirt, etc.

Count the windows in the room.

Count the chairs.

Count pennies.

B. Number Order

Use ten 4" x 3" cards.

Draw one circle on the first card, two on the second, etc. Place cards on floor, mix them up and have children put them in the correct order.

C. More or Less

Use buttons, stones, etc.

Make two piles of buttons: in one pile use a few buttons, in other pile, use many.

Ask which pile has many? few? more? less?

VI. FINGERPLAYS

Objective: To develop memory and counting skill through repetition.

Evaluation: Most children remembered the words, actions and numbers, and were able to repeat them.

A. The Wind Came Out to Play

The wind came out to play one day
It swept the clouds out of the way
(sweeping motion with arms)
It blew the leaves and away they flew
(wiggle fingers away)
The trees bent low and their branches did too
(arms raised, then lowered)
The wind blew the great big ships at sea
(sweeping motion)
The wind blew my kite away from me.
(hide hands)

B. March Wind

The winds of March begin to blow
And it is time for kites you know
Here's the way I make my kite
Watch and help me do it right.

C. I cross two sticks so thin and long
(cross two pointers)
Tied together good and strong
(tying motion)
A string I fasten to each end
And across the middle to make it bend
I measure and cut the paper gay
(motion of measuring and cutting)
And paste along the edge this way
(pasting motion)

A ball of string to hold my kite
(make a circle)
When it sails almost out of sight
And here's my kite all ready to go
(make a diamond with pointers and thumbs)
Please, March Wind, begin to blow!
(blow)

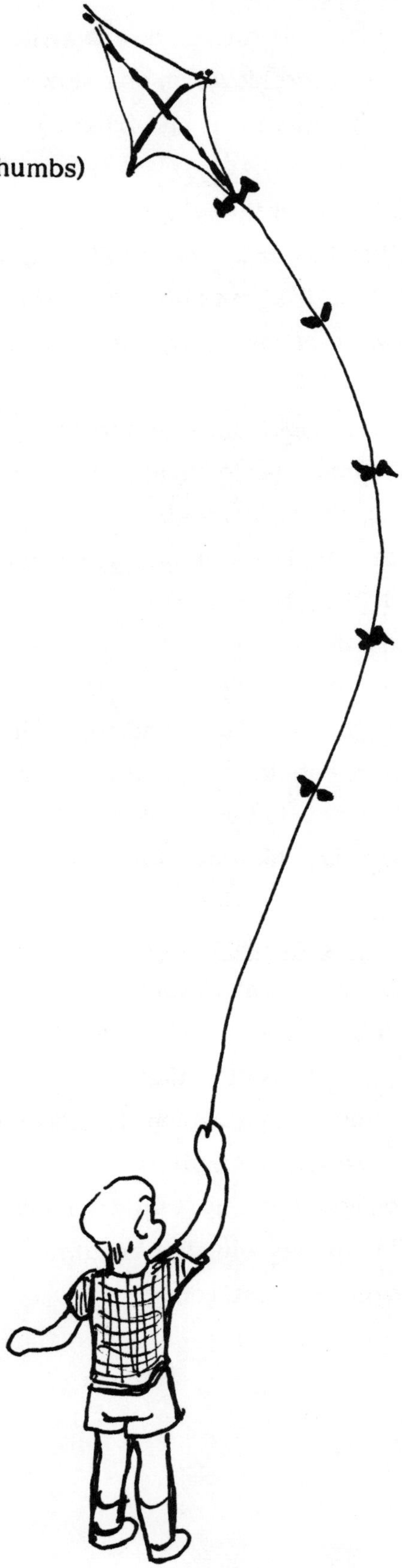

D. Wind Loves
A kite
To give
It flight
To whirl
To dip
To curl
To tease
And toss
And send
Across
Where clouds
Are thinned . . . .
A kite
Loves wind!!!

E. What's fluffy white and floats up high
(point upward)
Like piles of ice cream in the sky
(rub stomach)
And when the wind blows hard and strong
(move hands sideways)
What very gently floats along
(move hands slowly through air)
What brings the rain?
(flutter fingers downward)

What brings the snow?
(flutter fingers downward)
That showers down on us below?
(point to self and friends)

F. Who has seen the wind?
Neither you or I (shake hand sideways)
But when the trees bow down their leaves (bow)
The wind is passing by (move arms)

G. Bubbles, bubbles, large and small
(make large then small circle)
Sailing through the air.
I reach out to catch one (pretend to catch bubble)
and POP (clap hands)
It isn't there!

H. Blow a bubble (blow and form circle with hands)
Catch a bubble (pretend to catch a bubble)
Look, what do I see? (pretend to look in bubble)
It looks just like me! (point to self)

I. Fuzzy Wuzzy Caterpillar
Fuzzy wuzzy caterpillar
Into a corner will creep (children may creep)
He'll spin himself a blanket
And then go fast asleep (children curl up)
Fuzzy wuzzy caterpillar
Wakes up by and by (children awaken and dance about)
To find he has wings of beauty,
Changed to a butterfly.

J. <u>Good-bye Winter</u>

Good-bye winter, good-bye winter,
Good-bye winter, we wish you'd go away.

Good-bye snow!
Good-bye slush!
Good-bye puddles!
Good-bye snowsuits!
Good-bye cold wind!

Come back springtime.
Come back springtime.
Come back springtime.
We wish you'd come to stay.

Come back green grass!
Come back flowers!
Come back birdies!

Toward the end of March, children as well as adults get tired of winter and are looking forward to Spring.

This song could also be used when it's time to go home:

Good-bye Anna. Good-bye Anna.
Good-bye Anna. We'll see you another day.

K. <u>Safety</u>

Cut out 3 circles, red, yellow and green. Glue them on rectangle made of black construction paper.

Red on top
Green below
Red says stop
Green says go
Yellow says wait
Even if you're late!

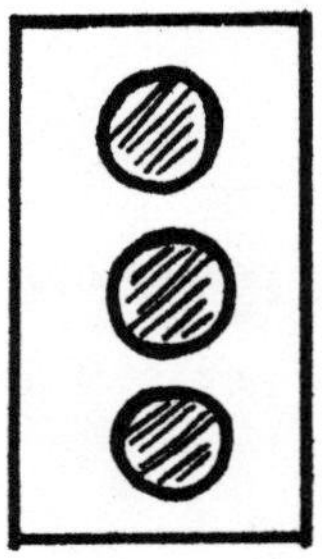

VII. SCIENCE

Objective: To understand what the wind does.

Evaluation: Children understood various things about the wind through experimentation.

A. Wind Experiences

Children can learn about the wind when they see flags waving, clouds floating, signs swinging. Moving air makes them move. We cannot see air or wind. We see what it does when it moves.

Feel air. Fan face. Wave arms, run. Listen to leaves rustle, clothes flap on a line, windows rattle. Moving air moves these things and the moving things make sounds.

We cannot taste or smell air or wind, although the wind does bring smells to us.

Read Gilberto and the Wind by Ets; Kenny and His Kite.

Use a hair dryer to give a dramatic presentation of wind.

B. Balloons

Blow or pump up with a ballon "pumper".

C. Air

You will need:

- squares of wax paper
- straws
- food coloring
- water

Place teaspoon of colored water in the middle of waxed paper. Children blow at the water, causing it to move, separate, etc. More than one color can be used, and by blowing two colors together, a new color will be formed.

D. Air

"Catch" air to prove it is everywhere. Using large plastic bags, open ends and pull it through the air and close quickly. Have children take them to different parts of the room to see if they can "catch" air there.

E. Tornado

You will need:

- 1 jar with cover 8" high
- enough water to fill jar (8 to 10 ounces)
- dash of yellow food coloring
- dash of liquid detergent

Put everything in jar and tighten lid. Hold jar by both ends turning it away from you smoothly and rapidly. Quickly hold it upright and watch your tornado.

F. Pussywillows

Pussywillows in the spring are fun to look at. If any are available around school, pick and bring in, put in water and they will last a long time. Discuss how they feel, smell, etc.

Objective: To understand what magnets do.
Evaluation: Children enjoyed experimenting with magnets.

G. March is a good month to have a unit on magnetism. Have good sized magnets available. Have each child play with magnets and verbalize what is happening. Discuss North and South poles.

1) Unlike magnetic poles attract.
2) Like magnetic poles repel.

H. Magnets and Their Properties

Encourage children to spread different objects out on a table. Let them explore with the magnets to see which objects can be picked up and which won't be. Will the magnet pick up everything, why not? Encourage children to sort objects into two different trays, according to whether they attract or repel.

I. <u>Magnets</u>

Line up some paper clips. How many paper clips can your magnet pull? The number of paper clips a magnet can pull gives a measure of the strength of the magnet. The stronger the magnet, the longer the train.

J. Try to pick up different types of keys with magnets. Which one does the magnet lift? If the magnet lifts the key, the key is made of iron, if the magnet does not lift the key, it might be brass, aluminum, etc.

K. Try the book, <u>Mickey's Magnet</u> by Branley. It's fun to read and do the experiments.

L. We can find a way for magnets to pick up paper and cloth; put the cloth on top of the paper clip. Point the magnets toward the cloth and paper clip. The magnet will lift them. This is simple for pre-schoolers.

VIII. PHYSICAL DEVELOPMENT - GAMES

Objectives: To improve large motor coordination, develop good sportsmanship, and have fun.
Evaluation: Large motor coordination and good sportsmanship were improved, and the children had fun.

A. Windy

Place a ping pong ball at the center of a table. Each player attempts to blow the ball off opponent's end of the table by being as windy as possible.

B. Clouds that Float

For a cloud, use a white balloon. Inflate it and tie. Have children strike it underneath with their hands to make cloud float in the air.

C. Fly Ballon

Blow up balloon. When adult gives signal, release balloon and see how far the balloon will fly. Blow more air into the balloon and more wind will be released making balloon fly farther.

D. Catch the Wind

Have two children hold opposite sides of the open end of a large trash bag. Then walk or run to make bag inflate. Close bag quickly and catch the air.

E. Windmill Exercise

Have children stand with their arms extended forward. Move arms forward and backward to form small circles, larger circles, and giant circles.

F. Parachute Games

Parachutes can be purchased at a military surplus store. If a chute isn't available, use a light blanket or a sheet. An adult gives directions and children respond together. Children hold chute with both hands.
Example:

Air conditioning: all lift and lower chute together.

Pop corn: bounce nerf balls on top of chute

Circle Games: Ring around Rosie, Merry-Go-Round, change directions, etc.

Record: "Parachute"

G. Dramatic Play

Go on a butterfly hunt; make butterfly nets by bending out hangers into a circle and attaching netting (citrus fruit bags). Paper butterflies thrown into the air make good props, too.

H. Elephants

One elephant went out to play,
All on a bright and sunny day.
He had such enormous fun,
He called another elephant to come.

Have one child pretend to be an elephant while the rest of the group makes a circle around the elephant. Repeat the song, adding another elephant each time (two elephants went . . .). Each elephant attaches to the previous one by holding onto the shoulders or waist. Let the last one in the line each time choose the next elephant.

H. Name Game

Children just love this. It is well worth your effort.

Materials: enough multicolored poster board to cut out each child's name in VERY LARGE individual letters - 12" to 18". For economy, use heavy brown shopping bags.

Ahead of time: Draw letters block style, cut out. Hide each child's name in a different spot, each letter tucked in a special hiding place. With the children: have children each help one another find their letters, one child's name at a time.

IX. FIELD TRIPS

Objectives: To develop an awareness of their surroundings.

Evaluation: The children were made more aware of their surroundings.

Visit a hospital - help children to become acquainted with hospital.

Airport

Pet shop

Visit a farm to see maple syrup being tapped

X. BOOKS

The Cloud Book	De Paolo
One Wide River to Cross	Emberly
Pete's Puddle	Foster
Curious George Rides a Bike	Rey
Curious George Flies a Kite	Rey
Little Pieces of the West Wind	Garrison
Staying Home Alone on a Rainy Day	Iwasaki
Caps for Sale	Slobodkina
Follow the Wind	Tresselt
When it Rained Cats and Dogs	Turner
Gilberto and the Wind	Ets
Kenny's Kite	Shapiro
Green Eggs and Ham	Seuss
Mickey's Magnet	Branley
Little Yellow and Little Blue	Lionni
It Looked Like Spilt Milk	Charles Shaw
Jonathan Plays with the Wind	Gallant
The Wind Blew	Hutchins
Where Does the Butterfly Go When it Rains?	Garrilick
Who Has Seen the Wind?	Conger
I See the Winds	Mizumora
"My Playmate the Wind"	Young People's Record
"My Playful Scarf"	Young People's Record
A Letter to Amy	Keats
The Storm Book	Zolotow
Andy and the Lion	Daugherty
Magnets and How to Use Them	Pine
Secret Magnets	Schneider
The Very Hungry Caterpillar	Carle

APRIL

I. ARTS AND CRAFTS

Objective: To improve small motor coordination through pasting, cutting, painting.
Evaluation: Small motor coordiantion was improved through painting, pasting and cutting.

A. Paper Plate Bunny

Use small paper plates. Fold in half and glue together. Cut out ears and glue on. Glue on cotton balls for decoration.

B. Cut easel paper into bunny face or egg shape. Mix white paint into all colors for beautiful pastels.

C. Bunny Face

Give each child two large paper plates. Have them cut on dotted lines on one of them. On second plate, paste on ears and bow tie. Cover entire face with glued on cotton. Paste on pre-cut eyes, nose, mouth. Can be hung on wire or yarn.

D. Easter Bonnet

Use large paper plate. Punch holes on opposite sides and tie on ribbon or yarn. Have children decorate bonnet with small colored cupcake holders, tissue paper, plastic flowers, ribbon, glitter, etc. Read Jennie's Hat by Keats.

E. <u>Tube Bunny</u>

Toilet paper tube. Cover with white, pink, or tan colored paper. Have children cut out ears and put in face with magic markers. Glue on cotton ball for tail.

F. <u>Paper Bag Bunnies</u>

Use white 5 lb. bags. Draw a V at the open end for children to cut on to make ears. Open bag and stuff with wadded up newspaper. Staple shut between ears. Paste on precut facial features and cotton ball tail.

G. <u>Egg Carton Basket</u>

One plastic-foam egg carton will make three baskets. Cut off the top of the carton. Cut the carton into three sections, each containing four cups. One section makes a basket. Make small holes on 2 opposite sides of each basket. Twist 2 pipe cleaners together to form a handle. Push the ends of the handle into the holes. Fill basket with cellophane grass. Can decorate handle.

H. <u>Tomato Basket - Easter Basket</u>

Have children cut strips of colored construction paper and weave them in and out of tomato basket. Use pipe cleaner for handle.

I. Have children crush egg shells and glue to various surfaces for primitive mosaics. Children may color shells either before or after glueing. They can use magic marker, water colors, or crayons.

J. Make bunnies "hiding in the grass". On drawing paper, have children make a few quick strokes of green crayon for grass and several dots of glue atop which the youngsters pop their cotton balls. Count how many are hiding in each child's picture.

K. Seasonal Tree

The seasonal tree lends itself to Easter. Have children bring in eggs. At home, poke hole in either side and blow yellow and white out. Can be used for scrambled eggs, baking, etc. Then, string fine wire through egg. Children can paint eggs with pastel colored tempera paints. Be sure to put name on eggs, use masking tape. Children love to take home.

L. Tuna Cans

Collect tuna cans so that each child has one. Cover them with felt. Cotton balls can be used for a tail. Paper, felt markers, any combination, can be used to create the face and whiskers at the opposite end of the can. Put on paper ears and Presto! There is a bunny that can double as a jelly bean holder.

M. Fuzzy-Wuzzy Pins

To make the basic fuzzy-wuzzy pin, start with a cotton ball and glue on two "wiggle eyes". (These eyes can be bought at a craft store for a few cents). Basic fuzzy-wuzzies can be turned into different creatures by adding paper ears, yarn, whiskers, and whatever else you would like to add. Use a safety pin to attach the fuzzy-wuzzy to your shirt.

N. April showers bring May flowers. Have children show umbrellas they brought to school. Discuss variety in size, shape and colors and then make a rainy day picture. Make these shapes and children can cut out. Use black, shiny paper for boots.

O. <u>Doily Art</u>

The use of doilies during holiday seasons can give some attractive and different results. Paste doily on a white paper plate. Use construction paper for facial features.

P. <u>Crepe Paper Eggs</u>

An easy and exciting way for children to paint. Using crepe paper, teacher or parents will have to help cut out eggs of many colored crepe paper. Pin the crepe paper to a 9" x 12" manila sheet of paper. Using a large brush, apply water over <u>entire</u> area of the crepe paper. Let dry before removing pins from crepe paper. Remove crepe paper and a replica of the object will appear on manila paper - magic!

Q. Easter Necklace

Fun art for any season. You will need a bobbie pin, colored yarn approximately 14" long, colored straws cut into 1" pieces. Tie yarn onto bobbie pin and string with it. Egg shapes cut out of construction paper can be interspersed with the pieces of straws. This project can be used for any season by substituting pumpkins, hearts, turkeys, etc., with small hole cut in center.

R. Paper Easter Basket

At the top of a closed lunch bag, draw bunny ears along outside edges. Cut away space on inside of ears. Staple ears together.

Draw bunny face on bag.

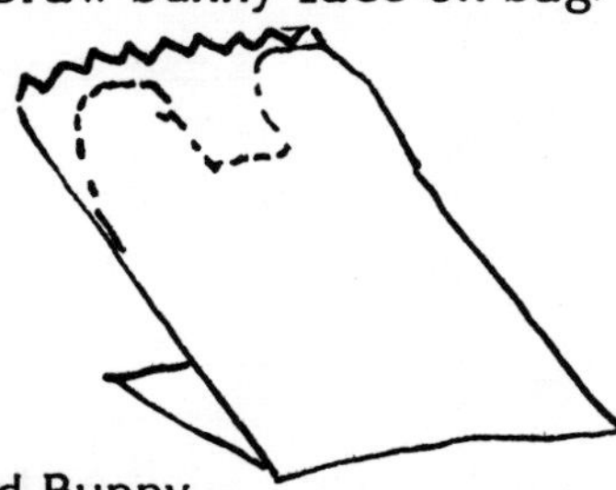

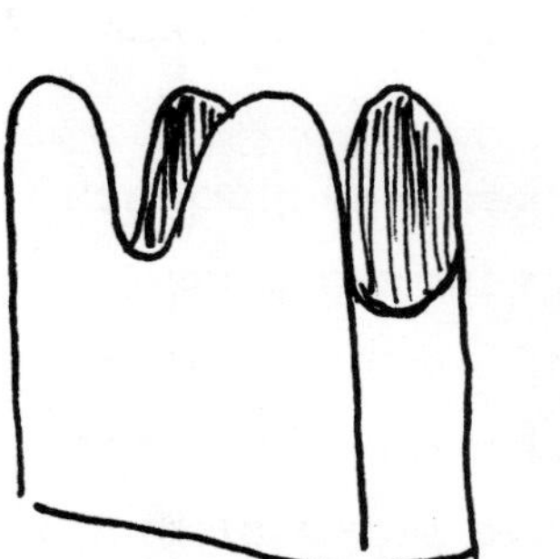

S. Stuffed Bunny

Stuff newspaper in paper bag. Tie yarn around middle and paint on face.

T. Cherry Tomato Carton Easter Basket

Have children cut out strips of pastel colored paper. Then have them weave paper in and out of tomato carton. Stuff with paper grass and tie yarn for handle.

U. Chick 'n Egg

Use individual egg containers filled with paper grass. Shake cotton balls in yellow powdered tempera. Glue on paper beak if possible. Put chick in container.

V. Fancy Easter Eggs

Mix 2 C. hot water, 2 Tbsp. vinegar, 2 tsp. food coloring. Dip eggs and enjoy unusual coloring.

W. Rabbit Ears Hat

Make a headband from a strip of paper. Cut it to fit the child's head. Have the children cut out bunny ears and glue them to headband.

X. Hickety, pickety, my black hen
She lays eggs for gentlemen.
Sometimes nine and sometimes ten.
Hickety, pickety, my black hen.

Fold five sheets of thin paper in fourths lengthwise and you will have ten eggs to give away.

Y. Rain on the green grass
And on the tree.
Rain on the house-top
But not on me.
Why not?
Because I have an umbrella.

Z. Mary, Mary, quite contrary,
How does your garden grow?
With silver bells and cockle shells
And pretty maids all in a row.

Make accordion folds in wide sheet of paper.

II. COLOR DAY

Objective: To recognize color yellow.
Evaluation: Children recognized color yellow.

Have children wear something yellow. Discuss yellow objects around room. Bring in forsythia, dandelions, daffodils, lemons, etc. Use yellow paint at easel, mix yellow with other colors and see new colors they can make.

Have lemon jello, cheese, hard-boiled eggs for snack.

III. STORY

Objective: To understand the story and customs of Passover.

Evaluation: The children understood story and customs of Passover

Passover is the Festival of Freedom, when Jews all over the world remember the historic exodus of the Hebrews from Egypt after 430 years of slavery under the cruel Pharoahs. The traditional family dinner, called the Seder, commemorates the Passover event and the approach of spring with special food, songs, and prayers. Parents and children read aloud from the Haggadah, which tells the story of the Exodus. The holiday lasts eight days. Matzoh (unleavened bread) is traditionally eaten all week.

Invite parents to class to explain how Jewish families celebrate Passover and show the special foods used for this celebration.

Have a matzoh hunt: wrap the matzoh in a napkin or plastic bag and hide at eye level for the children to find. This will be most successful if matzoh is available for all the children regardless of who finds the "afikoman".

Have matzoh for snack. Try it plain first, many children will eat it that way. Others may prefer it with butter, jam, jelly, or cream cheese.

Passover Foods

Matzoh (unleavened bread)
Matzoh meal pancakes or latkes
Soft yellow sponge cakes made with matzoh meal
Matzoh ball soup
Fried matzoh

Objective: To appreciate the joy of literature.

Evaluation: Children enjoyed stories.

The Rabbit and the Turtle (an old fable)

One day a rabbit met a turtle. "You are such a slowpoke," said the rabbit. "It takes you so long to go anywhere."

Just as the rabbit was ready to show how fast he could go, the turtle replied, "I will run a race with you anytime you like."

"Very well," answered the rabbit, "let us start at once."

The turtle immediately set off in his slow and steady way without waiting or looking back. The rabbit thought it was a great joke and decided to take a nap, being sure it would be easy to overtake the turtle at anytime.

The turtle plodded on while the rabbit slept. But the rabbit slept too long. When he awoke and dashed off, he found the turtle was waiting at the winning post.

(A good, dramatic type story for the children to act out.)

Easter Basket Story

When Tim woke up on Easter morning, he found a beautiful Easter basket.

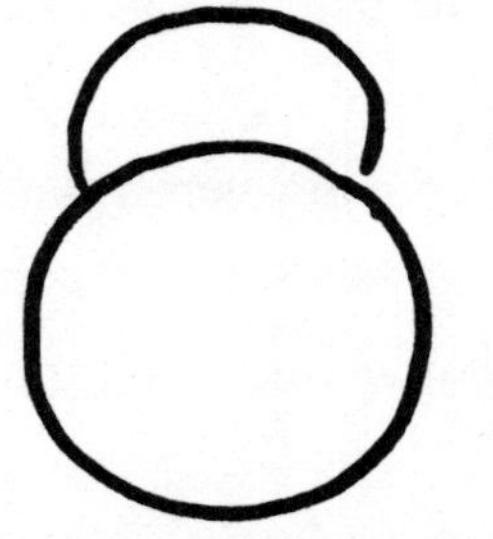

At the bottom of the basket was a beautiful Easter egg.

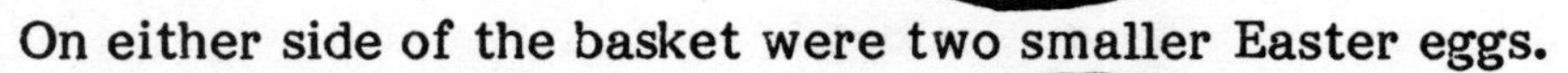

On either side of the basket were two smaller Easter eggs.

Tim wondered who left the beautiful Easter basket when suddenly two long ears appeared!

(This story is fun for the feltboard.)

The Egg Who Couldn't Decide

Once upon a time there was a little egg named Benedict who didn't know what color he wanted to be for Easter. He said, "I've always like the color of trees. Perhaps I should be a green egg. But then again, I like the color of carrots. Maybe I should be an orange egg. Of course, the color of water is very pretty, too. I wonder how I would look if I were a blue egg."

And then he thought of a duck in a meadow and decided there and then to be a yellow egg. But at that moment a great big fire engine drove by and Benedict said, "That's the color for me - I'll be a red egg." A moment later when he saw a squirrel eating a bunch of grapes he couldn't decide whether to be a brown egg or a purple egg. "Oh dear, oh dear," said Benedict, "I can't make up my mind. All these colors are so pretty."

Just then who should appear but the Easter Bunny. "Don't worry, Benedict," he said, "I know what to do." And what he did made Benedict very happy.

Do you know what the Easter Bunny did?

Draw figures on
tag board. Cover
with clear contact. Use
magnetic tape.

AMY

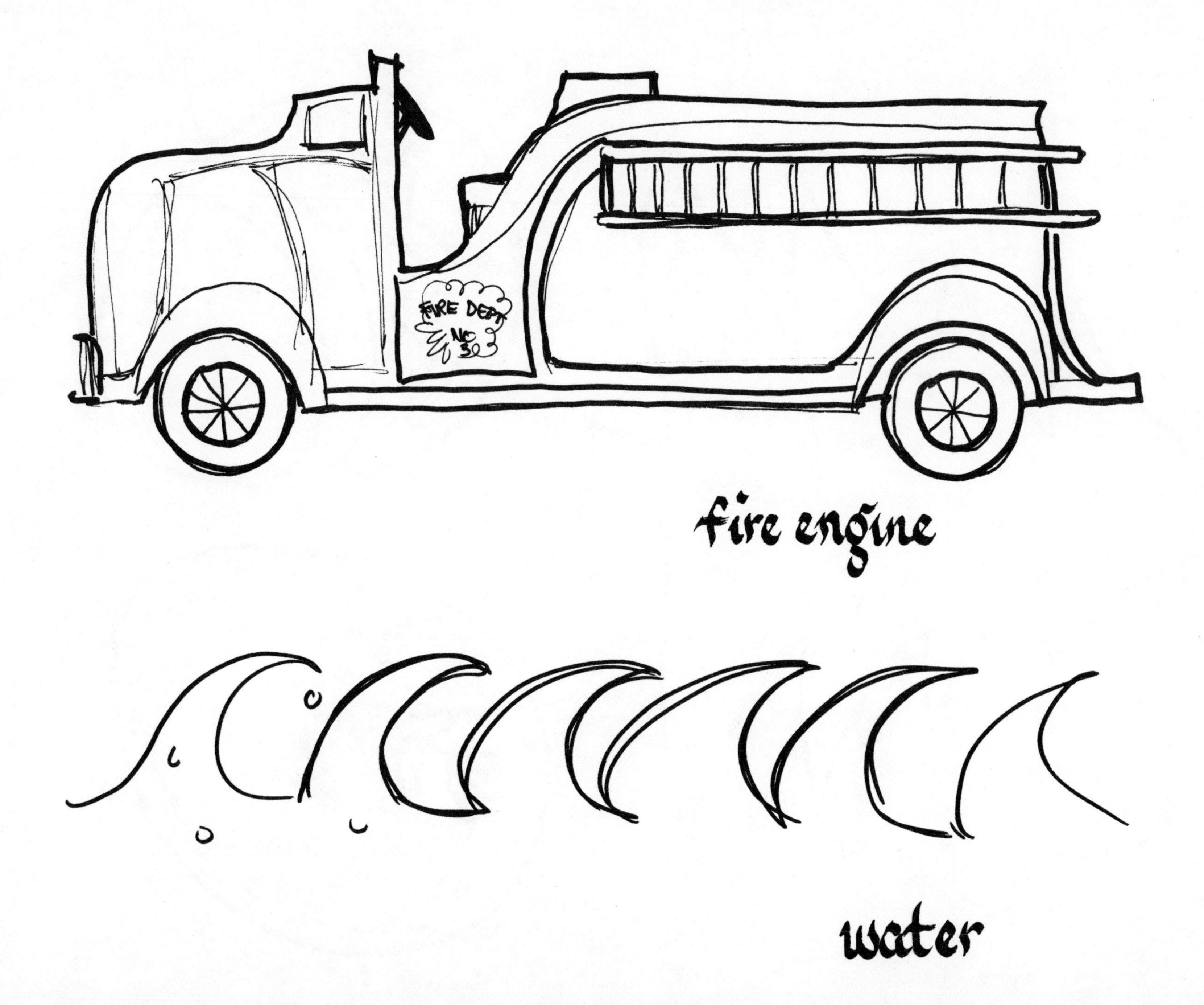
FIRE DEPT
fire engine
water

IV. COOKING

<u>Objective</u>: To increase fine motor coordination through mixing, kneading, decorating, etc. To develop math skills by counting and measuring ingredients.

<u>Evaluation</u>: Fine motor coordination was increased through mixing, kneading, decorating. Math skills were developed through counting and measuring.

A. <u>Dandelion Salad</u>

1. Blow a fuzzy dandelion puff into a pot of soil.
2. You will see a seed at the end of each piece of fuzz.
3. Some of these seeds will stick in the soil and begin to grow.
4. Keep the soil moist.
5. While the leaves are still small, pick them.
6. Toss them together in a bowl for a tasty salad.

B. <u>Ice Cream Cone Cupcakes</u>

Materials:

flat-bottomed waffle ice cream cones
cupcake mix
frosting
colored sprinkles
bread and butter knives

Method:

Ahead of time (best to do day before, can be done in class): heat oven to 350°. Make batter for cupcakes as directed on cake mix package. Place the waffle cones on a cookie sheet and fill a scant 1/2 full (about 1/4 cup batter). If you put in too much on too little the cones will not have a nice rounded top. Bake 15-18 min. Cool. Next day, with the children: give them their own spreading knives and container of frosing and sprinkles. Let them frost and decorate their own cones. For many, it may be more fun than the eating.

These cones will be wonderful for the Easter party. Use pastel colors in icing.

C. Biscuit Bunnies

Tube of 10 biscuits

1 for face
1 for ears

Pinch ears onto first biscuit. Use raisins for eyes, slivered almonds for whiskers.

Frosting:

1 T. milk
1/4 tsp. vanilla
3/4 C. confectioner's sugar
red food coloring

Bake at 350° 10 minutes.

D. Bunny Hop Salad

2 apples (wash and dice, do not peel)
2 large carrots, peeled and grated
1/2 C. diced celery
1/2 C. raisins
1/4 t. salt
1/4 C. mayonnaise
1/4 C. sour cream
1/4 t. vinegar or lemon juice

Have children peel and grate carrots. Dice apples and celery, and help measure rest of ingredients. Refrigerate until served.

E. No Cook Coconut Pastel Bonbons

1 3 oz. pkg. cream cheese, softened
2-1/2 C. confectioner's sugar
1/4 t. vanilla
dash salt
food coloring
1 C. grated coconut

No Cook Coconut Pastel Bonbons (continued)

As soon as children come in: Beat cream cheese with electric mixer until soft and smooth. Beat in confectioner's sugar gradually until well blended. Beat in vanilla, salt and food coloring. Let the children take turns adding ingredients and beating. Cover and refrigerate.

One hour later: Have the children shape the dough into small balls and roll in a plate full of the grated coconut. Line the cookie sheet with waxed paper and put the finished bonbon balls on that. Refrigerate several hours.

Variation: Omit food coloring and instead of coconut, roll in 1 C. chopped nuts.

F. Matzoh Meal Pancakes (Latkes)

1/2 C. matzoh meal	3/4 C. cold water
1 T. sugar	3 eggs

Combine matzoh meal, salt and sugar. Separate eggs, beat yolks slightly and combine with water. Add to dry ingredients. Let stand 1/2 hour. Beat whites stiff, fold into mixture. Drop by tablespoon onto a greased fry pan and brown on both sides.

G. Fried Matzoh

Soak two large matzohs in warm water and squeeze out. Beat one egg with milk, add salt. Add to Matzohs. Fry in butter (like scrambled eggs).

H. 1-10 Egg Drop Soup

2 10 oz. cans chicken broth	2 eggs
2 soup cans water	2 tsp soy sauce

Boil soup and water. Beat eggs and water in small bowl, add soy sauce. Pour eggs into hot soup and stir while you count to 10.

I. S'mores

8 graham crackers	Miniature marshmallows
2 small chocolate bars	

On cookie sheet, put graham cracker, chocolate bar, marshmallows and another graham cracker to cover. Put in 300° oven until melted. Umm.

J. <u>Spicy Muffins</u>

1-1/2 lbs. ground round
1 egg
1/2 C. bottled barbecue sauce
1/2 tsp. salt
1/2 tsp. chili powder (optional)

In bowl mix beef, egg, barbecue sauce and chili powder. Spoon mixture into 6 large muffin pan cups or 6-oz. custard cups. Bake at 350° for 40 minutes.

K. <u>Macaroons</u>

4 egg whites
3/4 cup sugar
1-1/2 tsp. matzo meal
1 cup coconut
1-1/2 tsp. lemon juice
1-1/4 tsp. potato starch
1 tsp. almond extract

Beat egg whites and sugar and add remaining ingredients. Spoon onto a greased cookie sheet and bake until brown, about 20 minutes at 325°.

L. <u>Paintbrush Cookies</u>

Cream: 3/4 C. margarine
1 C. sugar

add: 1 egg
1 tsp. vanilla

add: 2-1/2 C. flour mixed with:
1 tsp. baking powder
1 tsp. salt

Chill dough

<u>"Egg Yolk Paint"</u>

Blend well: 1 egg yolk with 1/4 tsp. water

1. Divide "paint" into small cups. Add a few drops of food color to each one to make them different. If paint thickens, add a few drops of water (you may want to mix the dough before involving the children as it might be too much to mix) and paint the cookies in one session.
2. Children help roll out cookie dough on floured board and cut out using cookie cutters.
3. Place on ungreased cookie sheet and paint with small, clean paint brushes.
4. Bake at 400° for 6-8 minutes. Should make 2 dozen cookies.

V. MATH

<u>Objectives</u>: To improve counting and matching skills.
<u>Evaluation</u>: Counting and matching skills were improved.

A. Egg Hunt

Fill egg carton "eggs" (two sections taped together) with surprises, such as candy, pennies, paper clips, small stones, beans, Easter grass, rice, buttons, etc. See who finds the heaviest, lightest, noisiest, sweetest, etc.

Variation: Matching eggs. Fill and hide pairs of eggs with identical objects and have children try to match the eggs. Trades can be made. Who has the most pairs?

B. Easter Basket

You will need 10 small Easter baskets, plastic Easter grass (enough to fill each basket so the grass will stick to the basket), jelly beans to fill each basket, numbered stickers for baskets, 1-10. Children can count ordering numerically.

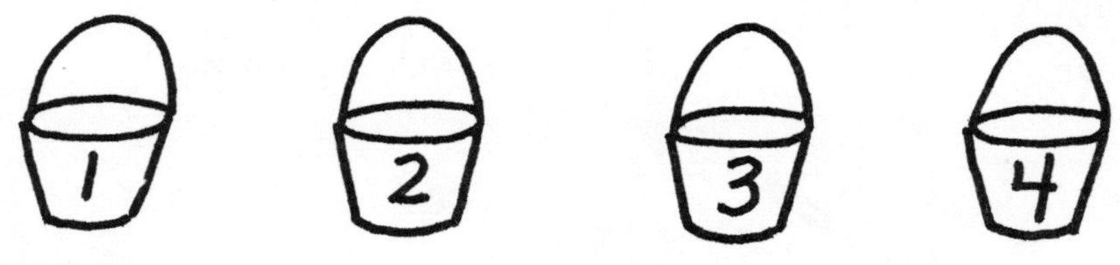

C. Flannelboard Groups

You will need a flannelboard, flannel shapes (10 patterns with a varying number of each shape), cut-out flannel numerals, and a container for the flannel shapes and numerals.

6 7 8 9 10

D. Paper Towel Rolls

Cut them to different heights and spray paint. The children can line them up according to height. Can glue them on cardboard, paint them, and create different sized buildings.

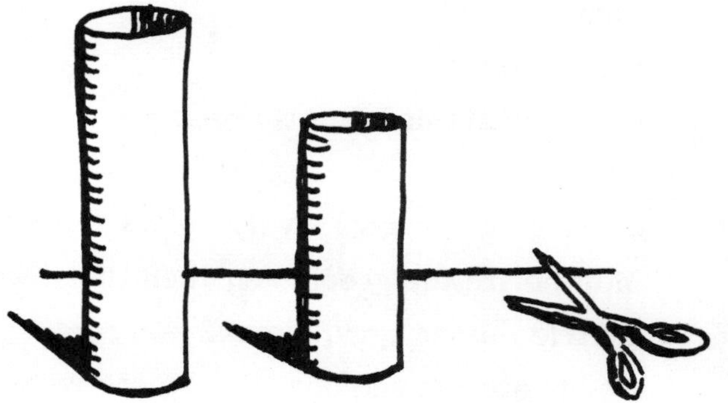

E. Compare sizes of milk cartons

Bring in gallon size, half gallon size, quart size, pint size, and half-pint size. Discuss which is largest, smallest, etc.

Gallon 1/2 Gallon Quart Pint 1/2 Pint

VI. APRIL FINGER PLAYS

A. Easter eggs are prettier
Than any I have seen
One is red, one is blue
One is white and one is green

B. 5 little Easter eggs lovely colors were
Mother ate the green one, then there were 4
4 little Easter eggs, 2 and 2 you see
Daddy ate the red one, then there were three
3 little Easter eggs, before I knew
Sister ate the orange one, then there were 2
2 little Easter eggs, oh what fun--
Brother ate the pink one, then there was one.
1 little Easter egg, see me run
I ate the very last one and then there were none.

C. <u>Rabbit</u>
I saw a little rabbit that went hop, hop, hop (make hand hop)
And he had big ears that went flop, flop, flop.
And this little rabbit was very, very queer,
He shook one leg and he wiggled one ear.

D. Here is a bunny with ears so funny
(hold up index and middle finger)
And here is his hole in the ground
(make hole with other hand)
When a noise he hears, he pricks up his ears
(extend 2 fingers)
And hops in his hole in the ground
(jump fingers into hole)

Pinky is a rabbit (hold up index and middle fingers)
His tail is fluffy white
Hop, hop, hop goes Pinky
All the day and night (hand hops)

E. <u>The Rain</u>

Pitter-patter raindrops (wiggle fingers to imitate falling rain)
Falling from the sky
Here is my umbrella (hands over head)
To keep me safe and dry!
When the rain is over
And the sun begins to glow (make large circle with arms)
Little flowers start to bud (cup 2 hands together)
And grow and grow and grow (spread hands apart slowly)

F. <u>Ten Fluffy Chickens</u>

Five eggs and five eggs (hold up 2 hands)
That makes ten.
Sitting on top is the mother hen
Crackle, crackle, crackle;
What do I see?
Ten fluffy chickens
As yellow as can be (hold up 10 fingers)

G. <u>Rain</u>

It rained on Ann, it rained on Dan,
(wiggle fingers over head)
It rained on Arabella
It didn't rain on Mary Jane,
She had a big umbrella!
(touch fingertips over head, forming circle)

H. <u>The Rain</u>

Put up your umbrella (Place forefinger of one hand against palm of other)
To keep yourself dry.
Put up your umbrella,
There's rain in the sky.
Patter . . . patter . . . patter.
(Make hands move up and down and make fingers wiggle)

I. Song (Tune of London Bridge)

Bunny rabbits have no tails, have no tails, have no tails
Bunny rabbits have no tails
They have powder puffs.

J. Song (Tune of London Bridge)

Little ducks go quack, quack, quack
Quack, quack, quack,
Quack, quack, quack
Little ducks go quack, quack, quack
In the springtime.

Little lambs go baa, baa, baa
Baa, baa, baa,
Baa, baa, baa;
Little lambs go baa, baa, baa
In the springtime.

Etc.

K. A Little Hole

Dig a little hole (dig)
Plant a little seed (drop seed)
Pour on a little water (pour)
Pull a little weed (pull up and throw away)

Chase a little bug (chasing motion with hands)
Heigh-ho, there he goes (shade eyes)
Give a little sunshine (cup hands)
Let it grow, grow, grow (smell flower, eyes closed, smiling)

LITTLE PETER RABBIT

Lit-tle Pe-ter Rab-bit had a fly up-on his ear,
(hands make rabbit ears)(fingers fly away)(point to ear)

Lit-tle Pe-ter Rab-bit had a fly up-on his ear
(same actions as above)

Lit-tle Pe-ter Rab-bit had a fly up-on his ear and he
(same actions as first line)

flicked it 'til it flew a-way.
(flick ear) (fingers fly a-way)

2. Leave out word "Rabbit" but do motions
3. Leave out "Rabbit" and "fly," do motions
4. Leave out "Rabbit," "fly" and "ear," do motions.

BABY BIRD (Scale Song)

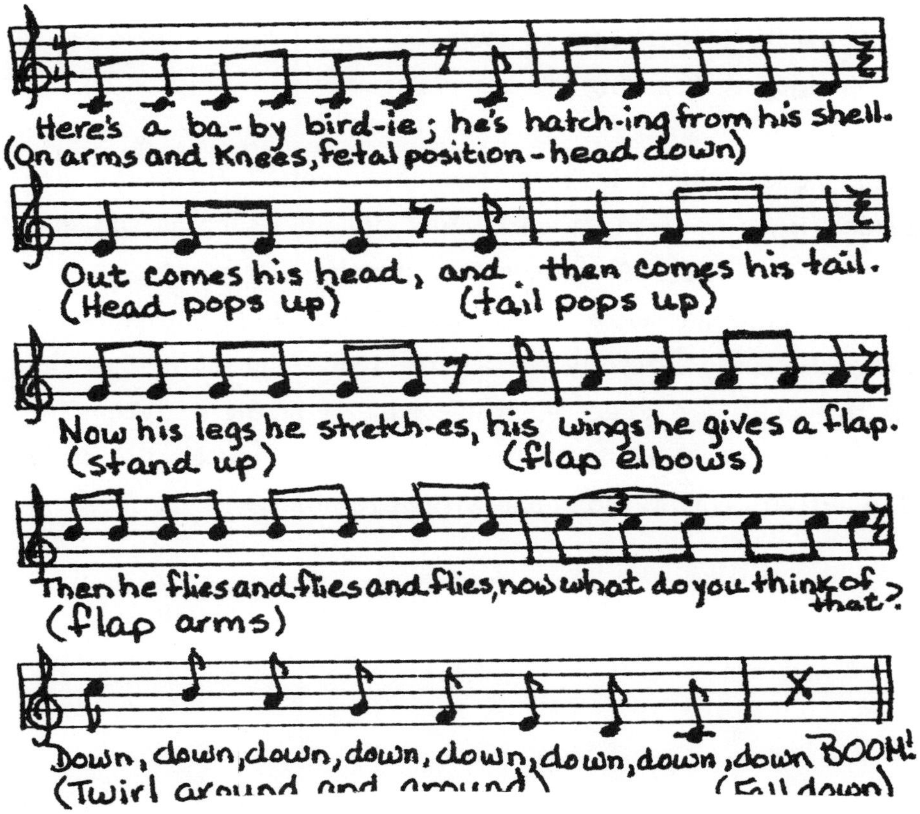

Here's a ba-by bird-ie; he's hatch-ing from his shell.
(On arms and Knees, fetal position - head down)

Out comes his head, and then comes his tail.
(Head pops up) (tail pops up)

Now his legs he stretch-es, his wings he gives a flap.
(stand up) (flap elbows)

Then he flies and flies and flies, now what do you think of that?
(flap arms)

Down, down, down, down, down, down, down, down BOOM!
(Twirl around and around) (Fall down)

VII. SCIENCE

Objectives: To plant seeds, water and watch grass grow.
Evaluation: Children were very excited watching the grass grow.

A. Watch "hair" grow on potato heads. Scoop out a hole in a large potato. Fill the hole with moist cotton. To make a funny face, push in bottle caps or use straight pins and glue to attach corks, buttons and other materials. Sprinkle quick-growing seeds, such as cress or mustard or grass on the cotton. Keep the potato upright and keep the cotton moist. In a few days sprouts will appear. As the sprouts grow, trim them and use them in salads.

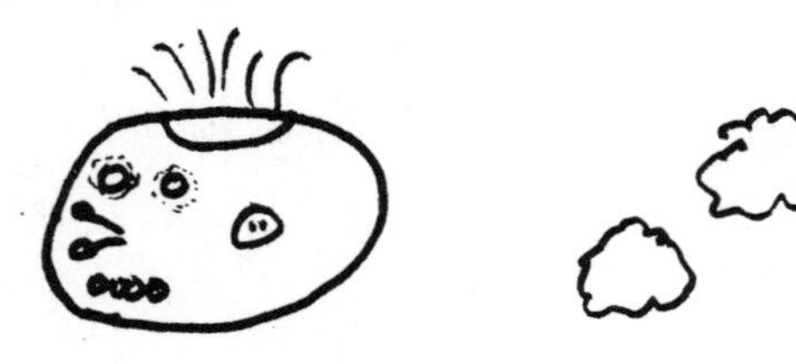

B. Read How a Seed Grows by Helen Jordan. Have children plant beans in egg shells and water them. Grass can also be planted in an egg shell to resemble hair. Draw face with magic markers.

Objective: To distinguish different types of seeds.
Evaluation: Children enjoyed observing the various seeds

C. Plants produce seeds which, in turn, produce plants. Different plants have different seeds. Have on hand an assortment of fruits such as apples, oranges, lemons, cantaloupes, piece of watermelon, peach, cherry, etc., a package of sandwich bags, a magic marker, and pictures of fruits cut from magazines.
Have children take turns carefully cutting the fruits and taking out some seeds. Discuss how the seeds are alike and different. Put the different seeds into plastic sandwich bags and label accordingly. Later, match the seeds to the pictures. The activity may also be done with vegetables.

Objective: To observe the different stages in the development of a bean plant.

Evaluation: Children enjoyed watching their seeds develop.

D. Growing Beans

Give each child a baby food jar or plastic see-through glass. Tape on child's name. Put cotton in the bottom of each jar (about 1/4 full). Put 2 beans between the cotton and the glass in each jar and 2 beans on top of the cotton. Dampen the cotton and keep damp. Place jars on window ledge so they will receive light and watch what happens.

Objective: To understand how a nest is made

Evaluation: Children enjoyed making their own nests

E. Bird's Nest

Have children go outside and pick up twigs and grass. On shirt cardboard, make paste of sugar, flour, and water. Form into nest. Make eggs from playdough or use cotton balls which have been shaken in a bag of blue tempera, or can stick in a paper bird on a toothpick. Read The Nest Book, The Lion in the Nest or Who Stole the Farmer's Hat?

Objective: To understand how plants "drink water"

Evaluation: Through the experiment, children were able to understand how a plant gets nourishment

F. Show how plants drink water: Place a stalk of celery in colored water for several hours and watch it change colors, bottom to top.

G. Watch for first robin.

Objective: To see how children have grown as compared to fall measurement.
Evaluation: Children were delighted to see how much they had grown.

H. Measure and compare the children's heights. Talk about "tall" and "small". It is fun to measure in the fall and again in the spring to see how they have grown. Record heights on poster board. Read The Growing Story by Ruth Kraus.

Objective: To understand the importance of vegetables, their parts and how they grow.
Evaluation: Children enjoyed learning about vegetables.

I. Vegetables

Vegetables help us grow and to keep well, they have different sizes, shapes, colors and tastes. Some grow above the ground, some grow below the ground.

Hold up different vegetables, have children name them while discussing the three parts of the plant (root, stem, leaf), color, size, shape, and if it grows above or below the ground.

Games: Who Can Find

a vegetable that is orange?
a beet?
a vegetable that grows below the ground? etc.

Guess What?

Place vegetables in a bag,
have children take turns reaching in and guessing what
they have by the shape

Songs to act out (Tune: Farmer in the Dell)

The farmer plants the seeds (put seeds in ground)
The farmer plants the seeds,
Hi, Ho the dairy-o,
The farmer plants the seeds.

The sun comes out to shine (make big circle with arms), etc.
The rain begins to fall (hands flutter to the ground), etc.
The seeds begin to grow (children begin to rise), etc.
The farmer digs them up (pretend to use a shovel), etc.
Now we'll have some to eat (pretend to eat), etc.

Grow a Carrot

Put carrot tops in a pie pan filled with water and wait for green leaves to appear.

Rainbows All Over

Carefully-placed prisms can create rainbows all over a room. Jump on a rainbow; read on a rainbow; dance on a rainbow; sit on a rainbow; sleep on a rainbow. The nice thing about these rainbows is that they are all created by the sun. They appear at different times each day and crop up in surprise places depending on where the prisms are.

Rainbows--Choose One Color, Please

Look at a rainbow. Invite each child to choose a color. It might be purple for one child, red for another, green for another. Encourage the children to create one-color, multi-texture pictures. Put out materials. If the choice was purple, you might put out a tray with all different shades of purple crayons, purple markers, purple paper, ribbon, paint, chalk . . . Give each child a large piece of paper, glue, scissors, and some encouragement.

LET'S LET LIGHT MAKE A RAINBOW

Window

Sun

Sunlight

Bowl of Water

Ingredients:
Bowl of water
Piece of white paper

Piece of white paper

Let's Let Light Make a Rainbow (Continued)

Fill the bowl almost to the top with clear cold water. Place the bowl so that it is half in and half off the edge of the table. Be sure the sun shines directly through the water and onto the piece of white paper which is on the floor.

Adjust both the bowl and the glass until a rainbow forms.

Teach the children that light is made up of many colors. When it passes through water the light is broken into pieces. These colors are seen as a rainbow.

Can make rainbow layered jello. Read the children Rainbow of My Own by Freeman. Use song Jenny Jenkins, making verses for the colors in the rainbow.

Jenny Jenkins (Suit actions to words. Allow children to answer for Jenny Jenkins.)

Will you wear white
Oh my dear, oh my dear?
Will you wear white, Jenny Jenkins?
No-o-o-o, I won't wear white
For the color's too bright.
I'll buy me a foldy, roldy,
Tiddle toldy, rufty, tufty
Girlie whirlie roll.
Roll, Jenny Jenkins roll.

Will you wear red
Oh my dear, oh my dear?
Will you wear red, Jenny Jenkins?
No-o-o, I won't wear red
It's the color of my head.
I'll buy me a foldy, roldy,
Tiddle toldy, rufty, tufty
Girlie whirlie roll.
Roll, Jenny Jenkins roll.

Will you wear green
Oh my dear, oh my dear?
Will you wear green, Jenny Jenkins?
No-o-o-o, I won't wear green
I would look like a bean.
I'll buy me a foldy, roldy,
Tiddle toldy, rufty, tufty
Girlie whirlie roll.
Roll, Jenny Jenkins roll.

Will you wear yellow
Oh my dear, oh my dear?
Will you wear yellow, Jenny Jenkins?
No-o-o-o, I won't wear yellow
I would look like jello
I'll buy me a foldy, roldy,
Tiddle toldy, rufty, tufty
Girlie whirlie roll.
Roll, Jenny Jenkins roll.

How do we taste our food?

The surface of the tongue shows many bumps and ridges all of which look alike. The tongue, however, is divided into areas specialized for different kinds of tastes - sweet, sour, salt, and bitter. In this activity, the children will discover how these areas are arranged on the tongue. Have the children look at their tongues with a magnifying mirror and see the small bumps which are called taste buds. To find out where the tongue tastes sweet, sour, salt, and bitter, we can do the following experiment:

Start with a sugar solution - take a small container and fill it about half full of water - put in ¼ tsp. sugar and stir. Have children dip a Q-tip in the solution and carefully swab their tongues all over. Have them close their mouths, wait a minute and try to locate the place where they get the strongest sensation of sweet taste. Hint: Ask them how an ice cream cone tastes and how they lick it. Have them rinse their mouths and make a sour solution by filling a small cup half way full of water and adding a little lemon juice. Use a second swab and have them swab tongue all over, close mouth, and wait a minute. Later you can try a salt solution with a small cup of water and a few pinches of salt and a bitter solution by mixing a little vanilla in water.

L. Air and Wind

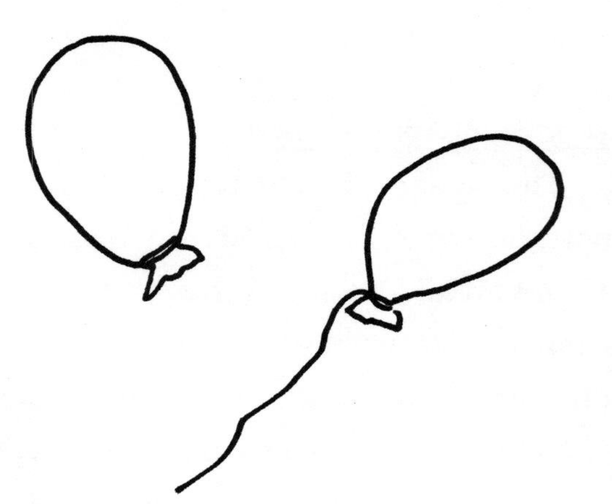

Materials

Balloons, pencil with eraser, stick pin, paper.

Directions:

Blow up several balloons - tie one with a string and let one go so air rushes out. As you let the air out, pull tightly on the mouth of it so it sings.

Using pinwheels is also fun on a windy day - to make one, cut a square of paper inward from each corner. Fold every other section in toward the middle and put a pin through all the layers and the center. Stick the pin securely into a pencil eraser. Run in the wind and watch them go!

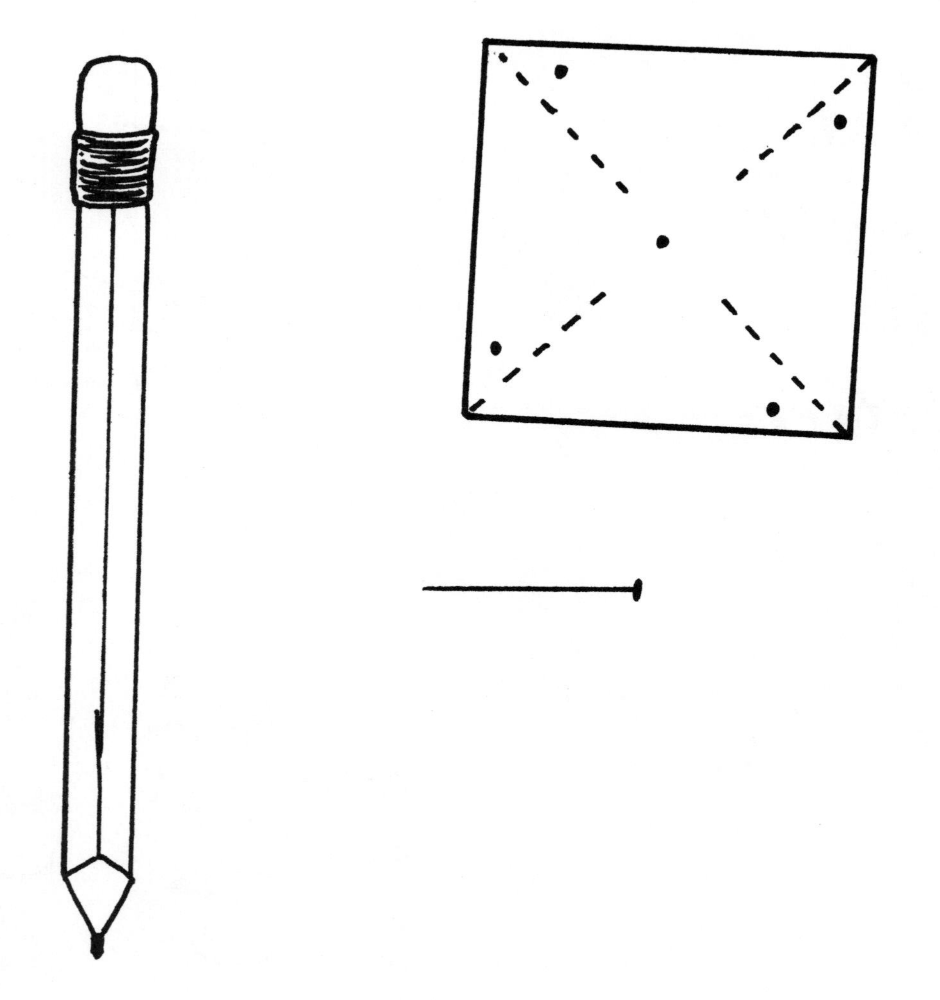

Static Electricity

You will need: a piece of wool. A good strong balloon. A small piece of paper and a comb.

Have the children sit in a circle - then blow up the balloon. This is a good time to explain to the children that only one person's mouth can blow in balloon because germs spread in this way. Now ask the children to put the balloon on the wool and see if it will stick. Let as many try as wish. Next rub the balloon on the wool. See if it sticks this time. Explain now that static electricity may be formed by friction.

Next use a pocket comb, ask a child to comb hair; it must be dry. Next ask the children to they use the comb as if it were a magnet to pick up small pieces of paper.

Help children to understand static electricity may be created by friction.

N. Activities

Take a field trip to a vegetable farm or garden

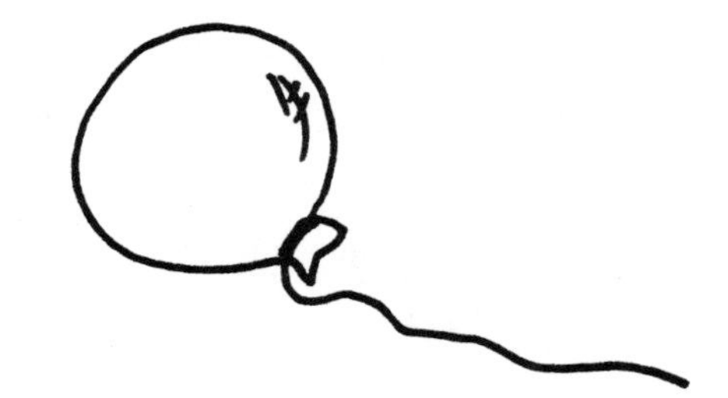

Taste different raw vegetables at snack time

Make vegetable soup to eat at snack time

Do vegetable prints

Have children plant carrot seeds. Read The Carrot Seed by Ruth Kraus

Read Stone Soup by Brown

Objective: To enjoy watching bulbs sprout.
Evaluation: Children enjoyed watching the various bulbs grow.

O. Grow Bulbs

Can use an onion, avocado, sweet potato, gladiola, etc.

Grow Bulbs (continued)

Stick 3 toothpicks into the bulb. Place the bulb on top of a clear glass or jar about 3/4 full of water with the pointed end down. Put the glass in a dark place for 2-4 weeks, or until the bulb sprouts and has roots. The bulb may split slightly. Add water when necessary, keeping the water level always about the same, 1/2 way up on the bulb. Once the bulb has sprouted, put it in a sunny place, and watch it grow.

Note: An onion will produce long green leaves and perhaps even a flower, but it may become smelly after awhile. Cut a gladiola bulb open and see the babies waiting to come out.

Seeds in pine cones will sprout when pushed into the soil.

Plant raw shelled peanuts in a large container and keep moist.

P. Grow seeds in sponges, can be natural or man made. Place sponge in bowl. Keep moist, full sun. Grass seed and bird seed work best.

Q. Seed Poster

To make a seed poster, you will need a big sheet of paper, paste, and as many interesting seeds as you can find. Paste the seeds on the paper and hang it on the kitchen wall. Ask everyone in your family to name the seeds.

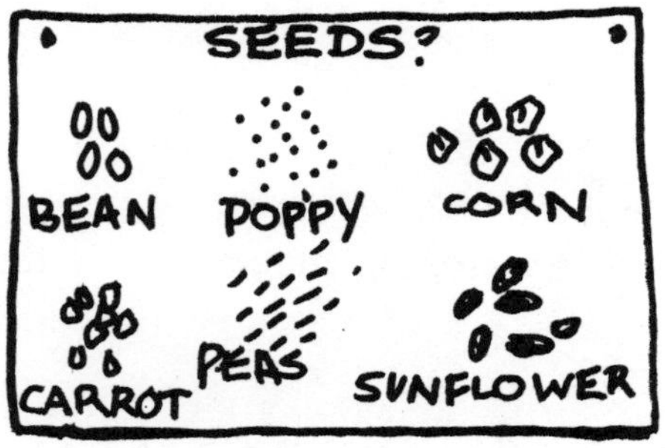

Discuss how seeds travel from one place to another in lots of interesting ways.

Q. Did You Know That . . .

Bread begins with grains of wheat
And cakes from corn are made?
Berries, grapes and oranges
Are what's in jam and marmalade?
Beans are ground for coffee?
Leaves are soaked for tea?
And lots of seeds make tasty treats
-- Like rye and sesame?

The mint and fruity flavors
of gum and candy bars
Aren't really made on the Milky Way
By little men from Mars.
For most of the tastes you've learned to love
Were plants not long ago.
Plants' seeds and leaves and flowers and fruits
Make many foods we know!!

Never eat a plant you don't know!
Some plants are not good to eat.
Some are even poisonous.

R. <u>Matzo Yeast Experiment</u>

Matzo (unleavened bread) is an important part of the observation of Passover. The story of Passover tells us that matzo originated thousands of years ago when the Hebrews fled Egypt in such a hurry that there wasn't time to let their bread dough rise. That's why Jews still remember the event by using matzo during Passover week.

To help you understand what happened, try this experiment. Fill two glasses half full of warm water. Stir some flour into one glass. In the other, dissolve a little yeast in the water; then add flour. Now set them both in a warm place for an hour and watch the result.

VIII. PHYSICAL DEVELOPMENT - GAMES

Objective: To improve large motor coordination, develop good sportsmanship, and have fun.

Evaluation: Large muscle coordination was improved as well as good sportsmanship. The children also had fun.

A. Egg Hunt

Hide paper or dyed eggs of various colors. Give each color a value: 5 for blue, 4 for yellow, 3 for red, 2 for green, etc. A silver foil egg could be worth the most (you can match the numbers right on the eggs). The one who gets the highest score is the winner.

B. White House Egg Roll

Give each player an Easter egg. He must push it with his nose around a set course on the floor or grass.

C. Egg Running Contest

Set up teams in relay fashion; each player in turn runs with an egg balanced on a spoon!

D. Another "Old-Timer"

Roll or push the eggs toward a shallow hole. A large tin can or a milk carton turned on its side can also be used as a target.

E. Twin Game

Paste duplicate pictures or draw identical pictures on shirtboards. Children match cards from pile, making sets of twins.

F. Shapes

Draw duplicate shapes (square, triangle, circle, diamond, rectangle, star, heart, cross) on shirtboards. Let children match cards.

IX. FIELD TRIPS

Objective: To provide firsthand, enriching experiences.
Evaluation: Enriching experiences were provided.

1. Visit a greenhouse.

2. Visit an "Old Folks Home". Bring small gifts, pieces of fruit or small cakes and cookies, Easter eggs; sing spring songs.

3. Visit a grocery store.

4. Visit an egg farm.

5. Go for a neighborhood walk. Read Going for a Walk by Schenk de Regniers.

X. BOOKS

All About Eggs	Selsam
Easter Kitten	Konkle
The Bunny Who Found Easter	Zolotov
The Egg Tree	Milhous
The Wonderful Egg	Scholar
Tell Me Little Boy	Foster
Peter Rabbit	Potter
Lilies, Rabbits and Painted Eggs	Barth
Look-inside Easter Egg	Bianco
Humbug Rabbit	Balian
Pink Paint	Dean
Easter Rabbit	Duvoisin
The Easter Bunny That Overslept	Friedrich
The Country Bunny and the Little Gold Shoes	Heyword
Happy Easter, Dear Dragon	Hillert
The Runaway Bunny	Brown
A Rabbit for Easter	Carrich
A Tale for Easter	Tudor
Jennie's Hat	Keats
Good Morning, Chick	Ginsburg
The Chick and the Duckling	Ginsburg
The Tale of Meshka the Kvetch	Chapman
Pitter Patter	Baruch
Rainbow of My Own	Freeman
Who Knows When Winter Goes	Simon
When it Rains Cats and Dogs	Turner
Umbrella	Yashima
The Passover Parrot	Zusman

MAY

I. ARTS & CRAFTS

Objectives: To improve small motor coordination through printing, painting, gluing, cutting.

Evaluation: Small motor coordination was improved through printing, painting, gluing, cutting.

A. Spring Bulletin Board

Uses sponges. Paint green grass on a long piece of paper and add art projects throughout the week (flowers, butterflies, etc.)

B. Inkblot Butterfly Pictures

Give the children butterfly-shaped paper with a fold in the middle and have them paint (eye-dropper dots, watercolor, etc.) on one side and then press together both halves of this picture.

C. Pastel Soap Painting

Add color (paint, food coloring) to Ivory Soap and water to use as fingerpaint.

D. Egg Carton Flowers

Divide egg carton (not sytrofoam) into sections. Have children paint them inside and out. Punch hole in bottom with pencil and attach pipe cleaner for stem. Can put several in a juice can and use for centerpiece for Mother's Day Luncheon.

E. Paint and construct barn and silo from boxes and cardboard and use for farm play.

F. Dip chalk in buttermilk and draw.

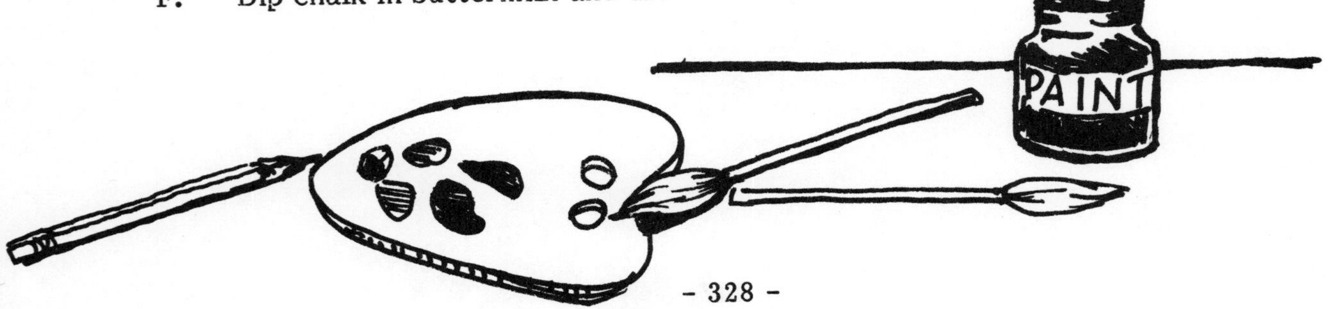

G. Printing

Use various fruits and vegetables dipped in paint and pressed on paper. Can use an apple cut in half; cut a potato in half and carve a simple shape in the flat end; carrots; celery.

H. Read Hamilton Duck's Springtime Story by Getz. Draw tree; give children pink and purple tissue paper squares to crumple and paste all over tree.

I. May Day Basket

Give each child a large paper plate. Have them fold it in half. Teacher puts slit in plate and staples basket sheet above slit. Children put ribbon through slit and teacher ties bow. Children insert flowers (either real or made) into the edges of the basket.

M. Monoprint with Fingerpaint

Use: Liquid starch

Powdered paint (in flour shakers)

white shelf paper 9" x 12" or larger

Pour a small amount of starch on the work surface; shake on color and mix with hands. Children create designs with fingers.

Help them press paper onto their design to make an imprint. You may do this two or three times with the same piece of paper using a different color for each addition.

The result is a superimposed picture with a silk screen appearance.

N. A nice gift for Mother's Day--handprints of their children. Use a large piece of white construction paper. Xerox or print on verse:

Sometimes you get discouraged
Because I am so small
And always leave my fingerprints
On furniture and walls.

But every day I'm growing--
I'll be grown up someday
And all those tiny handprints
Will surely fade away.

So here's a final handprint
Just so you can recall
Exactly how my fingers looked
When I was very small.

Love,

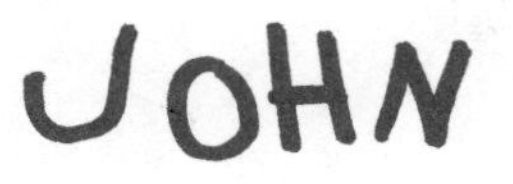

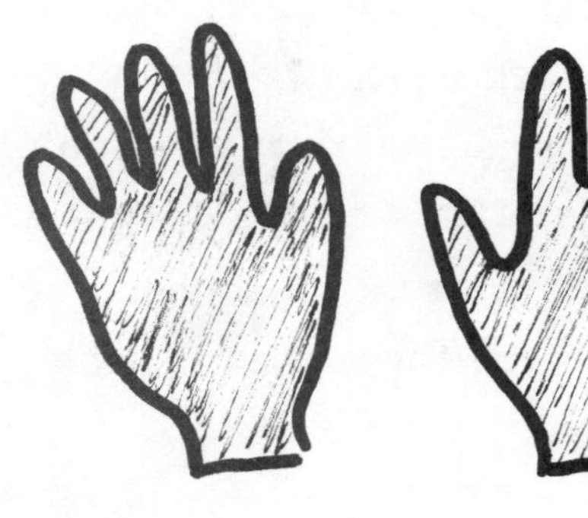

O. An invitation to Mother's Day Lunch

Dear Mom and Grandma,

I love you very much and want to do something really nice for you. My nursery school class decided we would make a lunch for our very special moms and grandmas. Mrs. _______ taught us how to cook so we can make almost everything ourselves. Please come to our "Happy Mother's Day Lunch" and eat with me.

Date _______

Time _______

Place _______

Love,

____

P.S. Fathers invited too!!

Read Monkey Face - Asch (do with flannelboard)

Ask Mr. Bear - Flack

P. Lemon-Cloves Sachet

Have each child bring in whole lemon. Give them each several whole cloves to stick in rind. Has a wonderful smell in any drawer!

Q. Mother's Day Corsage

Have children pick dandelions on way to school. Have them paste them to small round paper doilies and pin on mother with safety pin.

R. Flowers

Baking cup flowers. Flatten paper baking cups and glue them on a large sheet of construction paper. Have children cut out green stems and leaves and glue them on, or draw on with markers.

S. Sunflower

Have children cut out several yellow petals and paste on small paper plate. Fill center with sunflower seeds.

Plant remaining seeds in garden.

T. Button Flowers

Glue buttons on paper for the flower center. Make petals by drawing them with markers, gluing on petals they have cut out, or by dipping their fingertips into different colored paints and printing with them.

U. Cereal Flowers

Paste colorful cereals on paper plates in the shape of flowers. Children can complete flowers by coloring in stems and leaves.

II. COLOR DAY - PURPLE

Objective: To recognize color purple.
Evaluation: Color purple was identified.

Have children wear something with purple on it, if they do not have anything with purple on it, you can pin on a purple flower made out of construction paper.

Look for color purple in objects found in the room. Bring in an iris or lilac branch. Try mixing colors on the easel to get purple.

For snack, can have grape jello squares, peanut butter and grape jelly, purple grapes.

Read Harold and the Purple Crayon by Crockett Johnson.

III. STORY

<u>Objective</u>: To increase their appreciation of literature.
<u>Evaluation</u>: Children enjoyed the story very much.

The Gingerbread Boy

This is an excellent story to read, act out with felt, etc., or even have the children dramatize themselves. There are many versions of this story. It is easy to get at the library or even an inexpensive edition is simple to obtain. We've included the figures that we have used on the felt board.

(See recipe in May cooking section or in Special Day section)

Old man
horse

cow

fox

The Turnip

Once upon a time an old man planted a little turnip and said,

"Grow, grow, little turnip, grow sweet! Grow, grow, little turnip, grow strong!"

And the turnip grew up sweet and strong and big and enormous.

Then, one day, the old man went to pull it up. He pulled and pulled again, but he could not pull it up. He called the old woman.

The old woman pulled the old man.

The old man pulled the turnip. And they pulled and pulled again, but they could not pull it up. So the old woman called her granddaughter.

The granddaughter pulled the old woman.

The old woman pulled the old man.

The old man pulled the turnip.

And they pulled and pulled again, but they could not pull it up. The granddaughter called the black dog.

The black dog pulled the granddaughter.

The granddaughter pulled the old woman.

The old woman pulled the old man.

The old man pulled the turnip.

And they pulled and pulled again, but they could not pull it up. The black dog called the cat.

The cat pulled the dog.

The dog pulled the granddaughter.

The granddaughter pulled the old woman.

The old woman pulled the old man.

The old man pulled the turnip.

And they pulled and pulled again, but they still could not pull it up. The cat called the mouse.

The mouse pulled the cat.

The cat pulled the dog.

The dog pulled the granddaughter.

The granddaughter pulled the old woman

The old woman pulled the old man.

The old man pulled the turnip.

They pulled and pulled again, and up came the turnip at last.

turnip

Monkey Face

One day at school, Monkey painted a picture of his mother.

On the way home, he stopped to show it to his friend, Owl.

"Nice picture," said Owl, "but you made her eyes too small."

"How's that?" asked Monkey.
"Much better," said Owl.

When Monkey saw Rabbit sunning himself, he held up the picture for him to see.

"Looks just like her," said Rabbit, "except the ears are a bit short."

"How's that?" asked Monkey.

"Big improvement," said Rabbit.

At the river bank, Monkey found Alligator and showed the picture to her.

"Pretty," said Alligator, "but she hasn't got much of a mouth."

"How's that?" asked Monkey.

"Beautiful!" said Alligator.

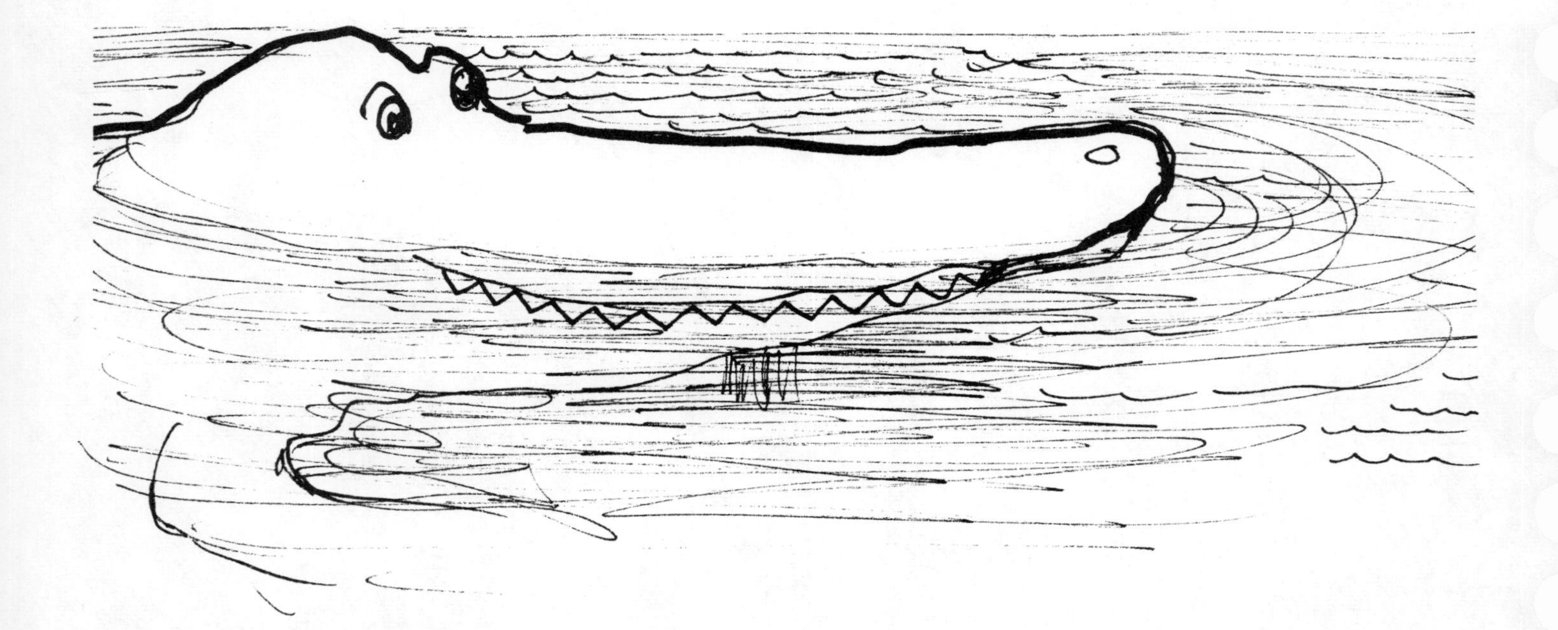

As he walked on, Monkey met Elephant and showed him the picture. "Good likeness," said Elephant. "But her nose is almost invisible."

"How's that?" asked Monkey.

"Unforgettable," said Elephant.

Monkey couldn't wait for Lion to see his picture.

"You're a born artist," said Lion, "except for one thing--you've forgotten her fluffy mane."

"How's that?" asked Monkey.

"Most becoming," said Lion.

When he was almost home, Monkey saw Giraffe and let him look at the picture. "Nearly perfect," said Giraffe, "but her neck needs to be a little longer."

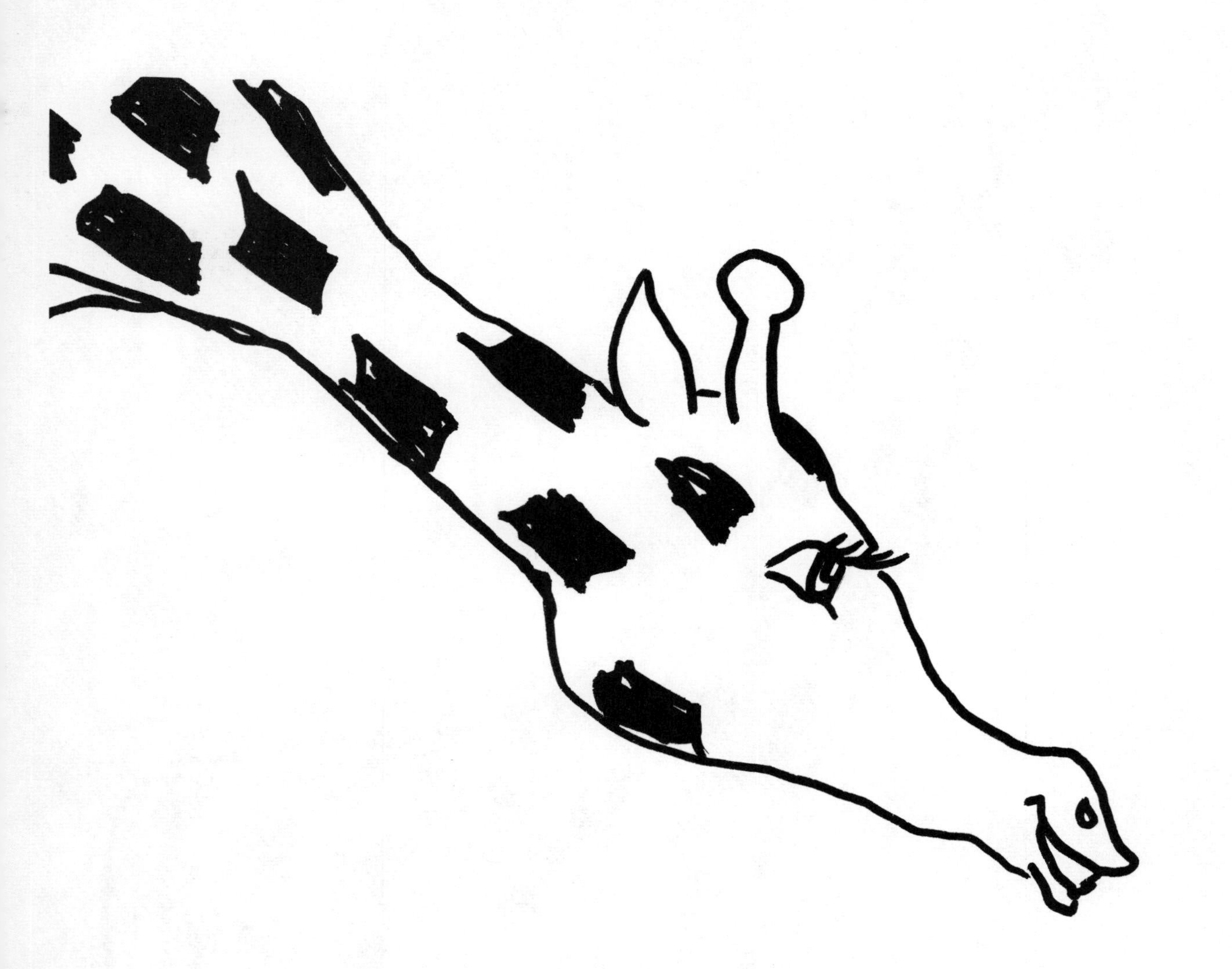

"How's that?" asked Monkey.

"Truly elevating," said Giraffe.

Monkey ran the rest of the way.

His lunch was all ready and his mother was waiting for him.

"Look what I made in school today," said Monkey. "A picture of you."

"I love it!" said his mother.

"Just the way it is?" asked Monkey.

"Just the way it is," said his mother. And she hung it on the refrigerator for everyone to see.

(An excellent story to use with the flannelboard!)

IV. COOKING

Objective: To improve small motor coordination through mixing, sifting, rolling, decorating. To improve math skills by counting and measuring.
Evaluation: Small motor coordination was improved through mixing, stirring, rolling, and decorating. Math skills were improved through counting and measuring.

A. Spinach Salad

(Children can make this for Mother's Day Lunch. They can cut with plastic knives with serrated edges.)
1 pkg. fresh spinach (rinsed and dried)
bean sprouts
sliced fresh mushrooms
sliced purple onion
bacon, fried crisp and crumbled (or Bacos)
croutons

Dressing
1/2 C. salad oil
1/3 C. catsup
1/3 C. sugar
1 T. Worcestershire

B. Butter

Divide one carton of whipping cream between a few containers (baby food jars) and shake, shake, shake. Separate the butter from the buttermilk. Sample each. You may want to salt the butter. Serve with crackers.

C. Gingerbread Boys

1 C. shortening
1 C. sugar
1 egg
1 C. molasses
2 Tbs. vinegar

5 C. flour	1-1/2 tsp. soda
1/2 tsp. salt	2 tsp. ginger
1 tsp. cinnamon	1 tsp. cloves

Cream shortening and sugar. Stir in egg, molasses and vinegar, beat well. Sift dry ingredients. Stir in molasses mix. Chill Roll between waxed paper or on foil. Cut with cookie cutter or let children shape gingerbread boys. Provide raisins, colored sugars, candies, and icing for decorating. This is an excellent time to use a story or record of Gingerbread Boy.

D. Fresh Fruit Salad

(Good for Mother's Day Luncheon).

Have each child bring in one or two pieces of fruit to cut up for fruit salad. Use a little lemon juice to keep apples and bananas from turning brown.

E. Peanut Butter Smorgasbord

Brown bread, butter, peanut butter

Toppings:

honey, jam, fruit butters, pickles, sliced bananas, apples or pears

1. Set out plates and plastic knives for everyone
2. Make a line up of sandwich ingredients
3. Have children create their own sandwich

F. <u>Make-Your-Own Sundae</u>

Give each child a scoop of yogurt in a cup. Set out an assortment of fruit, nuts, and seeds. Invite everyone to create their own special yogurt sundae.

G. <u>Popsicles</u>

Mix and pour into popsicle mold:

1 C. hot water

2 C. lemonade

1 pkg. strawberry jello

Freeze and enjoy

H. <u>Special Fruit Salad Kids Can Make</u>

(For Mother's Day Luncheon)

Use half a peach or a pear (canned or fresh) for a face. Make eyes, nose and mouth with cloves, raisins, small cheese cut-outs or pieces of olive or pimento. A lettuce leaf can be a skirt; and celery or carrot strips make arms and legs.

Let each child make his own.

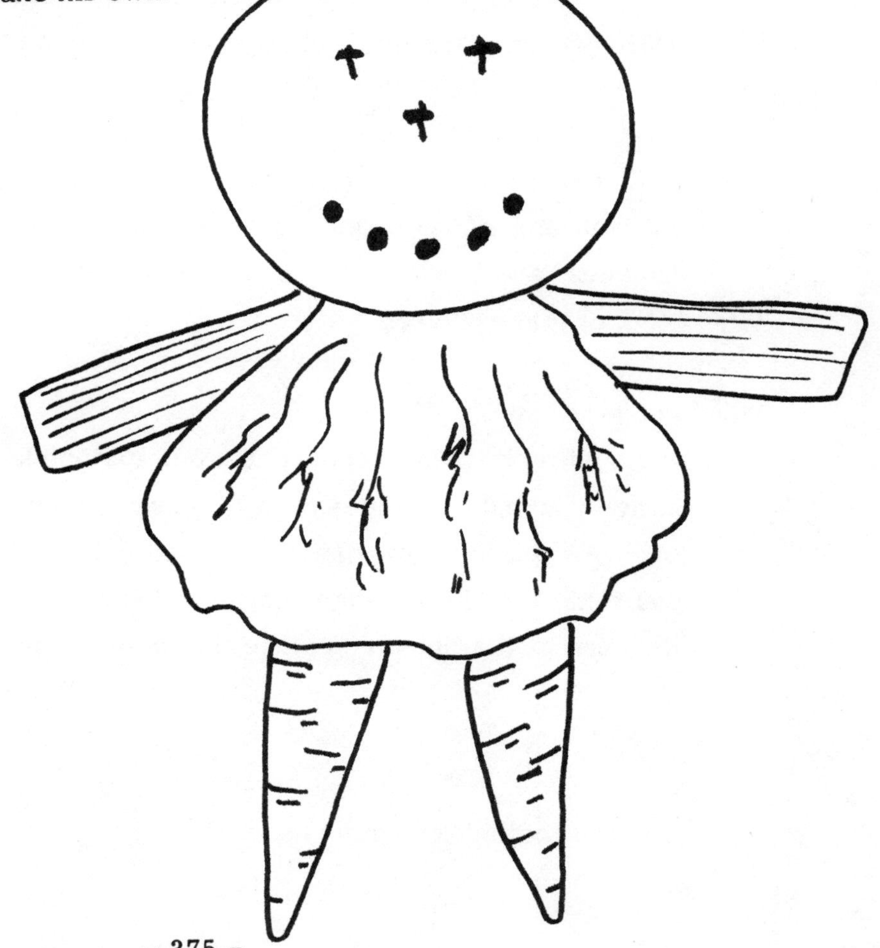

V. MATH

Objectives: To improve matching skills, make patterns.

Evaluation: Matching skills and pattern skills were greatly improved through these activities.

A. Farm Lotto

Using pictures from magazines or inexpensive books, make several boards and cards to match. Make two sets of cards: one with pictures to match and the other with names of the animals to match.

B. Baby Animals

Using pictures from magazines or inexpensive books, make one set of cards with their babies to match. Or, make a set of cards to match to a board of corresponding animals.

Fruit and Vegetable Boards

Using pictures from garden catalogs, make a set of cards to match to a board of common fruits and vegetables. The pictures do not have to be identical.

C. Food Dominoes

Using stickers from a stationery store, or magazine pictures, paste an item on each end of rectangle cards and match as dominoes. Remember to make "doubles" and blanks. You can make several sets of these and group by type of food, or make one set.

D. Patterns

With children watching, lay out toothpicks according to a set pattern. The design you make should consist of a regular pattern repeated over and over.

As you lay down the toothpicks, help children perceive the pattern. After you think they have caught on, ask, "What comes next?" See if they can select the correct toothpick and place it according to the pattern.

Colored toothpicks can be used.

VI. FINGERPLAYS

Objective: To improve counting and memory skills.

Evaluation: Counting and memory skills were improved

5 enormous dinosaurs letting out a roar;
One went away, And then there were four.
4 enormous dinosaurs munching on a tree;
One went away, And then there were three.
3 enormous dinosaurs didn't know what to do;
One went away, And then there were two.
2 enormous dinosaurs having lots of fun;
One went away, And then there was one.
1 enormous dinosaur afraid to be a hero
He went away, And then there was zero.

Five Little Farmers

5 little farmers (fist)
Woke up with the sun
For it was early morning
And the chores must be done (open)

The first little farmer
Went to milk the cow. (close fingers, move up and down)
The second little farmer
Thought he'd better plow. (close fingers, move side to side)
The third little farmer
Fed the hungry hens. (toss feed from one hand)
The fourth little farmer
Mended broken pens. (hammer up and down)
The fifth little farmer
Took his vegetables to town. (hold reins or steering wheel)
When the work was finished (fist)
And the evening sky was red
5 little farmers
Tumbled into bed.

Five Little Ducklings

One little duckling, yellow and new
Had a fuzzy brother and that made two.
Two little ducklings now you can see
They had a little sister and that made three.
Three little ducklings - will there be more?
A friend came along and that made four.
Four little ducklings went to swim and dive
They met a little neighbor and that made five.
Five little ducklings, watch them grow,
They'll turn into fine big ducks you know.

Sing: "Old MacDonald's Farm"
Can make animal puppets. Trace and cut out different animals. Paste on flat part of small paper bag. Have children hold up their animal when it is called out in the song.

Animals
We'll hop, hop, hop like a bunny
And run, run, run like a dog
We'll walk, walk, walk, like an elephant
And jump, jump, jump like a frog
We'll swim, swim, swim like a goldfish
And fly, fly, fly like a bird
We'll sit right down and fold our hands
And not say a single word.

Little Green Frog
"Gung, gung" went the little green frog one day.
"Gung, gung" went the little green frog.
"Gung, gung" went the little green frog one day.
And his eyes went "aah, aah, gung."
(fingers around eyes, stick out tongue.

YOU ARE MY SUNSHINE

You are my sun-shine, my on-ly sun-shine, you make me hap-py when skies are gray. You'll nev-er know, dear, how much I love you - please don't take my sun-shine a-way.

Old MacDonald had a Farm

Old MacDonald had a farm, E-I-E-I-O.

And on his farm he had some chicks, E-I-E-I-O.

With a chick, chick here and a chick, chick there,

Here a chick, there a chick, everywhere a chick chick

Old MacDonald had a farm, E-I-E-I-O.

2. duck - quack (flap arms) Repeat chick sounds.
3. cow - moo (milk cow) Repeat duck, chick sounds.
4. turkey - gobble (make turkey tail) Repeat cow, duck, chick sounds.
5. pig - oink (push up tip of nose) Repeat turkey, cow, etc.
6. donkey - hee haw (hands on either side of head) Repeat pig, etc.

LITTLE GREEN FROG

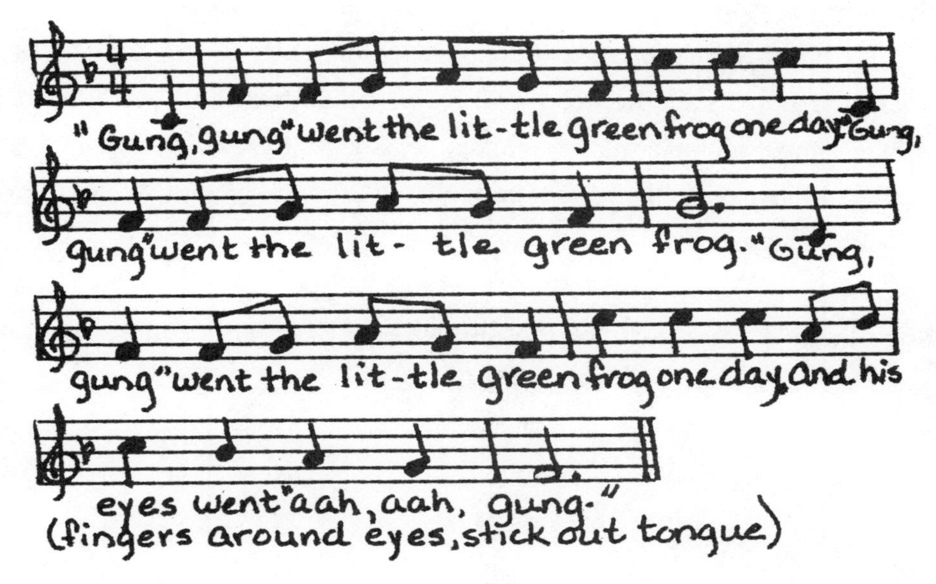

VII. SCIENCE

Objective: To develop an interest in dinosaurs.

Evaluation: An interest in dinosaurs was developed.

Dinosaur Unit

Dinosaurs lived on earth a long time ago. There were no people on earth at that time. We know about dinosaurs from bones we have found--some were very, very large, and some were as small as a person. They ate plants and other animals. Some of the common dinosaurs were:

Brontosaurus
Tyrannosaurus Rex
Brachiosaurus
Trachodon
Triceratops

To help children grasp an idea of the size of a large dinosaur, cut a lenght of string 70 feet long and see if a Brontosaurus could fit into your classroom.

Make a Bone Collage

Plan ahead in order to accumulate enough bones. Ask parents to save chicken bones--they should be well boiled and all traces of meat removed. They can also be bleached to ensure sanitation. Have children glue them onto sturdy dinosaur cut-outs. Some of the children may enjoy studying the skeleton pictures in dinosaur books before trying this activity.

Have some dinosaur models on hand. A good place to find them is in a museum gift shop. Or, trace some on heavy paper, color both sides and cover with clear contact or laminate. Stand them up on bits of playdough and let harden. Add a few "trees" (pipe cleaner trunks, paper fronds, in dough bases), a volcano (paper cone), some "grass", and water (shiny blue paper). The children enjoy maneuvering these materials in play situations.

A "bone band" is fun during dinosaur week. Have children bring in bigger bones (steak, spare rib) for a rhythm experience.

The children will enjoy moving like dinosaurs: slow and heavy steps for Brontosaurus; on feet only with arms out like Tyranosaurus; "flying" like Pteranodon.

For older fours' "Dinosaur in the Dell" can be played. This gives the children an opportunity to say those names and to "Be" a dinosaur!

(See Fingerplays and Book List for May)

SENSORY PLAY

Objective: To increase knowledge of their senses through tasting, feeling, smelling and listening,

Evaluation: The children became more aware of their senses through tasting, feeling, smelling and listening.

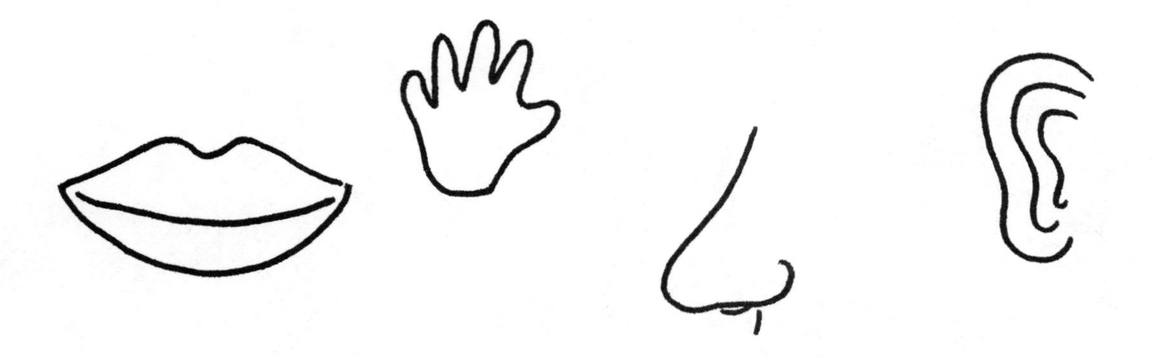

Young children take great pleasure in exploring their five senses: seeing, tasting, smelling, touching, and hearing. There are many innovative things that you can do with your children to stimulate their senses. Intriguing guessing games can be played on the spur of the moment--just use your imagination to conduct a variety of activities to learn about your body.

TASTING ACTIVITIES

What Is It?

Without looking, the child tries to guess what familiar food he is eating. For the young child offer him a chance to look at the foods first. Then, one at a time, offer him such foods as:

chocolate chips	raisins
orange slices	bread
marshmallows	pickle
dry cereal	bologna
banana slices	olives

cooked spaghetti	grapes
cookies	candy

First let him guess by tasting, then let him feel and smell.

Tasting Opposites

Assemble foods with opposite tastes

sweet vs sour	honey vs lemon juice
sweet vs bitter	chocolate chips vs unsweetened chocolate
salty vs unsalty	salted crackers vs cookies

Smelling Activities

Assemble a bunch of containers that look more or less alike, such as baby food jars, pill bottles. Put a small amount of each smelling substance into a container (one substance per container).

Possibilities include:

cinnamon	coffee grounds
vanilla	tea leaves
cloves	black pepper
tobacco	vinegar
perfume	talcum powder
chocolate chips	garlic
mint leaves	onion
lemon peel, dried	alcohol
orange peel, dried	

Let the children try to guess what each substance is by smelling it, have them blindfolded.

Feeling Activities

Put familiar household objects in a bag or use a box with a hole cut in the lid.

Possible objects:

toothbrush	comb
sponge	spoon
small doll	fork
toy car	stone
paper cup	crayon

Let the child reach in and try to guess what he feels before pulling object out.

Variations:

Play the game using only fruits or vegetables

Feel Board

Search for objects around the house that are of different textures, such as:

sandpaper
aluminum foil
pieces of fur
split peas
corregated cardboard
fabric
sponge
rice

Glue pieces of such objects on a large piece of cardboard. When the child is familiar with the various textures, he may wish to try to identify them while blindfolded.

Fabric Feeling

corduroy
velvet
burlap
vinyl
fur
carpet
silk
terrycloth

Listening Activities

Outdoor sounds: Go outside, close your eyes and listen for sounds. What do you hear?

Inside sounds: Close your eyes and listen. What sounds do you hear inside? Music? Water running? Footsteps?

Noisemaking Objects: Assemble a bunch of objects that can be used to make noise, such as:

pan lids
sandpaper
bells
blocks
rice
pot and spoon

VIII. PHYSICAL DEVELOPMENT GAMES

Objective: To improve large motor coordination, concept of taking turns.
Evaluation: Coordination was improved and children took turns.

A. Farmer in the Dell: To speed up game, start with two farmers, they take two wives, etc. Can hang cards around their necks showing pictures of animals until they are familiar with the game.

B. Bluebird

Bluebird, bluebird, in and out my window
Oh, Johnny, aren't you tired? (3 times)

Touch a little boy/girl and tap him
on the shoulder (repeat 3 times)
Oh, Johnny, aren't you tired?

Attach colored paper birds to children's shirts (blue, red, yellow). Sing first verse only, and have all the bluebirds go in and out, then change the color to the redbirds, etc.

C. Two in a Box: Tune of "10 Little Indians"

Two children face each other and make a "rowboat". Class sings:
"Two in a rowboat and the boat keeps rowing" (3 times)
Teacher calls two more children--
Each gets on the boat behind the first two.
"Four in the boat...etc.
All tip over!

D. Button Toss

Have a large supply of buttons, a large paper grocery bag, and a yardstick or adhesive tape to use as a line on floor to stand behind. Fold down the top of the paper bag and place it on the floor. A book in the bottom of the bag will keep it from toppling over. Have children stand behind line and throw one button at a time . See how many they can get in the bag. When all the buttons have been thrown, count the number of buttons in the bag. That's the score.

IX. FIELD TRIPS

<u>Objective</u>: To provide firsthand enriching experiences.

<u>Evaluation</u>: Enriching experiences were provided.

1. Visit zoo
2. Visit farm
3. Visit a florist
4. Visit a dairy
5. Visit a veterinarian
6. Visit a pet store

X. BOOKS

Little Farm	Lois Lenski
A Treeful of Pip	Label
Our Animal Friends at Maple Hill	Provensen
Old MacDonald Had a Farm	Quackenbush
Animals on the Farm	Rojandovsky
Great Big Animal Book	Rojankovsky
Come to the Farm	Tensen
Butterwich Farm	Webb
Baby Farm Animals	Williams
Goodmorning, Farm	Wright
Whose Eye Am I?	Ylla
The Chicken Book	Garth
Of Course a Goat	Bornstein
Mr. Tall and Mr. Small	Brenner
Boy Who Didn't Believe in Spring	Clifton
Belinda's New Spring Hat	Clymer
Three Friends Find Spring	Delton
The Chick and the Duckling	Ginsburg
Springtime for Hamilton Duck	Getz
The Gingerbread Boy	Galdone
Who Took the Farmer's Hat?	Nodset
All About Dinosaurs	Andrews
In the Days of the Dinosaurs	Andrews
Dinosaur Story	Cole
Dinosaur Time	Parish
Giant Dinosaurs	Rowe
Pele's New Suit	Beskow
Ask Mr. Bear	Flack
Monkey Face	Asch
Going for a Walk	Schenck de Rigneirs
What is a Plant?	Darby
The Growing Story	Kraus
The Carrot Seed	Kraus
Creepy the Caterpillar	Smith
Things that Grow	Eggleston
Bird Talk	Gans

Martin Luther King

Martin Luther King was born in Atlanta, Georgia in 1929. His father and grandfather were both ministers. As a small child he realized that white children could not play with him because he was black. His mother tired to explain to him that he was "as good as anyone." When the school bully hit him, he would not hit back, thus showing his hatred for violence.

Martin decided to become a minister also. He went to a school that only had six black students out of 100. He studied very hard and graduated first in his class and was the first black to be president of his class.

His main objective in life was for the black people to have the same equal opportunities as the white people and to obtain these rights peacefully, without fighting. He said, " I have a dream." He was shot and killed on April 4, 1968.

Harriet Tubman

Harriet Tubman was born in Maryland. She was born a slave, 1 of 11 children. She was a homely, willful child and never went to school, but she was in constant pursuit of freedom. Besides gaining her own freedom, she helped her family, friends and even people she did not know to escape from the South. She returned to the South as many as 19 times and brought more than 300 people to freedom.

Frederick Douglass

Frederick Douglass was born in 1817 in Maryland. He was born a slave and was brought up by his grandmother while his mother worked in the fields of the plantation where they lived. When he was seven, he was taken away from his grandmother and mother and sent to another plantation. He was so unhappy and angry that he made himself a promise never to be a slave when he was grown up.

The first thing he had to do was learn to read but being a slave, he was not allowed to go to school. He learned from his white playmates on the street. They taught him what they learned in school.

By the time he was 13, he was reading important speeches about freedom and wishing he could be free.

When he was 21, he escaped and traveled to the North where he would be free. He studied and read all that he could and began giving his own speeches about his slavery and his people in the South. He studied and spoke in England and edited a paper, The North Star, which spoke out against slavery.

When the Civil War began, President Lincoln called him in for advice. Frederick Douglass worked in the United States Government.

He wrote many important books about slavery and the people who read them could not believe he was an escaped slave.

Frederick Douglass was truely an Afro-American Hero.